THEODORE ROOSEVELT AND THE RHETORIC OF MILITANT DECENCY

Theodore Roosevelt, circa 1900. Photograph reproduced courtesy of Theodore Roosevelt Collection, Harvard College Library.

THEODORE ROOSEVELT AND THE RHETORIC OF MILITANT DECENCY

Robert V. Friedenberg

Foreword by Halford R. Ryan

Great American Orators, Number 9
Bernard K. Duffy and Halford R. Ryan,
Series Advisers

Greenwood Press
New York • Westport, Connecticut • London

Library of Congress Cataloging-in-Publication Data

Friedenberg, Robert V.
    Theodore Roosevelt and the rhetoric of militant decency / Robert
V. Friedenberg ; foreword by Halford R. Ryan.
    p.   cm. — (Great American orators, ISSN 0898-8277 ; no. 9)
    Includes bibliographical references (p.) and index.
    ISBN 0-313-26448-1 (lib. bdg. : alk. paper)
    1. Roosevelt, Theodore, 1858-1919—Oratory. 2. Political oratory
—United States—History. 3. United States—Politics and
government—1865-1933. I. Title. II. Series.
    E757.F84   1990
    973.91′1′092—dc20   90-3648

British Library Cataloguing in Publication Data is available.

Library of Congress Catalog Card Number: 90-3648
ISBN: 0-313-26448-1
ISSN: 0898-8277

First published in 1990

Greenwood Press, 88 Post Road West, Westport, CT   06881
An imprint of Greenwood Publishing Group, Inc.

Printed in the United States of America

The paper used in this book complies with the
Permanent Paper Standard issued by the National
Information Standards Organization (Z39.48-1984).

10 9 8 7 6 5 4 3 2 1

It is exceedingly interesting and attractive to be
a successful business man, or railroad man, or
farmer, or a successful lawyer or doctor; or a
writer, or a President or a ranchman, or the
colonel of a fighting regiment, or to kill grizzly
bears and lions. But for unflagging interest and
enjoyment, a household of children, if things go
reasonably well, certainly makes all other forms
of success and achievement lose their importance
by comparison.

Theodore Roosevelt 1913

For the unflagging interest and enjoyment you have provided,
this book is lovingly dedicated to David and Laura. Things
have indeed gone reasonably well, and all other forms of
success and achievement have most assuredly lost their
importance by comparison to the two of you.

Contents

Acknowledgments   ix

Series Foreword   xi

Foreword   xv

Preface   xvii

PART I: CRITICAL ANALYSIS

1. The Early Years   1

2. The Rhetoric of Militant Decency   15

3. The Rhetoric of Militant Decency and Foreign Policy   37

4. The Rhetoric of Militant Decency and Civic Virtue   57

5. The Rhetoric of Militant Decency and
   Progressive Reform   73

Epilogue   95

PART II: COLLECTED SPEECHES

The Duties of American Citizenship   103

Washington's Forgotten Maxim   115

The Strenuous Life   129

The Man with the Muck-rake   139

viii Contents

The New Nationalism   147

This Nation's Needs   161

Chronology of Speeches   167

Bibliography   201

Index   207

Acknowledgments

The oft quoted phrase "no man is an island" is particularly true of those doing scholarly research. This book owes much to the librarians of Miami University and Harvard University. My debt to Becky Zartner and her associates at the Miami University libraries and Wallace Daily, curator of the Theodore Roosevelt Collection at Harvard University, is considerable. It is with sincere gratitude that I acknowledge those debts.

Special thanks are due Halford Ryan, co-editor of the Great American Orator series, whose reading of the manuscript appreciably strengthened my efforts. Roosevelt has been the subject of an extensive body of scholarship. The thoughts of two Roosevelt scholars, Edmund Morris and Frederick W. Marks III, have contributed substantially to my own thoughts about Roosevelt.

In the course of my work I have received grants from the Miami University Faculty Research Committee and the Miami University-Hamilton Faculty Research Fund, both of which defrayed the costs of travel, duplication services, clerical help, and similar expenses associated with this project. These are simply the most recent examples that have caused me, in each of my books, to acknowledge the supportive atmosphere that I have found at Miami University.

I would be terribly remiss not to acknowledge the subject of this study, Theodore Roosevelt. There may be rhetorical critics who have studied finer speakers or more significant figures, but few if any rhetorical critics have had the opportunity to study a man whose exuberant personality makes him an absolutely captivating figure, even seven decades after his death. Thank you, Teddy. It was always provocative.

Finally, and Teddy would well understand why I say most importantly, I was fortunate to be raised by parents, Florence and Aaron, who encouraged my interests in politics, speaking, and history. To them, and to my wife, Emmy, whose skills at proofreading, indexing, and word processing seem to grow with each of my publications, I owe a special debt of gratitude that can be acknowledged, but never repaid.

Series Foreword

The idea for a series of books on great American orators grew out of the recognition that there is a paucity of book-length studies on individual orators and their speeches. Apart from a few notable exceptions, the study of American public address has been pursued in scores of articles published in professional journals. As helpful as these studies have been, none has or can provide a complete analysis of a speaker's rhetoric. Book-length studies, such as those in this series, will help fill the void that has existed in the study of American public address and its related disciplines of politics and history, theology and sociology, communication and law. In books, the critic can explicate a broader range of a speaker's persuasive discourse than reasonably could be treated in articles. The comprehensive research and sustained reflection that books require will undoubtedly yield many original and enduring insights concerning the nation's most important voices.

Public address has been a fertile ground for scholarly investigation. No matter how insightful their intellectual forebears, each generation of scholars must reexamine its universe of discourse, while expanding the compass of its researches and redefining its purpose and methods. To avoid intellectual torpor new scholars cannot be content simply to see through the eyes of those who have come before them. We hope that this series of books will stimulate important new understandings of the nature of persuasive discourse and provide additional opportunities for scholarship in the history and criticism of American public address.

This series examines the role of rhetoric in the United States. American speakers shaped the destiny of the colonies, the young republic, and the mature nation. During each stage of the intellectual, political, and religious development of the

United States, great orators, standing at the rostrum, on the stump, and in the pulpit, used words and gestures to influence their audiences. Usually striving for the noble, sometimes achieving the base, they urged their fellow citizens toward a more perfect Union. The books in this series chronicle and explain the accomplishments of representative American leaders as orators.

A series of book-length studies on American persuaders honors the role men and women have played in U.S. history. Previously, if one desired to assess the impact of a speaker or a speech upon history, the path was, at best, not well marked and, at worst, littered with obstacles. To be sure, one might turn to biographies and general histories to learn about an orator, but for the public address scholar these sources often proved unhelpful. Rhetorical topics, such as speech invention, style, delivery, organizational strategies, and persuasive effect, are often treated in passing, if mentioned at all. Authoritative speech texts are often difficult to locate and the problem of textual accuracy is frequently encountered. This is especially true for those figures who spoke one or two hundred years ago, or for those whose persuasive role, though significant, was secondary to other leading lights of the age.

Each book in this series is organized to meet the needs of scholars and students of the history and criticism of American public address. Part I is a critical analysis of the orator and his or her speeches. Within the format of a case study, one may expect considerable latitude. For instance, in a given chapter an author might explicate a single speech or a group of related speeches, or examine orations that comprise a genre of rhetoric such as forensic speaking. But the critic's focus remains on the rhetorical considerations of the speaker, speech, occasion, and effect. Part II contains the texts of the important addresses that are discussed in the critical analysis that precedes it. To the extent possible, each author has endeavored to collect authoritative speech texts, which have often been found through original research in collections of primary source material. In a few instances, because of the extreme length of a speech, texts have been edited, but the authors have been careful to delete material that is least important to the speech, and these deletions have been held to a minimum.

In each book there is a chronology of major speeches that serves more purposes than may be apparent at first. Pragmatically, it lists all of the orator's known speeches and addresses. Places and dates of speeches are also listed, although this is information that is sometimes difficult to determine precisely. But in a wider sense, the chronology attests to the scope of rhetoric in the United States. Certainly in quantity, if not always in quality, Americans are historically talkers and listeners.

Because of the disparate nature of the speakers examined in the series, there is some latitude in the nature of the bibliographical materials that have been included in each book. But in every instance authors have carefully described original historical materials and collections and gathered critical studies, biographies and autobiographies, and a variety of secondary sources that bear on the speaker and the oratory. By combining in each book bibliographical materials, speech texts and critical chapters, this series notes that text and research sources are interwoven in the act of rhetorical criticism.

May the books in this series serve to memorialize the nation's greatest orators.

Bernard K. Duffy
Halford R. Ryan

Foreword

The motion picture industry was in its infancy and the quality of the film footage was often poor, but who could fail to be impressed with Theodore Roosevelt's delivery before a crowd? His head bobbing vigorously, his hands punctuating important ideas, and his whole body thrusting and parrying with the audience, Roosevelt awed his audiences with his dynamism.

Yet the people of New York and later of the United States did not elect Roosevelt to his public offices on the basis of his physical presence, however forceful it was. Roosevelt addressed late nineteenth-century and early twentieth-century exigencies with political proposals that persuaded audiences. It might be added that most of his policies have served well into the late twentieth century.

To parse the factors that innervated Roosevelt's persuasive entreaties to his contemporaries, and that still capture the imaginations of Americans, is a strenuous task. Professor Robert Friedenberg is well adapted to the work. Attuned to the nuances of public persuasions, which he has explicated in numerous studies of political and religious communication, Friedenberg brings to this study of Theodore Roosevelt a thorough grounding in the criticism of American public address. Basing his findings on his own close reading of Roosevelt's speeches, and supplemented by his own research in the primary collections of Roosevelt's manuscripts, Friedenberg reveals the reaches of Roosevelt's fascinating rhetorical career.

The foremost criticism of the art of public speaking is a keen analysis of invention, arrangement, style, delivery, and the modes of proof. Friedenberg does not disappoint the traditional reader. For instance, he demonstrates how

Roosevelt created his own admixture of Aristotle's three means of persuasion: ethical, emotional, and logical appeals (ethos, pathos, and logos). He also demonstrates that Theodore Roosevelt recurrently used rhetorical topoi, to use the classical Greek word that denoted a topic to be discussed, in his long career as a bully pulpiteer. Friedenberg's study of Roosevelt's speaking is a testament to the efficacy of classical or neo-Aristotelian rhetorical criticism.

Halford R. Ryan

Preface

Between the death of Lincoln and the ascendancy of Theodore Roosevelt to the presidency, the United States endured thirty-five years of relatively weak presidential leadership. Yet, the United States prospered and grew. The passing of the Western frontier signaled America's emergence as an urban industrial power. Victory over Spain signaled its emergence as a nation with worldwide responsibilities and obligations. The ascendancy of Theodore Roosevelt to the presidency signaled the emergence of the United States' first modern rhetorical president.

Roosevelt, more than virtually any of his predecessors, seemed to realize the rhetorical power inherent in the office of the presidency. Calling the White House a "bully pulpit," he utilized a rhetoric of militant decency to advance his arguments and persuade on the public policy controversies of his day. Repeatedly Roosevelt spoke directly to the American people as he attempted to mobilize support on the public issues of his day. Theodore Roosevelt had clear conceptions of right and wrong. Those conceptions remained consistent from his early years in the New York state legislature to his final days as an ex-president. Roosevelt's conceptions of right and wrong formed the basis of his rhetoric of militant decency.

Unlike many national leaders, Roosevelt won the begrudging admiration of even those who opposed him. His dynamic personality, unbounded zest for life, and unquestionable integrity, made him almost impossible to dislike. Moreover, the training and education he had received from his family and schools contributed to making him one of the most appealing speakers in American history.

Roosevelt spoke as the twentieth century opened. Many of the issues on which he spoke, such as the respective roles of labor, management and government in the nation's economic life, or the role the United States should play in international affairs, remain unresolved as the twentieth century closes. Yet the depth of Roosevelt's understanding of those issues, and most importantly, the depths of his desire to speak and do what was right and just, distinguished him from the vast majority of both his contemporaries and his successors.

Roosevelt remains among the most beloved of national leaders not only because of his engaging personality but also because of his countrymen's recognition of his desire to speak and act on behalf of what was right. No one questioned Theodore Roosevelt's motives. He spoke and acted out of sincere beliefs about what was best for his nation. Theodore Roosevelt frequently found guidance and inspiration in the writings and speeches of the two nineteenth-century leaders he most admired, George Washington and Abraham Lincoln. Americans facing the twenty-first century, might do well to look for guidance and inspiration in the writings and speeches, the rhetoric of militant decency, of the man who led the United States into the twentieth century.

I
CRITICAL ANALYSIS

1
The Early Years

Theodore Roosevelt was not always the man speaking softly and carrying a big stick. He was not always the man who was so often the subject of caricatures by the nation's editorial page cartoonists. His development as a public figure, and most especially as a public speaker, was a consequence of many early influences. Four influences stand out. They strongly shaped the values to which Roosevelt gave voice throughout his career. Moreover, they greatly enhanced his ability to give voice to those values in a memorable, forceful, and articulate fashion.

The four aspects of his early life that dramatically impacted on Roosevelt's later speaking were: (1) the influence of his family; (2) the diverse and eclectic reading that he engaged in throughout his life, particularly as a child; (3) his educational experiences at Harvard University; and (4) the experiences he acquired in his early twenties as the youngest member of the New York state legislature. These four intertwined influences markedly affected Theodore Roosevelt's development as a public speaker

FAMILY INFLUENCES

Roosevelt was born on October 27, 1858, and reared with his two sisters and brother in New York City. His first training as a speaker was a function of the religious life of his family. By the age of three he was not only learning the alphabet, but he was also beginning to memorize hymns and psalms. Within a few years the Roosevelt children spent an hour every Sunday evening with their father, examining the sermon they had heard earlier in the day. Roosevelt's father taught him to listen to a sermon so that he could subsequently outline the major points and discuss the legitimacy of the content, forcing Roosevelt to become familiar with the Bible at an early age. All those who knew Roosevelt in later years claimed that his knowledge of the Bible was extraordinary. These sermon discussions soon came to focus not only on the sermon content, but also on the manner of expression used by the sermonist.[1]

Roosevelt claimed that his father, also named Theodore, "was the best man I ever knew." Recalling his father, Roosevelt observed that "he combined strength and courage with gentleness, tenderness, and great unselfishness." Roosevelt's father taught by example. Righteousness became attractive to young Theodore, no doubt in large part because he associated it with the life and personality of his father.   The elder Roosevelt was a successful businessman who taught Sunday school and was a leader in the New York City philanthropic community. He constantly spoke, both within the family and in public, on patriotism, good citizenship, and manly morality.[2] It is not accidental that those topics were so often addressed in the speeches of his son.

The strength of the elder Roosevelt's personality was not the only reason that he had an especially strong influence on his son. Young Roosevelt was a sickly child, suffering badly from asthma. Consequently, his early education was at home, provided by his parents and particularly his mother, Martha's, sister, Annie Bulloch. His father, a physically strong man, stayed up long nights with Theodore during his asthma attacks and encouraged his son to build up his body, especially his lungs and chest, as a means of resisting the asthma. Although Roosevelt exercised regularly throughout his teenage years, it was not until his late teens that his asthma subsided. By then he had begun to develop the strong upper torso that subsequently allowed him to project his voice to the back reaches of the largest halls.[3]

Learning at home under the direction of his family, Roosevelt was able to pursue his own interests. Hence, by the age of fifteen his education was very uneven.   He began studying seriously under the tutelage of Arthur Cutler in order to enter Harvard. A tutor was needed because, as Roosevelt himself observed, "I could not go to school because I knew so much less than most boys of my age in some subjects and so much more in others. In science and history and geography and in unexpected parts of German and French I was strong, but lamentably weak in Latin and Greek and mathematics."[4]

More important than any specific knowledge that Roosevelt acquired in his early years, the fact that he learned at home imbued him with attitudes and values to which he remained true throughout his public life. Reflecting on his early education, Roosevelt observed that he had been taught, both consciously and unconsciously, that "pretty much the whole duty of man lay in thus making the best of himself." His training, Roosevelt continued, involved "insistence upon individual responsibility."[5] Roosevelt's early education had provided him with a good background in a variety of subjects and extensive overseas travel. But it was the attitudes and values that he absorbed from his family that were to effect Roosevelt most throughout the remainder of his life.

His father's example served Theodore as a constant reminder of the importance of righteousness. It was an exaggeration to suggest, as did a Republican campaign document in 1904, that Roosevelt "born as a weakling . . . acquired by the sheer exercise of an iron will, through Spartan training, a body like spring steel-for one purpose only: to do his duty to his country."[6] However, in helping young Theodore overcome his asthma, Roosevelt senior made evident to his son the importance of physical strength, self-discipline, and self-reliance. The influence of Roosevelt's family, most notably his father, cannot be overestimated, for unlike most children who by the age of ten have been exposed to the ideas of others, and continue to be so exposed through schoolmates, teachers, and friends, in Roosevelt's formative years his family provided an essentially unchallenged influence on his intellectual development.

EARLY READING

The severity of Roosevelt's asthma meant that for much of his childhood he was a semi-invalid. Sitting up in bed, constantly wheezing, frequently changing his plans because of health problems, often traveling for the sake of his health, Roosevelt's early life was scarcely what one might expect of the vigorous cowboy who ranched in the Bad Lands of North Dakota and became a war hero on San Juan Hill. The enforced physical limitations of his boyhood caused the man who is best remembered for his energy, vigor, and action to become a bookish child.

Young Roosevelt's bookishness was encouraged by his Aunt Annie Bulloch, who lived with the Roosevelt family and payed for her expenses by teaching all of the Roosevelt children. The Bullochs were a prominent southern family whose ancestors included the first president of revolutionary Georgia. During the Civil War, Roosevelt's mother and aunt often reminded him of that southern heritage even as his father worked ardently on behalf of the Union. Most importantly, his aunt encouraged his early interest in reading history, as his father encouraged his early interest in reading natural science.

Roosevelt later recalled that it was from reading about the people he admired, "ranging from the soldiers of Valley

Forge and Morgan's riflemen, to the heroes of my favorite stories, and from hearing of the feats performed by my southern forbearers and kinsfolk, and from knowing my father," that he gained his admiration for men who were fearless. As a boy Roosevelt favored stories of action and adventure. Novels of the sea, Ballantyne's novels, and the Leatherstocking tales of James Fenimore Cooper were all among his favorites. Longfellow's epic poem, "The Sage of King Olaf," to which Roosevelt attributed his lifelong interest in Scandinavian literature, was a particular favorite.[7]

Roosevelt's early readings inspired him with examples of physical bravery and adventure. They also reinforced the values he absorbed from his family. The most notable of his readings in this regard was the magazine that he began to read regularly by the age of ten, Our Young Folks. "As a small boy," Roosevelt believed Our Young Folks "to be the very best magazine in the world." It was a belief, he wrote years later, "which I have kept to this day unchanged, for I seriously doubt if any magazine young or old has ever surpassed it." As an adult Roosevelt kept bound volumes of Our Young Folks from his childhood. The magazine presented stories that according to Roosevelt, were interesting and also taught "manliness, decency, and good conduct." Our Young Folks presented articles and stories of four types: natural history, outdoor life, manly enterprise, and womanly virtue. The shape of Roosevelt's developing mind and values is readily apparent in his observation that this publication "taught me much more than any of my textbooks," because, he continued, "everything in this magazine instilled the individual virtues, and the necessity of character as the chief factor in any man's success."[8]

By the age of twelve, Roosevelt had become an insatiable reader and a prolific writer. His childhood diary includes entries that sometimes run a thousand words a day. Although information on his childhood reading skills is lacking, they must have been remarkable, judging by accounts of his adult abilities. Repeatedly, observers were amazed at Roosevelt's ability to read rapidly with virtually total recall. Owen Wister, a close friend, recalled visiting Roosevelt before an evening's entertainment at the White House, loaning him a book, and being amazed to hear Roosevelt give a complete review of it over breakfast the next morning. Wister claimed that "somewhere between six one evening and eight-thirty the next morning, besides his dressing and his dinner and his guests, and his sleep, he had read a volume of three hundred and odd pages, and missed nothing of significance." Even in the midst of campaigning Roosevelt was an omnivorous reader. He was, for example, reported to have reread all of Macaulay's History of England, all of Rhodes' History of the United States, and

Dickens's <u>Martin Chuzzlewit</u> while campaigning in 1904. Associates claimed that Roosevelt read at the rate of two to three pages a minute and as an adult read at least one book a day, with two or three not being uncommon when he had little business in the evening.[9]

As a youth Roosevelt's reading reflected his remarkably versatile mind. John Morton Blum, one of his chief biographers, stated, "there was almost nothing that did not interest Theodore Roosevelt, almost nothing about which he would not or could not think." Moreover, not only did Roosevelt think and read about an enormous variety of topics as a youth, but he also had remarkable ability to recall what he read. Historian George Otto Treyelyan believed that Roosevelt's memory could be compared with the legendary memory of Thomas Babington Macaulay. Repeated stories of Roosevelt's astonishing memory have been told by associates. Roosevelt himself claimed that as he talked about a book "the pages of the book came before my eyes."[10]

Theodore Roosevelt's early reading, extensive because of his reading skills and semi-invalid boyhood, both reflected and helped to develop his mind. His diverse lifelong interests in history, men of action, the outdoors, and natural science were all stimulated by his early reading. Yet, while his early reading opened new frontiers for his mind and his imagination, it also reinforced the attitudes and values being instilled by his family, making him ever more certain of his fundamental moral beliefs.

HARVARD YEARS

Roosevelt entered Harvard University in the fall of 1896. He later summarized his career at Harvard by observing that "I am sure it did me good, but only in the general effect, for there was very little in my actual studies which helped me in after-life." He principally lamented his failure to gain more from his writing and forensic experiences at Harvard, no doubt realizing the value such experiences might have been to him in his subsequent career. He especially decried the practice of debating wherein students would switch sides without regard to their convictions:

> I had at the time no idea of going into public life and I never studied elocution or practiced debating. This was a loss to me in one way. In another way it was not. Personally I have not the slightest sympathy with debating contests in which each side is arbitrarily assigned a given proposition and told to maintain it, believe in it or not. I know that under our system this is necessary for lawyers, but I emphatically

disbelieve in it as regards general discussion of political, social, and industrial matters. What we need is to turn out of our colleges young men with ardent convictions on the side of the right; not young men who can make a good argument for either right or wrong as their interest bids them. The present method of carrying on debates on such as "Our Colonial Policy," or "The Need of a Navy," or "The Proper Position of the Courts in Constitutional Questions," encourages precisely the wrong attitude among those who take part in them. There is no effort to instill sincerity and intensity of conviction. On the contrary, the net result is to make the contestants feel that their convictions have nothing to do with their arguments. I am sorry I did not study elocution in college; but I am exceedingly glad that I did not take part in the type of debate in which stress is laid, not upon getting a speaker to think rightly, but on getting him to talk glibly on the side to which he is assigned, without regard to either what his convictions are or to what they ought to be.[11]

This passage is revealing in that it illustrates how strong Roosevelt's sense of values had become. They had taken such firm root that Roosevelt could not even justify speaking in debate contests for pedagogical reasons, if it meant that he might have to speak contrary to his sincerely held beliefs. Although Roosevelt's devotion to his beliefs is admirable, his relative closemindedness concerning the righteousness of those beliefs likely meant that the values he learned in his youth were rarely subject to serious examination in his later years. His Harvard classmate, historian Albert Bushnell Hart, claimed that the "intensity" of Roosevelt's convictions "sometimes blinded him to the sincerity and even to the justice of other points of view."[12] The relative consistency of ideas in Roosevelt's public speaking tends to confirm his closemindedness concerning many of the fundamental beliefs and values he learned in childhood.

The first public speech that Roosevelt gave was evidently delivered to the annual dinner of the Harvard Crimson, in 1879. Audience members would no doubt have been startled to learn that the speaker would subsequently address more audiences than any other orator of his time. Describing Roosevelt's maiden public speech, one audience member observed that "he seemed very shy. . . . He still had difficulty in enunciating clearly or even in running off his words smoothly. At times he could hardly get them out at all, and then he would rush on for a few sentences, as skaters redouble their pace over thin ice." This description of Roosevelt's early speaking is consistent with others, several of which suggest that his speaking was often deliberate and halting.[13] However, by his early twenties all such references disappear in accounts of Roosevelt's speaking.

Roosevelt did little at Harvard, or subsequently in his studies at Columbia University Law School, to contribute significantly to his development as a speaker. His college speaking experiences were limited to a few formal debates and some informal debates and addresses before clubs.[14]

If his Harvard years did little to directly improve his speaking, they did do much to improve his mind and reinforce his values. Roosevelt was an exceedingly able student who graduated with a Phi Beta Kappa key in the top tenth of his class. While at Harvard he learned the methods of both scientific and historical research and wrote what eventually became the opening chapters of his still-definitive naval history of the War of 1812. Moreover, while at Harvard, Roosevelt taught Sunday school and continued to exercise, gaining twelve pounds of muscle, which contributed to his enjoyment of sustained periods of good health. Popular with his classmates, Roosevelt's social life at Harvard was an active one that took a dramatic turn in October of his junior year when he met Alice Lee. Months after his graduation, they were married. The only blemish on Roosevelt's productive and enjoyable college years was the death of his father. If Roosevelt could look back on his Harvard years and regret not having gotten more from them that might have helped him in his subsequent political career, he could also write, as his senior year closed, that "my career at college has been happier and more successful than that of any man I have ever known."[15]

LEGISLATIVE EXPERIENCE

Roosevelt did not speak often as a student at Harvard. However he acquired extensive speaking experience a few short years later as a member of the New York State legislature. Graduating from Harvard in 1880, he and Alice returned to New York City, where he attended Columbia University's law school and joined the Twenty-first District Republican Association.

Until quite recently scholars have largely dismissed Roosevelt's legal studies as an undertaking which had little impact on his life. However, Robert Charles, based on his recent discoveries of over 1189 pages of Roosevelt's law school notes and related study, claims that "a substantial body of evidence" suggests that Roosevelt was a "trained lawyer."[16] Charles persuasively argues that Roosevelt had "an intimate knowledge of the law," equivalent to that of most practicing lawyers of the day. He was an industrious student, at what was then the nation's finest law school. His work at Columbia included successful moot court experience which provided Roosevelt with yet another early speaking experience.[17]

While at Columbia, Roosevelt also became active in New York City Republican politics. Men of Roosevelt's social status often complained of local government, but rarely participated. Well-bred, wealthy young men of old established families simply did not, in 1880, strive for careers in politics. Harvard graduates of this period might well have lended their energies to movements for civil service reform, or have written about corrupt municipal government, but they did not leave their businesses and social clubs to participate in political party activities. Roosevelt's decision to join the Twenty-first District Republican Association was remarkable. While Roosevelt surely must have shared many of the biases of his background, he claimed that he entered politics because he wanted to bring honesty to public life.

Noble as that purpose may have been, many students of Roosevelt suggest yet a second motive. Roosevelt was an ambitious man of action who loved to exert power. He recognized that ultimately power in a democracy rested with the people's elected office holders. Consequently, he aspired to office to exert power on behalf of improving the people's government. When his friends critized him for dirtying himself in politics, Roosevelt retorted that he "intended to be one of the governing class."[18]

Remarkably, even at the young age of twenty-two Roosevelt recognized that he had to start at the bottom and that he needed to cooperate with party leaders. Unlike many young men of wealth and education of his time, Roosevelt was willing to pay his dues in the party system, realizing that this was the way ultimately to gain sufficient power to be of service to his fellow man. Subsequently, he advised others who wished to get into politics to do it in the same spirit that

> their fathers went into the Federal armies. Begin with the little thing, and do not expect to accomplish anything without an effort . . . . If you keep on attending and try to form associations with other men whom you meet at the political gatherings, or whom you can persuade to attend them, you will very soon find yourself a weight.[19]

That Roosevelt became a Republican was only natural. Family background would have directed him to the party that in his youth had saved the Union and for whom his father and his father's friends had toiled. Moreover, a highly principled

New Yorker could scarcely be attracted to the Democratic organization. Although the Republican city machine was corrupt, at least by reputation, the Democrats of Tammany Hall were far worse.

The breadth of Roosevelt's enormous accomplishments, which include writing major volumes of natural history and American history, success as a state legislator, New York City police commissioner, civil service commissioner, assistant secretary of the navy, hero of San Juan Hill, governor of New York, vice- president, president, and international statesman, tends to obscure the central fact of his public life. As John Morton Blum stated, "Theodore Roosevelt was a professional Republican politician from New York. He made a career of seeking and holding public office."[20] Pragmatist that he was, Roosevelt's first exposure to politics in New York must have made it clear to him that a key to success in his choosen profession would be the ability to speak well.

Roosevelt's first election campaign did not require him to speak extensively. The Republican organization, delighted to have a candidate of his background and connections on the ticket, worked ardently on his behalf. Most of Roosevelt's communication during the campaign took place in small group meetings.

When Roosevelt first entered the legislature he suffered from an inordinate number of speaking problems. First was his initial ethos, or credibility. In addition to his origins of wealth, he was a Harvard man. He appeared effeminate, wearing eyeglasses on the end of a black silk cord and dressing in the high fashion of the first families of New York City. Even his first close friends in the state legislature, such as Isaac Hunt, recalled that initially "he was a joke . . . a dude the way he combed his hair, the way he talked-the whole thing."[21]

Additionally, Roosevelt's voice was rather high, and observers claimed that he was given to exaggerated yelling and desk pounding to make his points. Moreover, Roosevelt had a tendency to perceive issues as always offering choices between good and bad. As a result, he often sounded unbearably pious. One correspondent noted that "Mr. Roosevelt keeps a pulpit concealed on his person," and went on to report that "in his theology, God always resided with the Republicans, while the Devil was a Democrat." This criticism of Roosevelt, that he was pious and preachy, that he was always on the side of the angels, and that his foes were always on the side of the devil, would be made with some justification throughout Roosevelt's career.[22]

But while Roosevelt strove to correct many of his early shortcomings as a speaker, he was never alarmed at the criticism that he was a preacher. Roosevelt did perceive many issues as having an essential right and an essential wrong, and of course he was right and those who opposed him, regardless of the nobleness of their motive, were wrong. It was Roosevelt, not his critics, who called the White House a "bully pulpit" and rejoiced in the opportunities that pulpit presented him.[23]

Roosevelt remembered his years in the New York legislature as ones in which he "had considerable difficulty in teaching myself to speak." But, with the same perserverance that characterized his struggle against asthma, Roosevelt overcame his difficulties. He profited, Roosevelt claimed, from "the advice of a hard-headed old countryman," who told him, "Don't speak until you are sure you have something to say, and know just what it is; then say it, and sit down."[24]

By the end of his two years in the legislature, Roosevelt had become a much more polished speaker in several ways. First, he had become sensitive to the needs of his audiences. He used clear language that was readily understandable to both the Harvard graduate and the common man. Second, he began to use balanced sentences and the graphic, vigorous expressions that were so characteristic of his later speaking.

Third, during his Albany years Roosevelt began to realize the importance not only of his immediate audience, but also of the wider audience that read his remarks in the press. His growing awareness of audiences other than the immediate audience to whom he spoke and his penchant for picturesque language soon made Roosevelt a favorite of the Albany press corp.[25]

Fourth, Roosevelt's Albany speeches were characterized by sound use of evidence and well-developed logical argument. At Harvard, Roosevelt had developed a fondness for argument. His vast reading and his research skills readily enabled him to support his points. He soon became recognized in Albany as a formidable foe in legislative debate.[26]

Finally, the distracting mannerisms that characterized Roosevelt's initial speaking at Harvard and in the legislature, such as his hesitancy and his enunciating difficulties, gradually disappeared as he gained speaking experience. Whether these problems were eliminated because of his own growing confidence as a speaker, or because of persistent work on his own part, or for other reasons, the fact remains that by the end of his service in the state legislature, the delivery problems that had characterized Roosevelt's prior speaking no longer existed. Although his delivery would always prompt comments, marked as it was by vivid facial expressions, bold gestures, and his dramatic use of voice, by the end of his legislative years Roosevelt's delivery was no longer a liability but a positive asset to his career. By the close of his legislative service in 1884, twenty-four year old Theodore Roosevelt was able to communicate his ideas with sincerity, intensity, and conviction.

NOTES

    1. His second wife claimed that Roosevelt could "repeat at will long portions of scripture." His sister uses the term "extraordinary" to describe his knowledge of the Bible. For the comments of both see Edward H. Cotton, The Ideas of Theodore Roosevelt (New York: Appleton and Company, 1923), xi; 47. The major primary source on Roosevelt's early life is Theodore Roosevelt, An Autobiography (New York: Charles Scribner's Sons, 1926). This version of Roosevelt's autobiography serves as volume twenty in The Works of Theodore Roosevelt: National Edition (New York: Charles Scribner's Sons, 1926). Three excellent biographical accounts of Roosevelt's early life are Carleton Putnam, Theodore Roosevelt: The Formative Years (New York: Charles Scribner's Sons, 1958); Edmund Morris, The Rise of Theodore Roosevelt (New York: Coward, McCann and Geoghegan, Inc., 1979); and David McCullough, Mornings on Horseback (New York: Simon and Schuster, 1981). This discussion of Roosevelt's early training in sermon analysis is based primarily on the recollections of his sister, found in Christian F. Reisner, Roosevelt's Religion (New York: Abington Press, 1922), 31-32.

    2. Roosevelt, An Autobiography, 9-10. Also see chapters 1-3 of Morris, The Rise of Theodore Roosevelt for insight into the pervasive influence of Roosevelt senior on his son.

    3. The pervasive effects of Roosevelt's asthama on his childhood are evident in his early diaries and the letters of his parents. Both Putnam and Morris treat Roosevelt's asthma extensively. Most biographers suggest that Roosevelt acquired both discipline and tenacity in his childhood efforts to overcome his asthma.

    4. Roosevelt, An Autobiography, 23.

    5. Ibid., 28.

    6. Republican National Committee, Our Patriotic President (New York: Columbia Press, 1904), 1.

    7. See Roosevelt, An Autobiography, 18-30 for Roosevelt's recollections and comments on his childhood reading.

8.   See Putnam, Theodore Roooosevelt: The Formative Years, 28 for a description of the content of Our Young Folks. See Roosevelt, An Autobiography, 18 for his feelings about this publication.

9.   See Morris, The Rise of Theodore Roosevelt, 28-55 for accounts of Roosevelt's childhood reading and writing skills, as well as his adult abilities.   Owen Wister, The Story of a Friendship (New York: MacMillan, 1930), p. 89.   William Behl, "Theodore Roosevelt's Principles of Speech Preparation and Delivery," Speech Monographs 12 (1945): 114, cites the Indianopolis Star as the source for this account of Roosevelt's reading during the 1904 campaign.

10.   An excellent recent account of Roosevelt's intellectual attainments, which illustrates the eclectic and versatile nature of his mature mind, can be found in David H. Burton, The Learned Presidency: Theodore Roosevelt, William Howard Taft, Woodrow Wilson (Rutherford, N. J.: Fairleigh Dickinson University Press and Associated University Presses, 1988), 38-88.   John Morton Blum, The Republican Roosevelt (Cambridge Mass.: Harvard University Press, 1954), 24.   Morris, The Rise of Theodore Roosevelt, 26.   Roosevelt, An Autobiography, 24-25.

11.   Roosevelt, An Autobiography, 25.

12.   Hart is quoted in Richard Murphy, "Theodore Roosevelt," History and Criticism of American Public Address, III, Marie Hochmuth, ed. (New York: Russell and Russell, 1965), 322.

13.   This description was made by William Roscoe Thayer and is cited in Morris, The Rise of Theodore Roosevelt, 109.   Also see Charles C. Washburn, Theodore Roosevelt: The Logic of His Career, (Boston: Houghton Mifflin Company, 1916), 5 for additional accounts of Roosevelt's initial speaking.

14.   Behl, "Speech Preparation and Delivery," 112.

15.   Quoted in Morris, The Rise of Theodore Roosevelt, 129.

16.   The quoted statements throughout this paragraph are drawn from Robert B. Charles, "Theodore Roosevelt's Study of Law: A Formative Venture," paper presented at the Theodore Roosevelt Association-Hofstra University Cultural Center

Conference: Theodore Roosevelt and the Birth of Modern America, Long Island, New York, April 20, 1990. Charles will be publishing his work in the near future. All quotations used here are taken from the conference produced audio tape of Charles's remarks.

17. Ibid. New York state was among the first states to require three years of study for admission to the bar. New York changed this requirment after Roosevelt had started his studies at Columbia. Charles claims that Roosevelt had the training of most lawyers of his day, but primarily because of family demands and his increasingly demanding political career, he never finished New York's newly imposed third year and hence never received his degree.

18. Roosevelt is Quoted in Henry F. Pringle, Theodore Roosevelt: A Biography (New York: Harcourt Brace Janovich, 1956), 41. This interpretation is heavily reliant on Blum, The Republican Roosevelt 7-9. Also see G. Wallace Chessman, Theodore Roosevelt and the Politics of Power (Boston: Little Brown and Company, 1969), 24-26.

19. Theodore Roosevelt, "The Duties of American Citizenship" in The Works of Theodore Roosevelt: National Edition (New York: Charles Scribner's Sons, 1926), XIII, 286-87.

20. Blum, The Republican Roosevelt, 7.

21. For good descriptions of Roosevelt's initial impact on the legislature see Pringle, Theodore Roosevelt, 46-48; Behl, "Speech Preparation and Delivery," 113; and Richard Hofstadter, Anti-intellectualism in American Life (New York: Alfred Knopf, 1970), 192. Hunt is quoted in Hofstadter.

22. Behl, "Speech Preparation and Delivery," 112; Putnam, Theodore Roosevelt: The Formative Years, 288.

23. Roosevelt reportedly coined the expression "bully pulpit" while previewing a speech for friends in the White House. See Lyman Abott, Silhouettes of My Contemporaries (New York: Doubleday Page and Co., 1921), 95.

24. Roosevelt, An Autobiography, 66.

25. The best brief analysis of Roosevelt's relationship with the press is still the chapter on Roosevelt in James E. Pollard, The Presidents and the Press (New York: MacMillan Company, 1947).

26.   Aloysius A. Norton, <u>Theodore Roosevelt</u> (Boston: Twayne Publishers, 1980), 23.

2
The Rhetoric
of Militant Decency

If I wished to accomplish anything for the country," observed Theodore Roosevelt looking back on his career, "my business was to combine decency and efficiency; to be a thoroughly practical man of high ideals who did his best to reduce those ideals to actual practice." Roosevelt always perceived himself to be a lay preacher, as did those to whom he spoke. Once asked by students at Cambridge University to refrain from preaching to them, Roosevelt replied, "I will promise to preach as little as I can, but you must take your chances, for it is impossible to break the habit of a lifetime at the bidding of a comparative stranger." The essence of Roosevelt's lifetime of lay sermons was captured by his close friend William Allan White. "Over and over the theme is hammered into the mind and heart of the multitude: be good, be good, be good; live for righteousness, fight for righteousness, and if need be die for it. Nothing else matters but to be militantly decent."[1]

Theodore Roosevelt spent a lifetime in public service preaching the gospel of militant decency. Throughout his public career Roosevelt was always preaching. Philander Knox claimed that when Roosevelt retired from the presidency, "he should be made a bishop." Reports of his addresses often referred to them as ethical discourses. Roosevelt rejoiced in each political victory, recognizing that with each victory came yet a more prestigious "bully pulpit" from which to preach his gospel of militant decency.[2]

Three Rooseveltian characteristics informed on his speaking. First was his vigorously enthusiastic personality. Observers consistently spoke of Roosevelt's delighted enthusiasm for virtually any project he undertook or cause he addressed. One observer claimed that Roosevelt exhibited a "certain boyish zest" for everything he did. Nicholas Murray Butler felt that "no man in my time has been so happy" as Roosevelt. Roosevelt's enthusiasm for any cause for which he spoke is evident in virtually all of his speaking.

Yet, Roosevelt's highly animated delivery did not reflect an excited extemporaneous delivery. Rather, as one of Roosevelt's cabinet members claimed,

it was seldom that he spoke extemporaneously. The fire and animation which he imparted in the delivery of his speeches certainly conveyed no impression that they might have been carefully prepared and considered at a desk in a study. The pages of his manuscript were so small and inconspicuous that they did not interfere with his natural gestures. The effect was almost as if he spoke extemporaneously. The written address, printed on sheets about 3 x 6 inches and held in one hand, was completely lost sight of by the audience in those moments when Colonel Roosevelt became emphatic. In those moments he also interspersed extemporaneous remarks which brought out his argument more vividly and forcefully.[3]

Many factors contributed to Roosevelt's evident enthusiasm when he spoke. There is no doubt that one of them was Roosevelt's confidence that he was right. For the second characteristic of Roosevelt, which manifested itself in virtually all of his speaking, was his belief that answers to public questions involved fundamental rights and wrongs. He believed that underlying most public questions were questions of basic morality. Moral judgments reflect themselves in his speaking on a plethora of public issues. One of Roosevelt's principal biographers has observed that Roosevelt believed, "to begin with, that there was an absolute standard of right, second, that it was his duty to live by it to the letter, and third, that this duty included an obligation to lead others in the same direction."[4]

Roosevelt's pursuit of his standard of right, which manifested itself in much of his speaking, was tempered by an awareness of what could be accomplished. Roosevelt was, after all, among the consummate political figures of his age. Roosevelt's sense of the attainable, the practical, is the third overriding characteristic of his speaking, and they appear in speech after speech, on issue after issue. Roosevelt well recognized that good intentions were valueless without the means to achieve them. In an address at the Pacific Theological Seminary on March 24, 1911, Roosevelt urged potential clergymen to preach "realizable ideals," and "avoid preaching, as desirable, ideals which cannot be measurably attained."

Although Roosevelt's awareness of the need to temper the ideal with the attainable often resulted in his being criticized for compromising, he held to this belief throughout his life. In the last words he wrote for publication, Roosevelt claimed that he had nothing but "utter scorn for words that are not made good by deeds."[5]

Roosevelt's contagious enthusiasm, his belief that public questions involved elemental rights and wrongs, and his sense of the attainable, all informed his speaking. Roosevelt's speaking reflects what biographer John Morton Blum called his lifetime "quest for the moral." Exactly what Roosevelt meant by morality and decency might not always be precisely clear. Nevertheless, an analysis of his speaking suggests that probably without any design or plan, five basic themes, commonplaces, or topoi consistently appear in his speeches. These themes or topics constitute the basis of Roosevelt's beliefs that William Allan White so aptly characterized as militant decency.[6]

Many of the five basic themes that undergird his speaking were already evident by the time the twenty-four-year-old Roosevelt was first elected to the New York State Assembly. At different stages of Roosevelt's career he confronted different issues, and hence different themes were more fully developed at different periods of his public life. Nevertheless, by 1882 and the beginning of Roosevelt's public life in the New York legislature, through 1901 and his assumption of the presidency upon the assasination of William McKinley, and throughout the eighteen years of his life that followed, Roosevelt's public speaking consistently reflected five basic topoi. An examination of these themes, his gospel of militant decency, constitutes the remainder of this chapter.

POWER

Writing two years after he left the presidency, Roosevelt claimed that "our chief usefulness to humanity rests on our combining power with high purpose. Power undirected by high purpose spells calamity; and high purpose by itself is utterly useless if the power to put it into effect is lacking."[7] The acquisition and appropriate use of power was a lifelong concern of Theodore Roosevelt, and was reflected in his speaking in three ways. First, he frequently spoke about the importance of power for the individual. Second, he frequently spoke about the importance of power for the nation. Third, he frequently spoke about the importance of power for the proper conduct of the office of president.

Every student of Roosevelt is familiar with the chronic asthma that he spent his entire childhood and early manhood fighting. Striking him in infancy, his asthma steadily worsened throughout his childhood.   It became a family problem, dictating where and when the Roosevelts would travel and vacation, the nature of the education they provided their children, and a host of other family decisions.

Through the application of his own determination to the task of body building, Roosevelt acquired the stamina necessary to live a normal active life.   Recalling one of the crucial incidents that motivated him, Roosevelt provides us with a partial explanation for his emphasis on the importance of power for the individual:

> Having an attack of asthma, I was sent off by myself to Moosehead Lake.   On the stagecoach ride thither I encountered a couple of other boys who were about my own age, but very much more competent and also much more mischievous.   I have no doubt they were good-hearted boys, but they were boys!   They found that I was a foreordained and predestined victim, and industriously proceeded to make life miserable for me.   The worst feature was that when I finally tried to fight them I discovered that either one singly could not only handle me with easy contempt, but handle me so as not to hurt me much and yet to prevent my doing any damage whatever in return.
>
> The experience taught me what probably no amount of good advice could have taught me. I made up my mind that I must try to learn so that I would not again be put in such a helpless position; and having become quickly and bitterly conscious that I did not have the natural prowess to hold my own, I decided that I would try to supply its place by training.[8]

At this point in his life Roosevelt seriously began to learn to box.   Incidents such as these no doubt made him aware of the importance of physical and other forms of power for the individual.   His own helplessness motivated his physical development that culminated with his intensely physical experiences as a rancher in the South Dakota bad lands.[9]

One often forgets that when Roosevelt spoke about the importance of power for the individual and its acquisition through practicing the strenuous life, he spoke to a nation that was highly receptive.   Exercise and sport were coming of age in the late nineteenth century.   As Roosevelt urged physical fitness and strenuosness upon his countrymen, admonishing them to "hit the line hard," they were already doing so.   Roosevelt exhorted his countrymen to develop their physical prowess at the very time that James Naismith was inventing basketball to give them some means of channeling their impulses for sport and exercise during the winter. He preached physical fitness as the nation became so enamored of baseball that the nation's first professional baseball team, the Cincinnati Redstockings, spawned two entire leagues of professional teams and countless millions of players and fans. Even women were not exempt from the stress on physical development. A special "female frame" was developed to enable women to bicycle with their male friends. Women's equipment for a variety of sports soon followed. Indeed, as Roosevelt preached physical fitness, the nation's newsstands witnessed the introduction of a new publication <u>Physical Culture</u> with a motto Roosevelt no doubt found to be just bully, "Weakness is a crime."[10]

If weakness was a crime for individuals, Roosevelt found it even more of a crime for nations. His speaking clearly indicated that he believed that power was important for both individuals and nations to acquire and use appropriately. From almost the outset of his public career to his 1915-18 speaking campaigns on behalf of preparedness and the war effort, Roosevelt was constantly admonishing his countrymen to acquire the strong military necessary for national power. Moreover, he urged them to be willing, if necessary, to use their power.

Roosevelt's family heritage directed his early military interests to the navy. At Harvard he wrote the early chapters of what became his naval history of the War of 1812. The lesson of that war was simple: Be prepared. Roosevelt felt that the naval policies of the Jefferson and Madison administrations had been shortsighted. Those policies had resulted in the United States entering the War of 1812 with a decidedly inferior navy that placed the nation at an initial disadvantage that took considerable effort to overcome, and could well have proven fatal to the United States war effort.[11]

Roosevelt concluded his first address as assistant secretary of the navy, which many biographers claim was his first great speech, with a strong appeal for national power. Speaking at the Naval War College in June, 1897, he claimed that

> we ask for a great navy, we ask for an armament fit for the nation's needs, not primarily to fight, but to avert fighting. Preparedness deters the foe, and maintains right by the show of ready might without the use of violence. Peace, like freedom, is not a gift that tarries long in the hands of cowards, or of those too feeble or too shortsighted to deserve it; and we ask to be given the means to insure that honorable peace which alone is worth having.[12]

Passages such as these are typical of Roosevelt's development of the importance of national power, for they combine a call for appropriate arms with a recognition that such arms may ultimately serve best by avoiding the need to fight. Although Roosevelt's critics called him reckless and bellicose, both for his language and his actions (such as his role in building the Panama Canal and his show of American military strength by sending the Great White fleet around the world in 1907) the fact remains that under his stewardship the United States was never at war. Moreover, he remains the only sitting American president to win the Nobel Peace Prize.

There is a logical connection between Roosevelt's stress on the importance of physical power for the individual and his stress on the importance of military power for the nation. Military power was one important facet of national power. But national power also involved a healthy and physically strong population with a high birth rate. Moreover, for Roosevelt, national power required the development of the country's resources and the development of a strong industrial machine. Roosevelt believed that national strength involved much more than just a strong military machine.[13]

When Roosevelt assumed the presidency in 1901 he became the youngest man to have ever held that office. In subsequent years he proved himself to be among the most active men to have ever held the office. The acquisition and appropriate use of power by the president is the final aspect of power as a topoi in Roosevelt's speaking. Roosevelt claimed that as president "it was not only his right but his duty to do anything that the needs of the nation demanded unless such action was forbidden by the Constitution or by the law."[14]

Like many leaders, Roosevelt delighted in the exercise of power. As president, he had more power at his disposal than ever before. Frequently, in defending his actions as president, he found it necessary to share his perceptions of that office with his audiences. Recognizing that he had clearly broadened the use of executive power, Roosevelt typically defended his use of presidential power by asserting that he was acting for the public welfare.[15]

In sum, Theodore Roosevelt's speaking evidences a constant concern for the acquisition and appropriate use of power by the individual, by the nation, and by the nation's chief executive officer.

ORDER

Theodore Roosevelt's concern for power was often linked to his concern for order. Order is the second topoi of Roosevelt's gospel of militant decency. For Roosevelt, power

was a means of attaining order. Order was inseparably linked
in his belief system with justice, equality, and the need for
reform. This linkage was solidified in Roosevelt's mind by
Jacob Riis.[16]

The need to deal with legislation that came before the
New York State Assembly in the early 1880's had sensitized
Roosevelt to the plight of the working poor, as had his father's
many charitable works. That sensitivity was heightened, and
a lifelong friendship was forged, when Roosevelt read Jacob
Riis's How the Other Half Lives, which depicted life in the
tenement district of New York City in the 1880s. Riis described
their first meeting.

> He came into my office one day when I was out
> and left his card with the simple words written
> in pencil upon it: "I have read your book, and I
> have come to help." That was the beginning. .
> . . It was like a man coming to enlist for a war
> because he believed in the cause, and truly he
> did.[17]

Riis took Roosevelt throughout the city, acquainting him
with tenement life. The tenements touched Roosevelt deeply.
Residing in New York City, and serving as one of its police
commissioners, Roosevelt acquired firsthand experience with the
urban poverty portrayed in the writings of America's "new
realism" school of literature. Roosevelt read and associated
with many chroniclers of urban poverty. He numbered among
his friends William Dean Howells, Hamlin Garland, Richard
Harding Davis, Brander Matthews, Lincoln Steffens, and
Stephen Crane, as well as Riis.[18] This firsthand awareness of
the squalor of the working poor and the near impossibility of
their escape provided the undergirding rationale for Roosevelt's
concern with order and his linking of the need for order with
justice, equality, and reform.

The poverty of the tenements opened Theodore
Roosevelt's eyes to the need for reform. Indeed, he feared that
the terrible living conditions of the urban poor might well give
rise to social revolution if reform did not ameliorate the
situation. Roosevelt was a man who had been taught to
respect authority. He brooked no sympathy with radicals of
any stripe. He attacked men like John Peter Altgeld, William
Jennings Bryan, Eugene Debs, William Haywood, Edward
Bellamy, and Henry George with characteristic invective.[19]

Yet Roosevelt recognized that these reformers addressed
conditions that the industrial United States could not long
tolerate. Hence, although he constantly spoke against what he
perceived to be the wild-eyed revolutionary ideas of his day, he
called for acceptable changes made in an orderly fashion. "I
have always maintained," wrote Roosevelt,

> that our worst revolutionaries today are those
> reactionaries who do not see and will not admit
> that there is any need for change. . . . Some
> of these reactionaries are not bad men, but
> merely short-sighted and belated. It is these
> reactionaries, however, who, by standing pat on
> industrial injustice, incite inevitably to industrial
> revolt, and it is only we who advocate political
> and industrial democracy who render possible the
> progress of our American industry on large
> constructive lines with a minimum of friction.[20]

Importantly, Roosevelt sought to maintain order, as the above statement indicates, not simply by controlling radical social and economic reformers, but also by controlling their twin evil, men of great wealth who remained excessively conservative.

Roosevelt recognized that these twin evils at the extremes of society, radical social and economic reformers on one hand and those he termed "malefactors of great wealth" on the other, both had the potential to disrupt American society. In the name of maintaining order, Roosevelt could be honestly againt the abuses of big business, but also sincerely against indiscriminate trust-busting. He could be in favor of reform, but he could dislike militant reformers. Such equivocations are necessary for any practical politician. What is remarkable, as Richard Hofstadter has observed, is that while such equivocations "often sound weak and halting in the mouths of the ordinary politican, Roosevelt had a way of giving them a fine aggressive surge."[21] One student of Roosevelt's childhood claimed that

> if any youth could be said to have had an inborn
> perception of an orderly universe and of the duty
> of man to obey a fundamental law, that youth
> was Roosevelt. His father's teaching and example
> simply fortified it. And Roosevelt's thoroughness,
> his native zeal in this, as in all things, left no
> room for compromise.[22]

Thus, the second major theme found in Roosevelt's speeches is order. Roosevelt's speaking revealed a man, like the youth, seeking an orderly universe, desirous of obeying fundamental law. For Roosevelt, order was linked with justice and reform. Because of social and economic injustices, order could be threatened by social upheaval such as that advocated by radicals. Roosevelt, more than most leaders of his class, was sensitive to this problem. Order could also be threatened by men of great wealth who remained insensitive to the need to provide opportunity to the underclasses through social and economic reform. Roosevelt spoke to preserve order, but it was not order imposed by either radical reform or by sheer

economic might.   Rather, Roosevelt spoke on behalf of order
that balanced these twin evils by encouraging just social and
economic reform.

WORK

Speaking at the Quarter-centennial Celebration of
Statehood for Colorado at Colorado Springs on August 2, 1901,
Theodore Roosevelt gave voice to the third topoi of his gospel of
moral decency-work.   "We hold work," Roosevelt told his
audience,

> not as a curse but as a blessing, and we regard
> the idler with scornful pity. It would be in the
> highest degree undesirable that we should all
> work in the same way or at the same things, and
> for the sake of the real greatness of the nation
> we should in the fullest and most cordial way
> recognize the fact that some of the most needed
> work must, from its very nature, be
> unremunerative in a material sense. Each man
> must choose so far as the conditions allow him
> the path to which he is bidden by his own
> particular powers and inclinations. But if he is
> a man, he must in some way or shape do a
> man's work. If, after making all the effort that
> his strength of body and of mind permits, he yet
> honorably fails, why he is still entitled to a
> certain share of respect because he has made the
> effort. But if he does not make the effort, or if
> he makes it halfheartedly and recoils from the
> labor, the risk, or the irksome monotony of his
> task, why, he has forfeited all right to our
> respect, and has shown himself a mere cumberer
> of the earth. It is not given to us all to succeed,
> but it is given to us all to strive manfully to
> deserve success.[23]

For Roosevelt, if working was not itself a religious act
worthy of the highest praise, then surely indolence was a sinful
act, worthy of the highest scorn. Working, striving, exerting
effort, were expected of everyone by Roosevelt, just as he
expected them of institutions and nations.   In his
autobiography, Roosevelt virtually characterized work as an
eleventh commandment. "The law of worthy effort, the law of
service for a worthy end," he wrote, "without regard to whether
it brings pleasure or pain, is the only right law of life, whether
for man or for woman."[24]

Roosevelt's adherence to the work ethic is well known.
President at the age of forty-two and already a respected

historian, naturalist, military figure, and even cowboy, there was no task that he undertook without throwing himself wholeheartedly into it. The desire to work, to make worthy effort, is evident in many of his decisions. For example, pressed by his close friend Henry Cabot Lodge in early 1900 to indicate his intentions about seeking the vice-presidency, Roosevelt responded characteristically.

> The only thing for me to do is to do exactly as I always have done; and that is, when there is a chance of attempting a bit of work worth the trial, to attempt it. . . . Now the thing to decide at the moment is whether I shall try for the governorship again or accept the vice-presidency, if offered. . . . There is ample work left for me to do in another term-work that will need all of my energy and capacity-in short, work well worth any man's doing. . . . But in the Vice-Presidency I could do nothing. I am a comparatively young man yet and I like to work. I do not like to be a figurehead. It would not entertain me to preside in the Senate. . . . I could not <u>do</u> anything; and yet I would be seeing continually things that I would like to do, and very possibly would like to do differently from the way in which they were being done.[25]

Roosevelt's belief in the gospel of work, so evident in his own life, was manifest repeatedly in his speeches. Moreover, his comments on work often reflected his high regard for family life. He believed that women, like men, should strive to work on behalf of worthy causes. Roosevelt, reflecting the age in which he lived but showing surprising sensitivity to feminist concerns for a man of his generation, claimed that

> the woman must realize that she has no more right to shirk the business of wifehood and motherhood than the man has to shirk his business as bread-winner for the household. Women should have free access to every field of labor which they care to enter, and when their work is as valuable as that of a man it should be paid as highly. Yet normally for the man and the woman whose welfare is more important than the welfare of any other human beings, the woman must remain the housemother, the homekeeper, and the man must remain the bread-winner, the provider for the wife who bears his children and for the children she brings into the world. No other work is as valuable or as exacting for either man or woman; it must always in every healthy

society, be for both man and woman the prime
work, the most important work; normally all other
work is of secondary importance, and must come
as an addition to, not a substitute for, this
primary work. The partnership should be one of
equal rights, one of love, or self-respect, and
unselfishness, above all a partnership for the
performance of the most vitally important of all
duties. The performance of duty, and not an
indulgence in vapid ease and vapid pleasure, is
all that makes life worthwhile.[26]

Theodore Roosevelt believed in the work ethic and that belief
resounds throughout his speaking as the third principle topoi
of his gospel of militant decency.

SOCIAL RESPONSIBILITY

The fourth topoi that characterized Roosevelt's speaking
was his belief that each individual has social responsibilities.
This belief reflects the social gospel preaching of Roosevelt's
era. Preachers and theologians, championing the social gospel
movement during the period 1875-1915, claimed that the
Kingdom of God should be built through social reform. Russell
Conwell, John Ryan, Walter Rauschenbush, George Herron, and
others led a growing number of liberal ministers who sought to
apply religious principles in business and government to help
ameliorate the problems of the day.[27]

Roosevelt's speaking on behalf of individual social
responsibility is distinctly religious in character and reflects
three themes that were also commonly used in the social gospel
pulpits of his day: reform, service, and tolerance. These were
the key elements of the fourth topoi of Roosevelt's gospel of
moral decency-social responsibility.

The religious character of this theme is evident in many
of Roosevelt's comments about reform. He often referred to
those who opposed his favored reforms as evil, evildoers, or
the authors of evil. The spiritual virtue of reform is presented
in such passages as the one Roosevelt used to close a February
1912 magazine piece. "All reforms of first-class importance,"
Roosevelt wrote, "must look toward raising both men and
women to a higher level, alike as regards the things of the body
and as regards the things of the soul."[28]

Roosevelt championed a host of social and economic
reforms throughout his public life. He is best remembered for
his early reform advocacy of the conservation of natural
resources, the use of civil service laws, and of course, the
Progressive movement. His speaking on these issues assumed
a more religious tone than much of his other speaking. It was

entirely natural for Roosevelt, after an extensive explanation and defense of the Progressive governmental and economic reforms he advocated, to refer to his beliefs in these reforms as "a confession of faith." Similarly, it is characteristic of Roosevelt's speaking on reform to claim, as he did in his last speech before the Republican Convention of 1912, that he was "fighting for the loftiest of causes." "We fight," Roosevelt preached on that memorable Chicago evening of June 17, 1912, "in honorable fashion for the good of mankind; fearless of the future; unheeding of our individual fates; with unflinching hearts and undimmed eyes; we stand at Armageddon, and we battle for the Lord."[29] The Republican Convention nevertheless rejected him, thus giving rise to his Progressive party candidacy.

Although the religious tones of Roosevelt's speaking on social responsibility are perhaps most evident when he urged social and economic reform, he believed that social responsibility involved more than simple reforms. The second facet of social responsibility was service to society. Roosevelt gave voice to this theme in his February 23, 1907, address at the Harvard Union. "The religious man who is most useful," he claimed, "is not he whose sole care is to save his own soul, but the man whose religion bids him strive to advance decency and clean living and to make the world a better place for his fellows to live in."[30]

Roosevelt's belief in the importance of serving society is evident in his analysis of his own public life:

Almost immediately after leaving Harvard in 1880 I began to take an interest in politics. I did not then believe, and I do not now believe, that any man should ever attempt to make politics his only career. It is a dreadful misfortune for a man to grow to feel that his whole livelihood and whole happiness depend upon his staying in office. Such a feeling prevents him from being of real service to the people while in office.

In a passage whose truth rings more clearly today in an age of government by poll than it did in his own time, Roosevelt noted that a political figure should always have "some other occupation-I had several occupations-to which he can resort at any time he is thrown out of office." Only by maintaining his independence, Roosevelt concluded, can a political figure hope to provide true service to the people.[31]

The final component of Roosevelt's concept of social responsibility was tolerance. Roosevelt's tolerance manifested itself in both words and actions. Roosevelt believed firmly in the Judeo-Christian heritage. But within the broad ethical values of that heritage he was far more religiously tolerant than most Americans of his day. Moreover, while he had strong feelings for the contributions of the white Anglo-Saxon race, to which he attributed much of the world's progress, his belief in fair play and individual abilities made him far more tolerant of racial diversity than most Americans of his day.

Throughout his public career Roosevelt meet with religious leaders of all faiths. Consistently, he appointed men of all faiths to public office. In 1904 he claimed that the day would soon come when a Catholic would contend for the presidency and asserted that he would gladly support a Roman Catholic for the presidency if he was the best qualified candidate. In 1906 he appointed Oscar Straus to serve as his secretary of commerce and labor, making Straus the first cabinet appointee of the Jewish faith.[32]

Similarly, Roosevelt constantly consulted with and appointed blacks. He was heavily criticised for inviting Booker T. Washington, the famed black educator, to dine with him at the White House. Indeed, in 1884 Roosevelt delivered his first nationally reported speech when he spoke on behalf of the election of John R. Lynch of Mississippi, a black, to chair the Republican National Convention. Addressing the convention on June 3, Roosevelt noted that

> it is now, Mr. Chairman, less than a quarter of
> a century since, in this city, the great Republican
> party organized for victory and nominated
> Abraham Lincoln of Illinois, who broke the fetters
> of the slaves and rent them asunder forever. It
> is a fitting thing for us to choose to preside over
> this convention one of that race whose right to
> sit within these walls is due to the blood and the
> treasure so lavishly spent by the founders of the
> Republican party.[33]

Roosevelt's racial tolerance was further evidenced in his attitudes toward the Chinese. He used his Fifth Annual Message in 1905 to chastise those who would discriminate against the Chinese. He pointed out that while fear of Chinese coolies, unskilled laborers, might have some validity, Americans had done "grave injustice and wrong," to the people of China by acting as though the entire country was made up of unskilled laborers and discriminating against them accordingly in immigration and other policies. Importantly, Roosevelt observed that discriminatory policies hurt not only the Chinese, but ultimately they also hurt the United States as well.[34] Hence, although Roosevelt was a man of his time, subject to many of the prejudices that afflicted his era, he was far more tolerant than many of his contemporaries of those who had different religious beliefs and were born of different racial stock. Raised in the Dutch Reform Church, Roosevelt urged toleration for all whose beliefs fell within the mainstream of the Judeo-Christian heritage.   He admired the white Anglo-Saxons to whom he attributed much of civilization's progress, but he preferred to see people treated on their own individual merit, and spoke to that end.   A 1904 Republican campaign biography did not exaggerate when it claimed that Roosevelt "knows not race, creed, color, clique, class, descent or sectional divisions: he knows only Americans."[35]

In sum, the fourth topoi that characterized Roosevelt's rhetoric of militant decency, social responsibility, involved three basic themes.   First, social responsibility involved reform.   It was through reform, accomplished within the framework of fundamental religious principles, that social and economic problems of the day would be ameliorated.   Second, social responsibility involved service to society.   Finally, social responsibility involved tolerance for those of other faiths and other colors in the melting pot that was Roosevelt's America.

CHARACTER

The final and the paramount topoi that marked the speaking of Theodore Roosevelt was his belief in the importance of character.   "Alike for the nation and the individual," Roosevelt claimed, "the one indispensable requisite is character-character that does and dares as well as endures, character that is active in the performance of virtue no less than firm in the refusal to do aught that is vicious or degraded."   Virtually all Roosevelt scholars concur in claiming that if Roosevelt had one supreme belief, it was in character.   That belief in character manifested itself repeatedly in his speeches, taking two forms.   It manifested itself first in Roosevelt's speaking about the individual.   It manifested itself second in Roosevelt's speaking about the nation.[36]

Roosevelt felt that "the chief factor in any given man's success or failure must be that man's own character." Acknowledging that both individuals and nations can be affected by a variety of actions, beliefs, laws, and other factors, he nevertheless maintained that individual character must ultimately be recognized as the "most important" of all factors governing success.[37]

Roosevelt claimed that "there are three essential qualities going to make up character.   In the first place, there is honesty."   But honesty, Roosevelt continued, "is not enough. I don't care how honest a man is, if he is timid he is no good." Hence, Roosevelt claimed, "You need honesty and then you need courage; but both of them together are not enough."   So, Roosevelt concluded, "There is a third quality; that is, you must possess the saving grace of common sense."   If these were the three essential qualities of character, on other occasions Roosevelt added to them. Most notably, character also involved doing "a great many things which imply much effort of will and readiness to face what is disagreeable. . . . Perhaps there is no more important component of character than steadfast resolution."[38]

Honesty and moral virtue were always issues with Roosevelt. As one of his principal biographers has observed, "Clearly Roosevelt believed in the Decalogue and judged in its terms." But, as the passage above illustrates, Roosevelt also believed that one needed the courage to speak out and to act upon one's beliefs. He believed not simply in honesty and virtue, but in, as Roosevelt scholar Hermann Hagedorn has termed it, "heroic virtue." Continually, Roosevelt's speeches exhorted his fellow citizens to display character, heroic virtue. On occasion, as when he judged the merit of celebrated Russian writer Maxim Gorki's work on the basis of Gorki's private life, one might question whether Roosevelt always followed his own advice to balance the concern for honesty and courage with the saving grace of common sense. Nevertheless, if occasionally one questioned Roosevelt's action or judgment, his speeches reflected a salutary need to justify his behavior as consistent with what any man of character might have done.[39]

Roosevelt's concern with character went beyond a concern for the actions of individual citizens. He was equally concerned that nations act with character. "It is character," he suggested on April 27, 1900,

> that counts in a nation as in a man. It is a good thing to have a keen fine intellectual development in a nation, to produce orators, artists, successful businessmen, but it is an infinitely greater thing to have those solid qualities which we group together under the name of character-sobriety, steadfastness, the sense of obligation toward one's neighbor and one's God, hard common sense, and combined with it, the lift of generous enthusiasm toward whatever is right. These are the qualities which go to make up true national greatness.[40]

Roosevelt continually urged that the nation conduct its domestic policy in a manner befitting a country possessed of unusually strong character. As John Blum so incisively illustrated, Roosevelt felt that the central domestic issue of his time was the control of business. He was not concerned about the size of business, but about the policies of business. He was not concerned about the size of business profits, but about the manner in which businessmen made their profits. It was the morality of business, the character of its leaders as they carried out their professional activities, that worried him. The goal of Roosevelt's Square Deal was to make business act honestly, courageously, with common sense, and if sometimes necessary, to do what was disagreeable.

Similarly, Roosevelt continually urged the nation to conduct its foreign policy in a manner befitting a country of strong character. He summed up his own conduct of foreign policy by observing that

> during the seven and a half years that I was president, this nation behaved in international matters toward all other nations precisely as an honorable man behaves to his fellow man. We made no promise which we could not and did not keep. We made no threat which we did not carry out. We never failed to assert our rights in the face of the strong, and we never failed to treat both strong and weak with courtesy and justice; and against the weak when they misbehaved we were slower to assert our rights than we were against the strong."[41]

Although specific foreign policies of Roosevelt's administration might be subject to question, Roosevelt's speeches reflected a salutary need to justify his foreign policy as consistent with what a nation of character should do. Thus, the final topoi or theme of Roosevelt's rhetoric of militant decency is his belief, for both individuals and nations, in the importance of character.

CONCLUSION

Elihu Root, who served as his secretary of state, claimed of Theodore Roosevelt, that

> he did not originate great new truths, but he drove old fundamental truths into the minds and the hearts of his people so that they stuck and dominated. Old truths he insisted upon, enlarged upon, repeated over and over in many ways with quaint and interesting and attractive forms of expression, never straining for novelty or originality, but always driving, driving home the deep fundamental truths of public life, of a great self-governing democracy, the eternal truths upon which justice and liberty must depend among men.[42]

Five old, deep, fundamental truths characterized the vast body of Theodore Roosevelt's public speaking. These truths served as topoi for his speaking. As Root observed, Roosevelt insisted upon them, enlarged upon them, and repeated them over and over in many ways, for he perceived them to be an appropriate basis for dealing with virtually every issue upon which he spoke. Internally consistent among themselves, collectively these five topoi can be characterized as a belief in militant decency.

Theodore Roosevelt's rhetoric was militant because he was not bashful about seeking power. He spoke of empowering the individual, the nation, and the president, who best embodied the nation. Roosevelt's rhetoric was decent because once empowered, he urged individuals, nations, and their leaders, to use those powers for just ends.

Theodore Roosevelt's rhetoric was militant because Roosevelt actively pursued social order, attacking both the radical reformer and the malefactor of great wealth, for fear that their policies would ultimately disrupt the social order. Roosevelt's rhetoric was decent because Roosevelt was among the first Americans, and perhaps the first of major stature, to recognize how the economic changes of his day impacted on political freedom. He spoke to maintain an orderly political democracy, while treating those at both ends of the economic spectrum, the poor and the wealthy, with justice and equality.

Theodore Roosevelt's rhetoric was militant because he recognized that few things of value were ever attained without worthy effort, without work. He urged his countrymen to strive to fulfill their ambitions, to live the strenuous life, to work. Roosevelt's rhetoric was decent because he believed that the work of both men and women should be directed towards the development of society.

Theodore Roosevelt's rhetoric was militant because he beseeched his countrymen to actively assume their social responsibilities. He urged them to be militant in seeking reform, in seeking to serve, in tolerating those of different faiths and colors. Roosevelt's rhetoric was decent because one's social responsibilities were for eminently decent goals: equality in the voting booth, in the workplace, under the law; service to the nation; and tolerance of one's fellow man.

Theodore Roosevelt's rhetoric was militant, finally, because he exhorted men and nations to strive to exemplify nobel character. For Roosevelt character involved not simply beliefs, but also actively pursuing and speaking for those beliefs. Roosevelt's rhetoric was decent, finally, because for Roosevelt good character, in its essence, involved belief and action that was consistent with those two most fundamentally decent guideposts of Western Civilization-the Decalogue and the Golden Rule.

NOTES

1.   Theodore Roosevelt, An Autobiography (New York: Charles Scribner's Sons, 1926), 91. This edition of Roosevelt's autobiography serves as volume twenty in The Works of Theodore Roosevelt: National Edition (New York: Charles Scribner's Sons, 1926. Theodore Roosevelt, The Strenuous Life (New York: Charles Scribner's Sons, 1926), 572. This edition of The Strenuous Life is in volume thirteen of The Works of Theodore Roosevelt: National Edition. William Allan White, "Saith The Preacher," in The Works of Theodore Roosevelt, 13, xi.

2.   William Behl, "Theodore Roosevelt's Principles of Invention," Speech Monographs 14 (1947): 95 for the comments of Knox and journalists. Roosevelt is reported to have coined his much quoted expression "bully pulpit" while previewing a speech for friends in the White House. See Lyman Abbott, Silhouettes of My Contemporaries (New York: Doubleday Page and Co., 1921), 95.

3.   Butler and other observers are quoted in Aloysius A. Norton, Theodore Roosevelt (Boston: Twayne Publishers, 1980), 143; Oscar Straus Under Four Administrations: From Cleveland to Taft (Boston: Houghton Mifflin, 1922), 209. Roosevelt's enthusiastic delivery is also evident when one listens to the sound recordings or views the movies made of his speaking. Existing recordings and movies are virtually all of his presidential and post-presidential speaking.

4.   Carleton Putnam, Theodore Roosevelt: The Formative Years (New York: Charles Scribner's Sons, 1958), 603.

5.   Roosevelt's attempts to balance the ideal with the attainable have been recognized by all of his principal biographers. For an occasionally critical analysis of this characteristic of Roosevelt see Daniel Aaron, Men of Good Hope (New York: Oxford University Press, 1951), pp. 245-52; Theodore Roosevelt, "Realizable Ideals," The Works of Theodore Roosevelt: National Edition, 13, 615-29. For his last words see Edward H. Cotton, The Ideals of Theodore Roosevelt (New York: Appleton and Company, 1923), 204.

6.   John Morton Blum, The Republican Roosevelt (Cambridge, Mass.,: Harvard University Press, 1954), 85. It is unlikely that Roosevelt was aware of the classical concept of topoi for rhetorical invention. On this see Behl, "Invention," 94.

7. Theodore Roosevelt, "The Peace of Righteousness" in Works 16, 319.

8. Roosevelt, An Autobiography, 30-31.

9. Roosevelt, An Autobiography, 96-133 and Edmund Morris, The Rise of Theodore Roosevelt (New York: Coward, McCann & Geoghegan, Inc., 1979), 320-41 provide accounts of Roosevelt's exploits as a cowboy.

10. For insight into the growing importance of exercise and sport to Americans of Roosevelt's generation see Daniel J. Boorstin, The Americans: The Democratic Experience (New York: Random House, 1973), 404-06. For an exceptionally insightful analysis that suggests that Roosevelt was voicing the spirit of his times when he gave emphasis to physical prowess see Frederick Marks, Velvet on Ice: The Diplomacy of Theodore Roosevelt, (Lincoln: University of Nebraska Press, 1979), 15-16.

11. Roosevelt's maternal uncles had been Confederate navy officers and shared their experiences with Roosevelt during his boyhood. The importance of military preparedness is evident throughout Theodore Roosevelt, The Naval War of 1812, (New York: Charles Scribner's Sons, 1926). This edition of Roosevelt's study of the Naval War of 1812 is volume six in The Works of Theodore Roosevelt: National Edition (New York: Charles Scribner's Sons, 1926). For an excellent analysis of the relationship between Roosevelt and Admiral Mahan that suggests that it was Roosevelt who influenced Mahan's views on preparedness and not the reverse, see Peter Karstan, "The Nature of 'Influence': Roosevelt, Mahan and the Concept of Sea Power," American Quarterly 23 (October 1971): 585-99.

12. Theodore Roosevelt, "Washington's Forgotten Maxim," The Works of Theodore Roosevelt: National Edition (New York: Charles Scribner's Sons, 1926), 13, 198-99. All subsequent references to this speech are to this edition, which can be found among the collected speeches in this volume.

13. The best short analysis of Roosevelt's conceptions of national power is in Blum, The Republican Roosevelt, 125-26.

14. Roosevelt, An Autobiography, 347.

15. Roosevelt's most succinct explanation of his beliefs about presidential power can be found in Roosevelt, An Autobiography. See for example pp. 346-47; 375-76.

16. For insight on Roosevelt's relationship with Riis, see Jacob Riis, Theodore Roosevelt the Citizen (New York: The Outlook Company, 1904). Especially informative on the relationship between these two men is the section in which Riis treats Roosevelt's reactions to his book How The Other Half Lives and the section in which Riis discusses the two years when he reported on police activities and Roosevelt served as police commissioner.

17. Riis, Theodore Roosevelt the Citizen, 131-32.

18. Ellen Moers, "Teddy Roosevelt: Literary Feller," Columbia University Forum (Summer 1963): 10-16.

19. This explanation of Roosevelt's fear of radicals and his concern that social evils might give rise to radical change unless appropriate reforms were taken relies heavily on the work of John Morton Blum. See Blum, "The Years of Decision," in Elting E. Morison, ed. The Letters of Theodore Roosevelt, Vol. I: The Years of Preparation (Cambridge, Mass.,: Harvard University Press, 1951), 1492-93. Also see Blum, The Republican Roosevelt, pp. 108-09.

20. Roosevelt, An Autobiography, 475-76.

21. The phrase "malefactors of great wealth" was first used by Roosevelt in 1895. Richard Hofstadter, The American Political Tradition (New York: Vintage Books, 1948), 228.

22. Putnam, Theodore Roosevelt, 602.

23. Theodore Roosevelt, "Manhood and Statehood," in The Works of Theodore Roosevelt: National Edition, 13, 457.

24. Roosevelt, An Autobiography, 165.

25. Letter, Theodore Roosevelt to Henry Cabot Lodge, February 2, 1900, in Elting E Morison, ed., The Letters of Theodore Roosevelt: Years of Preparation. 2, 1160.

26. Roosevelt, An Autobiography, 167.

27. For an excellent overview of social gospel preaching see William Bos and Clyde Faries, "The Social Gospel: Preaching Reform 1875-1915," in Dewitte Holland, ed., Preaching In American History, (Nashville, Tenn.: Abington Press, 1969), 223-38.

28. Theodore Roosevelt, "Women's Rights: The Duties of Both Men and Women," The Outlook, February 3, 1912. This article is more readily available in Roosevelt, Works, 16, 208-19.

29. Theodore Roosevelt, "A Confession of Faith," Works, 17, pp. 254-99; Theodore Roosevelt, "The Case Against the Reactionaries," Works, 17, 204-31.

30. Theodore Roosevelt, "Athletics and Scholarship," Works, 13, 565-66.

31. Roosevelt, An Autobiography, 58. Also see 88-89.

32. Perhaps the best short discussion of Roosevelt's religious tolerance can be found in William H. Harbaugh, The Life and Times of Theodore Roosevelt, (New York: Collier Books, 1961), 214-17.

33. Theodore Roosevelt, "The Nomination for Temporary Chairman of the Republican Convention," Works, 14, 38.

34. Theodore Roosevelt, "Fifth Annual Message," Works, 15, 320-22.

35. Republican National Committee, Our Patriotic President (New York: Columbia Press, 1904), 1.

36. Theodore Roosevelt, "Character and Success," Works, 13, 386. On the primacy of Roosevelt's belief in character see Blum, The Republican Roosevelt, 33; David H. Burton, Theodore Roosevelt (New York: Twayne Publishers, 1972), 45-46; Carl A. Dallinger, "Theodore Roosevelt: The Preacher Militant," American Public Address: Studies in Honor of Albert Craig Baird, Loren Reid, ed. (Columbia: University of Missouri Press, 1961), 135; Harold Zyskind, "A Case Study in Philosophical Rhetoric: Theodore Roosevelt," Philosophy and Rhetoric, I (Summer 1968): pp. 228-30.

37. Roosevelt, An Autobiography, 165.

38. Theodore Roosevelt, The New Nationalism, (New York: The Outlook Company, 1910), 194-95; Roosevelt, Works 13, 384-85.

39. Blum, "Years of Decision," 1490; Hermann Hagadorn The Americanism of Theodore Roosevelt, (Boston: Houghton Mifflin Co., 1923), v.; Henry Pringle, Theodore Roosevelt: A

Biography, (New York: Harcourt Brace Janovich, 1956), 333-34; Marks, Velvet on Iron, 92-94.

40. Blum, The Republican Roosevelt, 116-121; Theodore Roosevelt, "Grant," Works, XIII, 437.

41. Roosevelt, An Autobiography, 491.

42. Root is quoted in the preface to Albert Bushnell Hart and Herbert Ferleger, eds., Theodore Roosevelt Cylopedia, (New York: Roosevelt Memorial Association, 1941), vi.

3
The Rhetoric
of Militant Decency
and Foreign Policy

Of all the aphorisms, bromides, platitudes and expressions coined or used by Theodore Roosevelt, surely the best remembered is: "Speak softly but carry a big stick." Understandably, Roosevelt, who argued vigorously throughout his public life for a strong military and who captured the public imagination as the gallant leader of the Rough Riders' charge up San Juan Hill, was readily identified with the second phrase of that statement. Editorial cartoonists pictured him countless times flourishing his big stick, or leaning ominously upon it. Editorial columnists reinforced the image of the aggressive, forceful, combative, pugnacious Roosevelt, brandishing his big stick.[1]

Historians have continued to foster and maintain Roosevelt's belligerent, combative image. Thomas Bailey has called Roosevelt "an apostle of Mars." Richard Hofstadter found that he stood for "the aggressive, masterful, fighting virtues of the soldier." I. E. Cadenhead has argued that the phrase "speak softly and carry a big stick," with the emphasis clearly on the "big stick," became the hallmark of Roosevelt's foreign policy.[2]

Yet, this emphasis on Roosevelt's "big stick" foreign policy, almost to the complete exclusion of the first statement, "speak softly," is neither accurate nor just. For Roosevelt's articulation and conduct of American foreign policy was governed by three topoi of militant decency that directed much of his public life.

First, his foreign policy speaking was marked by his emphasis on power. This aspect has often received undue attention, because it was not so much the use of power as it was the availability of power and the threat of power, that was important for Roosevelt. Roosevelt recognized that power, in the form of a strong military, gave the United States options. Though Roosevelt has been well remembered, and frequently criticized, for his militaristic cries for a big navy, a strong army, and the need for preparedness, the fact is that as president he never used that navy and army to make war. Throughout his administration, the United States was at peace. Roosevelt's most heralded use of the military was to send the Great White Fleet, the United States' battle fleet, around the world. His motives in doing so are revealing.

> In my own judgement the most important service that I rendered to peace was the voyage of the battle fleet around the world. I had become convinced that for many reasons it was essential that we should have it clearly understood by our own people especially, but also by other peoples, that the Pacific was as much our home waters as the Atlantic, and that our fleet could and would at will pass from one to the other of the two great oceans. It seemed to me evident that such a voyage . . . would make foreign nations accept as a matter of course that our fleet should from time to time be gathered in the Pacific, just as from time to time it was gathered in the Atlantic, and that its presence in one ocean was no more to be accepted as a mark of hostility to any Asiatic power than its presence in the Atlantic was to be accepted as a mark of hostility to any European power.

Roosevelt concluded by observing that when he left office, "we were at absolute peace," and "the cruise of the battle fleet was not the least of the causes which insured so peaceful an outlook."[3]

As historian Frederick W. Marks has ably illustrated, Roosevelt believed that nations were bound by moral codes, that powerful nations should act with restraint toward weaker nations, and, most importantly, that righteousness must come before peace. The readiness to employ force on behalf of righteousness, Roosevelt believed, would ultimately avoid the violence and injustice that weakness provoked. Roosevelt felt that the availability and threat of power was an essential element in the conduct of foreign policy, because it gave a nation a variety of otherwise unavailable options with which to secure righteousness.[4]

Second, Roosevelt's foreign policy speaking was marked by his emphasis on character. Roosevelt believed that the conduct of nations, like the conduct of individuals, should reflect sound moral character. A nation should be honest, it should have the courage to act, and it should act with common sense. These three components of character--honesty, courage, and common sense--should govern the actions of nations just as they governed the actions of individuals.

Third, Roosevelt's foreign policy speaking was marked by his emphasis on social responsibility. Just as individuals should behave in a socially responsible fashion, seeking reform, serving society, and behaving tolerantly toward others, so too should nations behave in a socially responsible fashion.

Thus, Roosevelt's foreign policy speaking was marked by reliance on three of the principal themes of militant decency. Though his statement, "Speak softly and carry a big stick," might well characterize Roosevelt's articulation and conduct of foreign policy, all too often undue stress has been placed on Roosevelt's "big stick diplomacy", reflecting his emphasis on national power. It should not be forgotten that Roosevelt first recommended speaking softly, appealing to character and social responsibility. The big stick should be used only if speaking softly failed. But he recognized that having the ability to fight might well be the best single deterrent to having to fight. These beliefs were evident in Roosevelt's foreign policy speaking throughout his career.

This chapter will illustrate Roosevelt's utilization of the themes of power, character, and social responsibility in his foreign policy speaking by focusing primarily on two of his foreign policy addresses. Biographer Edmund Morris has called "Washington's Forgotten Maxim," delivered at the Naval War College on June 2, 1897, "the first great speech" of Roosevelt's career, further characterizing it as "a fanfare call to arms."[5] The second address, "This Nation's Needs," was delivered on August 25, 1915, as the specter of World War I grew ever closer. Because of both the contents and circumstances of the speech, it attracted national attention and is highly representative of Roosevelt's preparedness speaking during the years preceding the United States'entry into World War I.

WASHINGTON'S FORGOTTEN MAXIM

Roosevelt was invited to address the students and faculty of the Naval War College by Rear Admiral Stephen B. Luce. The invitation was extended to Roosevelt both because of his position as assistant secretary of the navy and because of widespread recognition in the American naval establishment of Roosevelt's command of the concept of sea power. His first book, The Naval War of 1812, published fifteen years earlier, had established his reputation. In his subsequent writing, including letters, articles, reviews, and his biographies of Gouverneur Morris and Thomas Hart Benton, Roosevelt continued to demonstrate an appreciation and understanding of sea power rivaled by few Americans.   Though he was exceptionally well versed in his topic,   Theodore Roosevelt worked for over seven weeks on the address he presented at the Naval War College at Newport, Rhode Island, on June 2, 1897.[6]

Roosevelt opened his address to the faculty and students at the college by observing that "a century has passed since Washington wrote 'To be prepared for war is the most effectual means to promote peace.'" He claimed of Washington's remark that "the truth of the maxim is so obvious to every man of really far-sighted patriotism that its mere statement seems trite and useless; and it is not over-credible to either our intelligence or our love of country that there should be, as there is, need to dwell upon and amplify such a truism."   Nevertheless, Roosevelt continued his amplification of Washington's maxim by claiming that "in this country there is not the slightest danger of an overdevelopment of warlike spirit, and there has never been any such danger."   Roosevelt cited the American Revolution, the War of 1812, and a verse by James Russell Lowell, poet and diplomat, as he explicated Washington's remark through the first two pages of his address.[7]

Roosevelt's opening made use of one of the principal themes of his rhetoric of militant decency: power.   Roosevelt's claims that preparedness for war promotes peace and that preparedness never menaces peace were clearly designed to encourage the growth of American military power, particularly naval power.   This basic belief resounded through this speech and subsequently through much of Roosevelt's speaking, most notably in the years immediately prior to World War I. Moreover, his introduction reflected a variety of typically Rooseveltian rhetorical practices.   First, it was homiletic in nature. He opened with a text, in this case not from the Bible, but from Washington.   Like a clergyman, he devoted the opening passages of his address to amplifying, explaining, and illustrating the timeliness of his text. Second, the entire speech from the outset, as well as the principal sections of the speech, were organized deductively.   The speech started with a broad sweeping generalization, "To be prepared for war is the most effectual means to promote peace."   The remainder of the address moved deductively from this general claim to its specific applications.   Thirdly, though not as fully developed here as elsewhere in the speech, Roosevelt was already making use of his principal form of support material, historical example.

Following his introduction, Roosevelt moved to his first two major points in its amplification. "It is not only true that a peace may be so ignoble and degrading as to be worse than any war." he argued, "it is also true that it may be fraught with more bloodshed than most wars." Roosevelt spent almost four pages illustrating the first point by discussing the Turkish massacre of the Armenians, observing that it was facilitated by the reluctance of European leaders to resist Turkey. Moreover, he used the histories of England and Holland to laud people who have been willing to fight rather than tolerate an ignoble peace. Similarly, he cited Washington and Lincoln, our two most outstanding national leaders, as men who were also willing to fight if the alternative was an unjust, potentially bloody peace. The use of historical examples for support material was highly typical of Roosevelt's subsequent speaking. Indeed, throughout his life Roosevelt used historical example and his own assertions as the principal types of support material in his speeches.

Roosevelt's contentions reflected two of his basic topoi. That "a peace may be so ignoble and degrading as to be worse than any war," struck to Roosevelt's belief in character. Great nations, Roosevelt believed, were nations of character. Great character often involved the courage to act. The willingness to make war rather than accept an ignoble and degrading peace was a sign of national character. Moreover, the idea that peace "may be fraught with more bloodshed than most wars," struck to Roosevelt's belief in power. Nations with military power are able to wage quick and effective military campaigns, ending wars with less bloodshed than some peaces, such as those Roosevelt described.

In developing his contention that a peace may be so ignoble and degrading as to be worse than any war, Roosevelt made perhaps the most memorable statement in this address, and one that was frequently to be associated with him in subsequent years. "No triumph of peace," he claimed, "is quite so great as the supreme triumphs of war." This eminently quotable line subsequently was often used by critics as an indication of his supposed love of war. It perfectly evidences the characterizations of Roosevelt as the jingoistic, militaristic, pugnacious leader. What is oft forgotten is that this line was uttered by Roosevelt in his first major foreign policy address and he never again made such a strong statement on war.[8]

Roosevelt returned to the topic of power with his third point, that the nation must prepare for war well in advance of its outbreak. In this section of the speech Roosevelt first discussed the military and naval strategists whose reluctance to prepare for the War of 1812 proved extremely costly. Then he observed that the Union entered the Civil War with a navy, but the Confederacy lacked a navy and could not overcome this lack of preparedness. In 1897, Roosevelt observed, warships took upwards of two years to build. The message was clear. Modern warfare demanded extensive advance preparation.

The development of his third major point, that the nation must prepare for war well in advance, evidenced yet another common characteristic of Roosevelt's speaking, his penchant for reliance on either/or reasoning. Each of the examples Roosevelt discussed illustrated the point that either we prepare for war in advance, or we will suffer humiliation and defeat. In his later speaking Roosevelt consistently made use of either/or reasoning, casting an argument so that it seemed that one must either agree with him or expect dire consequences. Whether the topic was military preparedness, economic reform, or the conservation of natural resources, Roosevelt frequently utilized either/or reasoning, effectively presenting his listeners with but one viable option, that which he advocated.

Roosevelt's fourth major contention in this speech no doubt had considerable appeal for his immediate audience. He argued that the nation's first line of defense must be our navy and further, that an effective navy must have well-trained skilled personnel as well as considerable offensive capacity. Roosevelt acknowledged the importance of personnel, fortifying our harbors, and maintaining a fleet of swift torpedo boats and similar defensively oriented ships. However, he continued,

> no master of the prize ring ever fought his way to supremacy by mere dexterity in avoiding punishment. He had to win by inflicting punishment. If the enemy is given the choice of time and place to attack, sooner or later he will do irreparable damage. . . . In the last resort we must trust to the ships whose business it is to fight and not to run, and who can themselves go to sea and strike at the enemy when they choose, instead of waiting peacefully to receive his blow when and where he deems it best to deliver it. If in the event of war our fleet of battleships can destroy the hostile fleet,then our coasts are safe from the menace of serious attack; even a fight that ruined our fleet would probably so shatter the hostile fleet as to do away with all chance of invasion; but if we have no fleet wherewith to meet the enemy on the high seas, or to anticipate his stroke by our own, then very city within reach of the tides must spend men and money in preparation for an attack that may not come, but which would cause crushing and irredeemable disaster if it did come.

In this and similar passages in which he argued on behalf of a two-ocean navy with both defensive and offensive ability, national power as a topoi permeated Roosevelt's rhetoric.

This passage evidenced several rhetorical practices that subsequently became characteristic of Roosevelt's speaking. The passage opens with a vigorous and graphic metaphor, likening the fleet to a boxer. Such metaphors are legion in Roosevelt's speaking. This passage also evidenced Roosevelt's reliance on either/or reasoning. Either the nation followed his lead in developing a two-ocean navy with offensive capacity, or it was likely to ultimately suffer a crushing and irredeemable disaster.   Roosevelt returned to the theme of character in the final main point in this address. "Much of what is best and highest in national character," Roosevelt claimed, "is made up of glorious memories and traditions." Hence, he continued,

a rich banker may be a valuable and useful citizen, but not a thousand rich bankers can leave to the country such a heritage as Farragut left, when, lashed in the rigging of the Hartford, he forged past the forts and over the unseen death below, to try his wooden stem against the ironclad hull of the great Confederate ram. The people of some given section of our country may be better off because a shrewd and wealthy man has built up therein a great manufacturing business, or has extended a line of railroad past its doors; but the whole nation is better, the whole nation is braver, because Cushing pushed his little torpedo-boat through the darkness to sink beside the sinking Albemarle. . . . All of us lift our heads higher because those of our countrymen whose trade it is to meet danger have met it well and bravely.

This passage clearly evidenced several traits of Roosevelt's speaking. It was built around historical examples. It was developed with highly concrete, vivid images: the rich banker, the shrewd and wealthy man, Farragut lashed in the rigging of the Hartford, trying his wooden stem against the ironclad hull of the great Confederate ram, the little torpedo-boat pushing through the darkness. This final section of the speech was also organized deductively, opening with the broad general statement that "much of that which is best and highest in national character is made up of glorious memories and traditions." Roosevelt then illustrated that generalization with specific examples, and finally concluded this section by applying that generalization to our current situation; finding that "all of us lift our heads higher because those of our countrymen whose trade it is to meet danger have met it well and bravely."

Like a clergyman, Roosevelt concluded his speech by returning to his text and applying it to the specific situation he had been discussing. "In closing," Roosevelt stated,

> let me repeat that we ask for a great navy, we
> ask for an armament fit for the nation's needs,
> not primarily to fight, but to avert fighting.
> Preparedness deters the foe, and maintains right
> by the show of ready might without the use of
> violence.   Peace, like freedom, is not a gift that
> tarries long in the hands of cowards or of those
> too feeble or too short-sighted to deserve it; and
> we ask to be given the means to insure that
> honorable peace which alone is worth having.

The homiletic nature of Roosevelt's speaking, his constant amplification, extolling, and application of a gospel to a current problem, was evident in this speech as it subsequently proved evident throughout many of the major speeches of his career.

Roosevelt's speech was printed in full in many major newspapers in Boston, New York, Washington, Chicago, New Orleans, San Francisco, and a variety of other cities. Reaction to it was largely favorable, although Roosevelt was not without detractors. In his home town, The New York Herald called it a "grand" address, claiming it was "trenchant" and lauding its "decisive   conclusiveness."   The   Herald   concluded   that Roosevelt's address "can scarcely fail to inspire the youth of America with the same lofty spirit of devotion to our country's honor, glory, and prosperity that actuated its utterance by the speaker."   The New York Sun praised Roosevelt for "a very eloquent address," which was "a manly, patriotic, intelligent and convincing appeal to American sentiment in behalf of the national honor."   The Sun went on to praise Roosevelt's reasoning, and concluded that he was entirely correct in arguing that "the building of a powerful navy must therefore be the intermitted business of a time of peace; and such a navy is the best safeguard of peace."[9]

Praise for Roosevelt's address was also lavish from other parts of the nation. The Washington Post, in an editorial titled "Mr. Roosevelt Is All Right," observed that the assistant secretary of the navy had "honored both himself and the country of which he is now a conspicuous and distinguished representative."   The Post editorialized that Roosevelt had presented the country with a "welcome and refreshing message," and concluded by addressing Roosevelt directly: "Well done, nobly spoken: Theodore Roosevelt, you have found our proper place at last-all hail."   The Daily Picayune of New Orleans claimed that Roosevelt had voiced "the sentiments of the great majority of thinking people," and reserved special praise for the wisdom of his call for twenty new battleships. The Call of San Francisco found "nothing of a jingo tone in this speech," telling its readers that they, like Roosevelt, "must recognize the truth that we are living in a world where evil exists and where men must be always prepared to meet it and conquer it." In words Roosevelt might have used himself, The Call concluded that "America desires peace, but she cannot afford to accept it unless accompanied by justice and honor."[10]

Predictably, Roosevelt's remarks were criticized in Democratic papers. The Hartford Times found that Roosevelt was "cultivating a spirit of foolish bluster" that might needlessly involve the United States in "international quarrels--possibly war." The Brooklyn Eagle found that Roosevelt "takes what we believe to be a greatly exaggerated view of conditions." The Eagle observed that "to accomplish all that the assistant secretary would have us accomplish we would require a navy so big that the oceans verging on our territory would hardly suffice to hold it." Roosevelt, The Eagle concluded "belongs to the fire-eating school of American Statesmen."[11]

"Washington's Forgotten Maxim" was a hammer blow on behalf of naval preparedness and against isolation. Not only did it attract the attention of the nation's press, but perhaps more importantly it fell on receptive ears in both Newport and Washington. Speaking to a highly sympathetic audience of naval policy-makers, just as Hawaii and Cuba were becoming growing issues, Roosevelt clearly hoped to help make policy with his address. Learning of Roosevelt's remarks in Washington, President William McKinley was reported to have stated: "I suspect that Roosevelt is right and the only difference between him and me is the greater responsibility." Clearly, Roosevelt had signaled the path that future American policy would follow.[12]

Thus, Roosevelt's address to the Naval War College was significant for a variety of reasons. Though often thought of as the earliest of his major national addresses, it was built around two of the topoi that characteristically permeated all of his subsequent rhetoric--power and character. Second, it illustrated many of Roosevelt's characteristic rhetorical practices. It evidenced a homiletic approach involving the initial presentation of an old text and the application of that text to current problems. The overall organization of the speech was deductive, as was the organization of many subsections of the speech. Roosevelt relied heavily on either/or reasoning and his principal form of support material was historical example. Finally, even in this, his first major national address, he showed a penchant for using vivid, concrete, memorable images and metaphors. Unlike most of the speeches commonly associated with Roosevelt, this speech was made prior to his assumption of the presidency. It was made while Roosevelt was a comparatively obscure assistant secretary of the navy, not a United States president, a former president, or a presidential candidate. The dramatic impact of

"Washington's Forgotten Maxim" on the development of American foreign policy was a result of Roosevelt's ideas and language, not his position or prominence.

THIS NATION'S NEEDS

In 1914 former President Theodore Roosevelt again raised his voice on behalf of preparedness and national defense. By May of 1915, after the sinking of the Lusitania, the former president was not only championing preparedness, but strongly suggesting the need for American intervention in the European war. During the summer of 1915 he made a speaking tour across the United States, urging preparation for what he perceived as the inevitable war with Germany. As Americans learned of the sinking of the Lusitania and the invasion of Belgium, Roosevelt called on his countrymen to "wake up America." Vigorously, Roosevelt attacked the foreign policy of President Woodrow Wilson and his isolationist secretary of state, William Jennings Bryan, for maintaining neutrality and failing to arm the United States. No doubt Roosevelt's speaking was also prompted by the personal and political rivalry that existed between Wilson and himself. Nevertheless, Roosevelt's preparedness speaking, dating from 1914 and continuing beyond the United States' entry into World War I until the end of his life in January of 1919, has caused even his harshest critics to acknowledge that he preformed a crucial service to his nation, serving as "The Bugle that Woke America."[13]

It was toward the end of his first major speaking tour on behalf of preparedness, on August 25, 1915, at an officer's training camp near Plattsburgh, New York, that Roosevelt delivered "This Nation's Needs." This speech was highly representative of Roosevelt's foreign policy speaking throughout the last five years of his life. Moreover, it created a tempest in a teapot.

The commanding officer of the Plattsburgh camp, by 1915 a major general, was none other than the man who had served as Colonel and commanding officer for Lieutenant Colonel Theodore Roosevelt and the rest of the Rough Riders, Leonard Wood. Wood had invited his long-time friend to address the soldiers-in-training at Plattsburgh. What they heard from the former president was a sharply worded call for preparedness that, like virtually all of Roosevelt's preparedness speaking prior to the war, was also an attack on President Woodrow Wilson's foreign policy. Inadvertently, Roosevelt had placed his old friend Wood in an awkward position. As an army officer, Wood's speaking invitation to Roosevelt seemed to be encouraging criticism of his civilian superiors, the president and secretaries of war and state. Secretary of War Lindley M.

Garrison publicly rebuked Wood for allowing Roosevelt to speak. This incident, in which an American general was rebuked for inviting the former commander-in-chief of the American armies to speak on a military base, was widely reported.   It drew considerable attention to Roosevelt's remarks at Plattsburgh.[14]

Roosevelt relied on three of the topoi of militant decency in his Plattsburgh address.   The men he was addressing were completing a voluntary two-month program in military training. Hence, in his introduction Roosevelt commended his audience for illustrating both social responsibility and character in volunteering for military training.   In preparing themselves to serve their society, Roosevelt claimed, "You have done your duty," and acted in a socially responsible fashion.   In addition to lauding his audience for the social responsibility they had shown in volunteering for military training, Roosevelt also commended their character.   They had ministered "to their own self-respect."   Roosevelt found that in preparing itself for military training his audience had evidenced common sense and the courage to act, two requisites of good character. Roosevelt concluded his introduction by presenting the "text" of his address.   In a typically Rooseveltian balanced sentence, he proclaimed, "No man is fit to be free unless he is not merely willing but eager to fit himself to fight for his freedom, and no man can fight for his freedom unless he is trained to act in conjunction with his fellows."[15]

This statement served as Roosevelt's text.   Here, in first presenting his text, Roosevelt spoke of men.   Subsequently in the speech he spoke interchangeably about both men and nations.   Thus, while the above statement is the explicit text of the address, the implicit text would be: No nation is fit to be free unless it is not merely willing but eager to fit itself to fight for its freedom, and no nation can fight for its freedom unless it is trained to act in conjunction with its fellow nations.

Having used his introduction to commend his audience for their social responsibility and character, Roosevelt turned to the first major point of his address, and the passages from which the address received its name.

> The greatest need for this country is a first-class
> navy. Next, we need a thoroughly trained regular
> or professional army of 200,00 men if we have
> universal military service; and of at least half a
> million men if we do not have such universal
> military service.

Roosevelt claimed that Germany and Japan were far more powerful than the United States.   He suggested that these nations could, if they wished, ferry a fighting force across the oceans and "take New York or San Francisco and destroy them or hold them to ransom with absolute impunity, and the United

States at present would be helpless." In addressing what he perceived as an imbalance of power between the United States and its likely military foes, Roosevelt developed the third theme of militant decency that he used in this speech: power. As he did in his first outstanding foreign policy speech eighteen years earlier at the Naval War College, Roosevelt still perceived the basis of American national power to be a first-class navy. Thus by the conclusion of his introduction and his first major point, Roosevelt has already touched on the three topoi of militant decency that undergirded this speech.

He returned to character to develop his second major point. A nation may have the military power it needs, but it also needs character, the courage to act. Roosevelt used some of the most intense language of this speech to vilify the Wilson administration's neutrality policies.

> The professional pacifist is as much out of place in a democracy as is the poltroon himself; and he is no better citizen than the poltroon. Probably no body of citizens in the United States during the last five years has wrought so efficiently for national decadence and international degradation as the professional pacifists, the peace-at-any-price men, who have tried to teach our people that silly all-inclusive arbitration treaties and the utterance of fatuous platitudes at peace congresses are substitutes for adequate military preparedness.

Such individuals lack the character to lead great nations. In contrast, using language and examples that harken back eighteen years to his first major foreign policy address, Roosevelt found that

> the greatest service that has ever been rendered mankind has been rendered by the men who have not shrunk from righteous war in order to bring about righteous peace, by soldier-statesmen of the type of Abraham Lincoln, whose work was done by soldiers. The men of the Revolution and the men of the Civil War, and the women who raised these men to be soldiers are the men and women to whom we owe a deathless debt of gratitude.

Roosevelt concluded this assault upon the character of the Wilson administration by observing that

> for thirteen months America has played an ignoble part among the nations. . . . We have tamely submitted to seeing the weak, whom we had covenanted to protect, wronged. . . . We have seen our own men, women, and children

murdered on the high seas, without action on
our part.   We have treated elocution as a
substitute for action.   During this time our
government has not taken the smallest step in
the way of preparedness to defend our own
rights. . . . Reliance upon high-sounding words
unbacked by deeds is proof of a mind that dwells
only in the realm of shadow and sham.

No doubt these passages in which Roosevelt used an
American military post as the setting for his attack on the
character of Wilson and his advisors particularly angered the
administration, causing the rebuke of Major General Wood.
However, though this speech was given at a United States
military instruction camp, the federal government did little
besides provide the physical facilities. The men themselves had
to purchase their own uniforms and food as well as pay for the
training they received, with some costs defrayed by the
contributions of private citizens.

Hence, Roosevelt's second major point was that in effect
the administration was abrogating its social responsibility.   A
socially responsible administration would have underwritten the
efforts of men such as those to whom Roosevelt spoke, who
wanted to improve their ability to serve society in time of war.
Moreover, a socially responsible government would have
recognized that camps such as the one at Plattsburgh which
"include men of every creed and every national origin--Jew and
Gentile, Catholic and Protestant, men of English and Irish,
German and French, Slavonic and Latin, and Scandinavian
descent," made us more tolerant of one another.   A socially
responsible administration would have encouraged the tolerance
bred by camps such as this which made Americans of every
background more willing to ignore their differences and work
toward common goals.   Such camps reduce the tendency
towards what Roosevelt frequently called "hyphenated
Americans."[16] Camps such as these, Roosevelt believed, "are
schools of civic virtue as well as of military efficiency.   They
should be universal and obligatory for all our young men."
The administration's failure to fund such camps, especially
"during the last thirteen months, the time when during all our
history it was most necessary to prepare for self-defense,"
clearly illustrated the administration's lack of social
responsibility.

The final major point Roosevelt made in this speech was
that the administration's failure to live up to the Hague
Convention, and its policies embargoing and discouraging the
export of munitions, illustrated a lack of character. Under the
Hague Convention, Roosevelt claimed,

it was our bounden duty to take whatever action
was necessary to prevent and, if not to prevent,
then to undo, the hideous wrong that was done
to Belgium. We have shirked this duty. We have
shown a spirit so abject that Germany had
deemed it safe to kill our women and children on
the high seas.

Moreover, those who claimed it was immoral to export arms
failed to recognize, claimed Roosevelt, that the morality of
selling arms depends upon the use to which the munitions are
to be put.

Exactly the same morality should obtain
internationally that obtains nationally. It is right
for a private firm to furnish arms to the
policeman who puts down the thug, the burglar,
the white slaver, and the blackhander. It is
wrong to furnish the blackhandler, the burglar
and the white slaver with weapons to be used
against the policeman. The analogy holds true in
international life.

The Wilson administration policies toward intervention
and arms sales illustrated an inability to act courageously in
the face of evil and danger. In his conclusion, Roosevelt found
that "the men of this camp and the men responsible for
starting this camp have shown our government and our people
the path along which we should tread."

In sum, "This Nation's Needs" clearly reflected three of
the major themes of Roosevelt's rhetoric of militant decency.
In August of 1915 Theodore Roosevelt believed that his nation
badly needed power, in the form of a first-class navy and a
standing army of 200,000 men with universal military service
or 500,000 men without such service. Second, it needed
character. Our national leadership lacked not only the power
to act, but perhaps more importantly, the character to act.
Rather than act by developing a national policy of
preparedness, our leadership was still relying on essentially
voluntary programs, such as the one at Plattsburgh, largely
funded by private individuals. Moreover, our leadership shirked
from acting on behalf of Belgium and the democracies of
Western Europe. The second of this nation's needs, according
to Roosevelt, was a leadership that was active in the
performance of virtue, a leadership with character. The third
of our national needs was social responsibility. In a time of
crisis, as in the preceding thirteen months, Roosevelt argued
that a socially responsible administration would have helped
individuals prepare themselves to serve society in time of war,
and would have encouraged military training camps as schools
of civic virtue and tolerance as well as military efficiency.

This address exhibited at least four characteristics of Roosevelt's speaking.   First, it was homiletic in nature. Roosevelt presented a text and then amplified, extolled, and applied that text to the current problem.   Roosevelt's text was that "no man [country] is fit to be free unless he [it] is not merely willing but eager to fit himself [itself] to fight for his [its] freedom, and no man [country] can fight for his [its] freedom unless he [it] is trained to act in conjunction with his [its] fellows."   Each of the three major points in the body of the address amplified the text.   He constantly extolled the wisdom of this text and he applied it to current American foreign policy. Though not repeating the text in his conclusion, Roosevelt suggested that his audience of soldiers-in-training had shown "our government and our people the path along which we should tread."   Clearly, his audience was fit to be free, for they were willing and eager to train themselves and to work with one another.

Second, Roosevelt relied on historical examples and his own assertions for evidence.   More than "Washington's Forgotten Maxim," this speech relied on Roosevelt's own assertions.   Given the nature of his audience, and the increased credibility that Roosevelt had by 1915, it is likely that Roosevelt's assertions were acceptable to his immediate audience, and to sizeable segments of the nation at large.

Third, Roosevelt relied heavily on either/or reasoning. Indeed, the basic thrust of this speech is identical to the basic either/or reasoning in "Washington's Forgotten Maxim."   Either the nation followed Roosevelt's advice and prepared, or it would suffer an unacceptable alternative--military defeat.   This point was vividly illustrated in the passage where Roosevelt asserted that Germany and Japan already had the ability to capture and destroy New York and San Francisco.

Fourth, Roosevelt made use of vivid language and concrete images.   In this speech he used such terms as:

To Chinafy--To ignore the rest of the world at one's own peril.

Hyphenated Americans--Americans of foreign birth or heritage, i.e., German-Americans, Irish-Americans

Peace-at-any-pricers--Those who will go to virtually any extreme to avoid fighting a war.

Roosevelt is often attributed with coining or popularizing the first two of these terms.   Moreover, Roosevelt's use of invective, so common that one student of Roosevelt's rhetoric has written an entire master's thesis on it, contributed appreciably to the vividness of his language in this speech.   For example, he called his foes "poltroons" and "professional pacifists," who rely on "silly" arbitration treaties, "fatuous platitudes," and "a debauch of indulgence."   He found his opponents and their actions "utterly contemptible," "selfish," "sissies," "possessed of minds that dwell in the realm of shadow and sham." [17]

In sum, "The Nation's Needs" well illustrated Theodore Roosevelt's foreign policy speaking. In it, Roosevelt utilized three basic topoi of his rhetoric of militant decency: power, character, and social responsibility. In doing so Roosevelt developed basic ideas that were evident in his earliest foreign policy speeches and carried through to the end of his life. Moreover, this speech made use of a variety of rhetorical strategies characteristic of Roosevelt. It was homiletic in nature. It relied on historical example and assertion for evidence. It made extensive use of either/or reasoning. Finally, Roosevelt's language in this speech was vivid. It was marked by the characteristic invective and scorn that Roosevelt so often directed at his foes. Moreover, in "This Nation's Needs," Roosevelt made characteristic use of balanced sentences and highly concrete language.

CONCLUSIONS

Theodore Roosevelt's speaking on American foreign policy clearly reflected his rhetoric of militant decency. As the two representative speeches examined in this chapter illustrate, he invariably utilized the topoi of power and character in his addresses on American foreign policy and frequently used the topoi of social responsibility as well. His foreign policy addresses illustrated the homiletic nature of his speaking. Moreover, they evidenced many of his common rhetorical practices, including the use of historical example and assertions for evidence, the use of either/or reasoning, and the use of concrete, vivid language.

NOTES

1. In a letter to Henry L. Sprague, January 26, 1900, Roosevelt first expressed his fondness for what he described as "a West African proverb: 'Speak softly and carry a big stick.'" Cited in Richard Murphy, "Theodore Roosevelt," History and Criticism of American Public Address 3, ed. Marie Hochmuth, (New York: Russell and Russell, 1965), 353.

2. Thomas A. Bailey, A Diplomatic History of the American People (New York: Appleton-Century-Crofts, 1964), 52; Richard Hofstadter, The American Political Tradition (New York: Vintage Books, 1948), 209; I. E. Cadenhead, Theodore Roosevelt: The Paradox of Progressivism (Woodbury, N. Y.: Baron's Educational Series Inc., 1974), 89.

3.   Theodore Roosevelt, An Autobiography (New York: Charles Scribner's Sons, 1926), 535; 544.   This version of Roosevelt's autobiography serves as volume twenty in the national edition of The Works of Theodore Roosevelt (New York: Charles Scribner's Sons, 1926).

4.   Frederick W. Marks compellingly argues that contemporaries and historians who stressed Roosevelt's "big stick diplomacy" have not done him justice.   See particularly chapter 3 of Frederick W. Marks, Velvet on Iron: The Diplomacy of Theodore Roosevelt, (Lincoln: University of Nebraska Press, 1978).

5.   Edmund Morris, The Rise of Theodore Roosevelt (New York: Coward, McCann & Geoghegan, Inc., 1979), 569.

6.   See Peter Karsten, "The Nature of 'Influence': Roosevelt, Mahan and the Concept of Sea Power." American Quarterly 23 (October 1971): 587-588 for discussion of Roosevelt's reputation within the United States naval establishment and his invitation to speak at the Naval War College.   Morris, The Rise of Theodore Roosevelt, 569 claims Roosevelt's preparation took seven weeks.

7.   The quotations and references in this paragraph and all subsequent references to this speech are drawn from the transcript found in Theodore Roosevelt, The Works of Theodore Roosevelt: National Edition (New York: Charles Scribner's Sons, 1926), 13, 182-99, which is reprinted elsewhere in this book.

8.   I am indebted to John A. Gable, executive director of the Theodore Roosevelt Association, for his observations on the harm that this line may have caused to Roosevelt's reputation, as well as the fact that he never subsequently spoke so strongly on the point.   Letter, John A. Gable to the author, July 27, 1989.

9.   The quotations in this paragraph are drawn from the clippings in Theodore Roosevelt Scrapbook: April 5, 1897-May 8, 1898, Theodore Roosevelt Collection, Harvard University. The clippings from both New York papers are labeled June 3, 1897.

10.   The statements quoted in this paragraph are drawn from clippings found in Theodore Roosevelt Scrapbook: April 5, 1897-May 8, 1898.   Clippings from The Washington Post are undated.   Those from The Call are dated June 4, 1897, and those from The Daily Picayune are dated June 7, 1897.

11. Press comments cited in this paragraph are all drawn from "Assistant Secretary of the Navy Roosevelt's Address at the Opening of the Naval War College," Public Opinion 22 (June 17, 1897): 1-9.

12. McKinley is quoted in Morris, The Rise of Theodore Roosevelt, 572-73. Also see Henry F. Pringle, Theodore Roosevelt: A Biography (New York: Harcourt Brace Jovanovich, 1956), 118-21. Richard H. Collin, Theodore Roosevelt, Culture, Diplomacy, and Expansion (Baton Rouge: Louisiana State University Press, 1985), 111-30 argues that Roosevelt did not shape subsequent naval policy towards Spain but rather gave effective voice to the policies of William Wirt Kimball, a key figure in United States naval intelligence.

13. For more on Roosevelt's feelings toward Wilson see Pringle, Theodore Roosevelt, 406-10 and John Blum, The Republican Roosevelt (Cambridge, Mass.: Harvard University Press, 1954), 151-53. Herman Hagedorn, a strong admirer of Roosevelt, coined the phrase with his book, The Bugle That Woke America: The Saga of Theodore Roosevelt's Last Battle For His Country (New York: John Day Company, 1940). William Harbaugh uses the same phrase as the title of Chapter 29 of his much more even-handed biography, The Life and Times of Theodore Roosevelt (New York: Collier Books, 1966). Even Roosevelt's more severe critics, such as Pringle and Beale, acknowledge the importance of Roosevelt's preparedness speaking during the last five years of his life.

14. For the best accounts of the incidents surrounding the Plattsburgh speech see Ralph Barton Perry, The Plattsburgh Movement (New York: E. P. Dutton Company, 1921), 43-45 and "The Ex-Presidential War on the War Department," Literary Digest (September 11, 1915): 514-15.

15. This and all future citations to this speech are taken from the text found in Current History (October 1915): 18-22 and reprinted elsewhere in this volume.

16. Hyphenated Americans, according to Roosevelt, were those Americans of foreign birth or ancestry who gave their first allegiance to their place of birth or ancestry, rather than to the United States.

17. For discussions of Roosevelt's ability to coin memorable words and phrases see Edmund Morris, "The Many Words and Works of Theodore Roosevelt," Smithsonian 14 (November 1983): 86-87; William A. Behl, "Theodore Roosevelt's

Principles of Invention," <u>Speech Monographs</u> 14 (1947): 108; and Richard Murphy, "Theodore Roosevelt," in <u>History and Criticism of American Public Address</u> ed. Marie Hochmuth, (New York: Russell and Russell, 1965), 353. Gordon W. Winks, "A Study of Theodore Roosevelt's Use of Invective in His Public Speeches," (unpublished M. A. thesis, Northwestern University, 1933).

4
The Rhetoric of Militant Decency and Civic Virtue

Addressing a New York State Chamber of Commerce banquet in 1902, Theodore Roosevelt delivered a definition of civic virtue. "The first requisite of a good citizen in this Republic of ours," claimed Roosevelt, "is that he shall be able and willing to pull his weight--that he shall not be a mere passenger, but shall do his share in the work that each generation of us finds ready to hand; and, furthermore, that in doing his work he shall show not only the capacity for sturdy self-help but also self-respecting regard for the rights of others."[1]   This definition was characteristic of Roosevelt's speeches on civic virtue because it stressed the two key topoi that undergirded all of Roosevelt's conceptions of civic virtue; work and character.   In addition to these two themes, Roosevelt's speaking on civic virtue also revealed his secondary reliance on the topoi of order and power.

Roosevelt preached on civic virtue frequently throughout his long career.   Civic virtue, and such related topics as citizenship and Americanism, were constant topics in his speeches.   Moreover, particularly prior to his assumption of the presidency, they often constituted the basic subjects of his addresses.   Many of his addresses on these topics, like the two upon which this chapter focuses, were delivered to civic clubs, often composed of prominent figures in the local community. During Roosevelt's generation, as discussed earlier, it was not common for men of Roosevelt's background and education to enter politics.   Hence, it is not surprising that when addressing educated and affluent community leaders, similar to himself, Roosevelt might urge them to fulfill their responsibilities as citizens in a democracy.

Two such addresses were "The Duties of American Citizenship, "which Roosevelt delivered to the Liberal Club of Buffalo, New York, on January 26, 1893, and "The Strenuous

Life," which Roosevelt delivered to the Hamilton Club of Chicago, Illinois, on April 10, 1899. Roosevelt's 1893 address in Buffalo was given while he was serving as a united states civil service commissioner. It reflects his lifelong beliefs about citizenship, as well as several concerns that were of uppermost importance to him during this period of his life. "The Strenuous Life," delivered three months after Roosevelt became governor of New York, also reflects his lifelong beliefs about civic virtue and is among the speeches most frequently associated with Roosevelt. Though here considered as a speech on civic virtue, Roosevelt's words cannot be studied without an awareness of the tumultuous times in which he spoke. For as he advocated civic virtue and domestic strength, the United States was becoming an international power. If the United States chose "The Strenuous Life" that Roosevelt advocated, it would hasten its emergence as a major international power.

In many respects "The Strenuous Life" reflects not simply Roosevelt's beliefs about civic virtue, but indeed, his entire philosophy of life.

THE DUTIES OF AMERICAN CITIZENSHIP

Roosevelt opened this address by observing that to be a good citizen a man must possess the "home virtues." He must be a good husband and father, honest in his dealings with other men and women. These virtues quickly acknowledged, Roosevelt observed that he wanted to talk about "the attitude of the American citizen in civic life," and then he moved immediately to the passage that serves as his text for this civilsermon. "It ought to be axiomatic in this country, " claimed Roosevelt, "that every man must devote a reasonable share of his time to doing his duty in the political life of the community.[2]

Roosevelt's text clearly indicated that civic virtue cannot be attained without work. He amplified his text in the early minutes of his address by claiming that neither business nor pleasure was an acceptable excuse for shirking one's civic responsibilities, and then he cited James Russell Lowell's statement "that freedom does not tarry long in the hands of the sluggard and the idler." Roosevelt found that our forefathers labored to acquire their freedom and claimd that labor such as theirs, "in combination with our fellows who have the same interests and the same principles" was essential for gaining and maintaining freedom.

Thus, Roosevelt's introduction was homiletic in nature. He presented his audience with a text, the axiom that "every man must devote a reasonable share of his time to doing his duty in the political life of the community." He amplified the text, reiterating it and illustrating it, to ensure audience understanding.

From the very outset, the topoi of work served as the basis for Roosevelt's remarks. The gospel of work undergirded the very text that Roosevelt uses as the basis for this address. Moreover, as he did frequently, Roosevelt accompanied his discussion of the importance of work and effort, with references to the importance of family life. Roosevelt consistently linked the gospel of work with family virtue. For Roosevelt, working to secure a healthy family life was not only in and of itself extremely important, but it also served as ideal preparation and training for assuming civic responsibilities. The virtues of character that were cultivated in dealing with one's parents, spouse, and children were the same virtues of character necessary to work in civic groups for the betterment of society.

Having thus indicated that family virtues and hard work were prerequisites for good citizenship, Roosevelt turned to the "Duties of American Citizenship," from which this speech derived its name.

> The first duty of an American citizen, then, is that he shall work in politics; his second duty is that he shall do that work in a practical manner; and his third is that it shall be done in accord with the highest principles of honor and justice. Of course, it is not possible to define rigidly just the way in which the work shall be made practical. Each man's temper and convictions must be taken into account.

In this quick preview of the remainder of the speech, Roosevelt clearly signaled the themes that undergirded his thought: work, character, order, and power.

Roosevelt spent little time in developing his first point. Evidently he thought that the need for individuals to work in politics was so obvious as not to warrant development. Other than his own assertions to this effect, most frequent in the opening passages of the speech, he did little to develop this point. Nevertheless it was central to all that followed.

In developing his second point, that one's political work should be practical, Roosevelt stressed the need to work with organizations. Roosevelt acknowledged that often one may not agree with everything that a political party or another civic organization might favor, but he concluded that practical concerns mandate that if one hopes to accomplish something one must work in concert with others. Roosevelt favored order, and political organizations are a means of securing orderly reform. Moreover, if one simply could not in good faith work with one of the two principal parties, "he can surely find a number of men who are in the same position as himself and

who agree with him on some specific piece of political work,"
and they could work together to secure their goal.

Roosevelt discussed a second aspect of practicality. "The
man who goes into politics should not expect to reform
everything right off, with a jump." Rather, he must recognize
the need to pay his dues, to work hard and long. Reform comes
slowly. "But," concluded Roosevelt, "if you keep on attending
and try to form associations with other men whom you meet at
political gatherings or whom you can persuade to attend them,
you will very soon find yourself a weight."

Roosevelt's third major point was that one must be
guided by the highest principles in doing his duty. "No man
can do both effective and decent work in public life," claimed
Roosevelt, "unless he is a practical politician on one hand, and
a sturdy believer in Sunday-school politics on the other."
Undergirding Roosevelt's third major point was the topoi of
character. Roosevelt presented several examples to illustrate
this point, including references to his own experiences in
Washington and the New York State Assembly.

In the course of his discussion of the importance of
being guided by character and high principles in preforming
civic duties, Roosevelt, then serving as a civil service
commissioner, advocated civil service reform. Civil service
reform was a pet Roosevelt project throughout his life,
exemplifying as it did the virtues of character that Roosevelt
admired. Civil service reform was the honest, courageous way
to award responsible government positions. Moreover, common
sense dictated that its use would improve the quality of
government employees.

The last major point that Roosevelt made in this address
was that "the man who wishes to do his duty as a citizen in
our country must be imbued through and through with the
spirit of Americanism." Essentially, as he developed this point
primarily with examples, Roosevelt was stressing tolerance. He
cited a variety of political associates with widely varying ethnic
and religious backgrounds who had all served their
communities well. Roosevelt also expressed his concern for
what he later frequently called "hyphenated Americans," who
put their country of origin ahead of the United States. Such
individuals could not be good citizens. "A man has got to be
an American and nothing else," he claimed.

Roosevelt concluded this speech by returning to his text.
Though he never explicitly repeated his text-that every man
must devote a reasonable share of his time to political duty-
that text is implicit in his closing passage. Noting that the
nation will no doubt confront many dangers and perils in the
coming years, Roosevelt concluded: "There is every reason why
we should recognize them, but there is no reason why we

should fear them or doubt our capacity to overcome them, if only each will, according to the measure of his ability, do his full duty, and endeavor so to live as to deserve the high praise of being called a good American citizen."

This address was built on Roosevelt's belief in work, character, and order. Those three topics animated this address on civic virtue. Moreover, this address reflected a variety of Roosevelt's most commonly used rhetorical techniques. First, it was homiletic in nature. Roosevelt presented a text early in the speech. He amplified and extolled it throughout the speech, frequently attempting to show its importance to his audience, largely by applying it to the problems and situations they confronted.

Second, Roosevelt used little evidence in this speech, relying instead on his own ethos. Virtually all the evidence that Roosevelt does use was in the form of examples. He made several historical references to Lincoln and the Union armies, but never developed his historical references. He did use examples drawn from his own experiences in public life, and he used several hypothetical examples. But both of these latter two forms of evidence derived their potency from Roosevelt's ethos. Essentially, Roosevelt relied on his own assertions rather than evidence.

Third, Roosevelt relied on either/or reasoning in this speech, though not to the degree that we have seen in his foreign policy speeches. Perhaps his most conspicuous use of either/or reasoning was early in his address, when he elaborated on his text.

Nothing worth gaining is ever gained without effort. You can no more have freedom without striving and suffering for it than you can win success as a banker or a lawyer without labor and effort, without self-denial in youth and the display of a ready and alert intelligence in middle age. The people who say that they have not time to attend to politics are simply saying that they are unfit to live in a free community.

As in his foreign policy speeches, here Roosevelt suggested that either his audience followed his advice, in this instance devoting a portion of their time to doing their civic duty, or an unacceptable alternative, in this instance the loss of their freedoms, might well result.

The predominant form of reasoning Roosevelt used in this speech is analogy. Although often the analogies were not fully developed, Roosevelt reasoned from analogy more in this address than in the foreign policy addresses previously examined. For example, at one point Roosevelt observed that:

Somebody has said that a racing-yacht, like a good rifle, is a bundle of incompatibilities; that you must get the utmost possible sail power without sacrificing any other quality, and yet that you cannot help sacrificing some other quality if you really do get the utmost sail power; that in short, you have got to make more or less of a compromise on each in order to acquire the dozen things needful; but of course, in making this compromise you must be very careful for the sake of something unimportant not to sacrifice any of the great principles of successful naval architecture. Well, it is about so with a man's political work. He has got to preserve his independence on one hand; and on the other, unless he wishes to be a wholly ineffective crank, he has got to have some sense of party allegiance and party responsibility, and he has got to realize that in any given exigency it may be a matter of duty to sacrifice one quality, or it may be a matter of duty to sacrifice the other.

Although this analogy was more fully developed than many, it was indicative of Roosevelt's reliance upon analogy reasoning in this address.

Finally, many of Roosevelt's characteristic uses of language were evident in this speech. Clearly speeches on citizenship do not lend themselves to the often emotionally intense and highly connotative language that characterized Roosevelt's speaking on controversial foreign and domestic policies. However, this address clearly evidenced Roosevelt's characteristic use of balanced sentences. For example:

* He must always strive manfully for the best, and yet,like Abraham Lincoln, must often resign himself to accept the best possible.

* The screaming vulgarity of the foolish spread-eagle orator who is continually yelling defiance at Europe, praising everything American, good and bad, and resenting the introduction of any reform because it has previously been tried successfully abroad, is offensive and contemptible to the ast degree; but after all it is scarcely as harmful as the peevish, fretful, sneering, and continual fault-finding of the refined, well-educated man, who is always attacking good and bad alike, who genuinely distrusts America, and in the true spirit of servile colonialism considers us inferior to the people across the water.

* Let him make up his mind to do his duty in politics without regard to holding office at all, and let him know that often the men in this country who have done the best work for our public life have not been the men in office.

In sum, "The Duties of American Citizenship" was typical of the speeches that Roosevelt gave on civic virtue and Americanism. It was based on the <u>topoi</u> of work, character and order. It was homiletic in nature. It reflected Roosevelt's characteristic reliance on his own ethical proof to support his otherwise largely unsupported assertions. Like his foreign policy addresses, it made use of either/or reasoning. But more than his foreign policy addresses, it relied on analogy reasoning.

THE STRENUOUS LIFE

On July 1, 1898, a day Theodore Roosevelt subsequently would call "the great day of my life," he led his beloved Rough Riders into history, as they headed the American charges at Kettle Hill and the San Juan Heights. Within two months his wartime exploits had made him, according to biographer Edmund Morris, "the most famous man in America." Within four months Roosevelt's wartime fame had catapulted him to the governorship of New York. He assumed office on January 2, 1899, and three short months later, the Midwest had its first look at the United States' newest national hero. Amidst much advance publicity, thirty-nine-year-old Governor Theodore Roosevelt had come to Chicago to speak to the Hamilton Club.[3]

The address that Theodore Roosevelt delivered to the Hamilton Club on April 10, 1899, well summed up his philosophy of citizenship. Roosevelt opened his speech by complimenting both Chicago, "the greatest city of the West," and Illinois, "which gave the country Lincoln and Grant." He then moved immediately to his text.

I wish to preach, not the doctrine of ignoble ease but the doctrine of the strenuous life, the life of toil and effort, of labor and strife; to preach that highest form of success which comes, not to the man who desires mere easy peace, but to the man who does not shrink from danger, from hardship, or from bitter toil, and who out of these wins the splendid ultimate triumph.

As in "The Duties of American Citizenship," the theme of work undergirded Roosevelt's text. Successful citizenship demanded "the doctrine of the strenuous life, the life of toil and effort."[4]

Roosevelt's first major point in this speech was little more than a restatement of his text and its application to the lives of individuals. It reflected his constant reliance on the topics of work and character.

> We admire the man who embodies victorious
> effort; the man who never wrongs his neighbor,
> who is prompt to help a friend, but who has
> those virile qualities necessary to win in the stern
> strife of actual life. It is hard to fail, but it is
> worse never to have tried to succeed. In this life
> we get nothing save by effort.

Roosevelt amplified this point with his own assertions and hypothetical examples. Characteristically, he also observed that women too have highly significant work as spouses and mothers.

Roosevelt's second major point was that his basic text applied to nations as well as individuals. For nations, as well as individuals, Roosevelt preached the strenuous life.

> As it is with the individual, so it is with the
> nation. It is a base untruth to say that happy
> is the nation that has no history. Thrice happy
> is the nation that has a glorious history. Far
> better it is to dare mighty things, to win glorious
> triumphs, even though checkered by failure, than
> to take rank with those poor spirits who neither
> enjoy much nor suffer much, because they live in
> the gray twilight that knows not victory nor
> defeat.

Roosevelt used examples to amplify this point. He lauded the Civil War generation of Americans who were willing to fight the strenuous fight to do what was right. In contrast, he cautioned that the current generation must avoid behaving like China, "content to rot by inches in ignoble ease."

Roosevelt's third major point was to indicate for his audience the challenges that confronted the United States, the tasks that Americans living the strenuous life must confront. Among them, he found that "we must continue to build and maintain a strong navy and a strong Army," and

> if we are to hold our own in the struggle for
> naval and commercial supremacy, we must build
> up our power without our own borders. We must
> build the isthmian canal, and we must grasp the
> points of vantage which will enable us to have
> our say in deciding the destiny of the oceans of
> the East and the West.

Clearly, Roosevelt's lifelong concern for power undergirded this section of the speech.

But, Roosevelt continued, there is yet another challenge that confronts the United States.   Moreover, "from the standpoint of international honor," Roosevelt claimed, it was an even more significant challenge than that of maintaining our military readiness.   "The guns that thundered off Manila and Santiago," Roosevelt observed,

> left us echoes of glory, but they also left us a legacy of duty.   If we drove out a medieval tyranny only to make room for savage anarchy, we had better not have begun the task at all. It is worse than idle to say that we have no duty to perform, and can leave to their fates the islands we have conquered.   Such a course would be the course of infamy. . . . The work must be done; we cannot escape our responsibility; and if we are worth our salt, we shall be glad of the chance to do the work. . . . We must demand the highest order of integrity and ability in our public men who are to grapple with these new problems.

The topics of order and character undergirded the second challenge Roosevelt perceives.

Having suggested that two principal challenges confronted the United States as the twentieth century opened—maintaining our military strength and governing our newly won empire in an orderly and just fashion-Roosevelt finally offered his suggestions for meeting those challenges.   Among them were: "complete reorganization" of the army; appropriate growth of both the army and the navy; "civic honesty, civic cleanliness, civic good sense in our home administration of city, state, and nation;" and governing "wisely and well" the Phillippines and West Indies.

In 1899, Roosevelt perceived that for the United States to live the strenuous life, it had to meet two challenges and not "sit huddled within our own borders." Although this speech seems, at first glance, to be an address on the responsibilities of American foreign policy, it is not.   It is a discussion of the strenuous life, the life to which worthy citizens and nations should aspire.   Perhaps, had this speech been delivered a decade later, Roosevelt would have chosen to argue that for the United States to live the strenuous life it had to implement domestic economic reforms.[5]

Years later, reflecting on this speech, Roosevelt claimed that he had "always wished that I had myself used 'The Vigor of Life' as a heading to indicate what I was trying to preach, instead of the heading I actually did use."[6]   Roosevelt's presentation of his philosophy focused on the issues of 1899 that just happened to involve foreign policy.   Roosevelt utilized the most pressing issues of the day as a means of illustrating what he perceived to be involved in living the strenuous life, the vigorous life, the life requisite for good citizenship in turn-of-the-century America. Predictably, the philosophy Roosevelt articulated in "The Strenuous Life" reflects his lifelong beliefs in work, character, power, and order.

This address, so characteristic of Roosevelt in thought, was also extremely characteristic of his rhetorical practices. First, it was homiletic in nature. Roosevelt even introduced his text by observing that "I wish to preach, [emphasis added] not the doctrine of ignoble ease, but the doctrine of the strenuous life." He then amplified and illustrated his text by portraying the importance of the strenuous life, first in the lives of individuals and second in the lives of nations. He then applied his text to current affairs, suggesting the challenges confronting the United States and the strenuous actions necessary to meet those challenges. In the closing moments of his address, Roosevelt returned to his text. "I preach to you, [emphasis added] then, my countrymen," he concluded, "that our country calls not for the life of ease but for the life of strenuous endeavor."[7]

The second rhetorical characteristic of Roosevelt's that was clearly evident in "The Strenuous Life" was his reliance on the two basic forms of support he most typically used: assertions supported by little more than his own credibility, and historical examples. Repeatedly, Roosevelt asserted his major points.

* A mere life of ease is not in the end a very satisfactory life, and above all, it is a life which ultimately unfits those who follow it for serious work in the world.

* No country can long endure if its foundations are not laid deep in the material prosperity which comes from thrift, from business energy and enterprise, from hard unsparing effort in the fields of industrial activity; but neither was any nation ever yet truly great if it relied upon material prosperity alone.

* The work must be done; we cannot escape our responsibility; and if we are worth our salt, we shall be glad of the chance to do the work-glad of the chance to show ourselves equal to one of the great tasks set before modern civilization.

Virtually the entire last 40 percent of the speech, in which Roosevelt details his specific recommendations of what the nation needs to do in order to live the strenuous life, was asserted. Clearly, assertions whose persuasive effect came from

Roosevelt's ethos constituted the principal form of support material used in this address.

Roosevelt also relied on historical example. He used two extended examples in this address. In the first he cited the Civil War generation and its leaders, Lincoln and Grant, as a generation willing to live the strenuous life, costly as that life proved to be in terms of lives and dollars. Roosevelt concluded his long description of the virtue of this generation by observing that "in the end the slave was freed, the Union restored, and the mighty American republic placed once more as a helmeted queen among nations." His second extended example was a discussion of presidential and congressional actions taken in the decades prior to the Spanish-American War to prepare the United States Navy for combat. Roosevelt praised the men who were willing to take the peacetime actions necessary to make ours "one of the most brilliant and formidable fighting navies in the entire world." He observed that it would have been far less strenuous to simply ignore the navy's peacetime requests. Roosevelt also used additional examples drawn from the Civil War, the policies of the Chinese government, and England's colonial policies in India and Egypt to support his points.

A third common characteristic of Roosevelt's speaking that this speech illustrated was his reasoning. Ultimately, as with many of his speeches, including several of those previously examined in this work, Roosevelt's argument rested on either/or reasoning. He reduced the choices to either living the strenuous life as he recommend, or the unacceptable alternative of passively watching "the bolder and stronger peoples" pass us by and "win for themselves the domination of the world."

Finally, this speech also evidenced some of Roosevelt's most characteristic uses of language-apt, often emotionally intense, highly connotative word choice and balanced sentences. The very phrase from which the speech derived its title, "the strenuous life," is an exceedingly appropriate summary for Roosevelt's philosophy of citizenship and life. Moreover the connotations of the word strenuous, "arduous, laborious, toilsome," all reflecting work, as well as "energetic and aggressive," reflecting power, made Roosevelt's choice of a title, his own later reflections notwithstanding, exceedingly apt.[8]

Moreover, throughout this address Roosevelt used emotionally intense language. For example:

* That nation is rotten to the heart's core.

* When men fear work or fear righteous war, when women fear motherhood, they tremble on the brink of doom; and well it is that they should vanish from the earth, when they are fit subjects

for the scorn of all men and women who are
themselves strong and brave and high-minded.

* Thank God for the iron in the blood of our fathers.

* We cannot . . . be content to rot by inches
in ignoble ease within our borders, taking no
interest in what goes on beyond them, sunk in
a scrambling commercialism.

* So at the present hour, no small share of the
responsibility   for   the   blood   shed   in   the
Philippines, the blood of our brothers, and the
blood of their wild and ignorant foes, lies at the
thresholds of those who so long delayed the
adoption of the treaty of peace, and of those who
by their worse than foolish words deliberately
invited a savage people to plunge into a war
fraught with sure disaster for them--a war too, in
which our own brave men who follow the flag
must pay with their blood for the silly, mock,
humanitarianism of the prattles who sit at home
in peace.

Clearly, Roosevelt's natural penchant for apt, emotionally
intense, highly connotative language was evident in this
address.   Moreover, this address also reflected the second
principle characteristic of Roosevelt's language-his frequent use
of balanced sentences.   In addition to the samples already
indicated in discussing other aspects of this speech, the
following are but a few examples.

* It is hard to fail, but it is worse never to have
tried to succeed.

* When once we have put down armed
resistance, when once our rule is acknowledged,
then an even more difficult task will begin, for
then we must see to it that the islands are
administered with absolute honesty and with
good judgment.

* Their motives may or may not have been good,
but their acts were heavily fraught with evil.

Thus, the language that Roosevelt used in this speech and his
sentence structure are both highly characteristic of his
speaking.   In sum, "The Strenuous Life" well deserves to be
identified with Theodore Roosevelt, for it exemplifies many of
the themes and rhetorical strategies that he used throughout
his life.

CONCLUSIONS

In 1902 when Theodore Roosevelt defined the good citizen as one who was "willing to pull his weight" and "do his share in the work that each generation of us finds ready at hand" with a "self- respecting regard for the rights of others," he was drawing on years of thinking and speaking about civic virtue. Almost a decade earlier, in "The Duties of American Citizenship," and three years earlier in "The Strenuous Life," he had more fully articulated his thoughts about civic virtue. Undergirding virtually every definition and speech Roosevelt delivered on citizenship was his belief in the work ethic. Indeed, Roosevelt believed that strenuous and vigorous effort was absolutely essential to becoming a good citizen in the American democracy. But, claimed Roosevelt in speeches such as the two just examined, such effort also needed to be accompanied by character: honesty, common sense, and the courage to act. Work and character were the two fundamental topoi upon which Roosevelt always relied in his discussions of civic virtue. Secondarily, as these speeches illustrated, he also relied upon the topoi of order and power.

Roosevelt's many addresses about civic virtue and related subjects such as Americanism, civil service reform, and the like, evidenced many of his characteristic rhetorical practices.

In the two addresses studied in this chapter the homiletic nature of Roosevelt's speaking was evident from the outset. Moreover, the speeches reflected his comparative lack of evidence and his heavy reliance on his own credibility as a means of proof. They also reflected a characteristic reliance on either/or reasoning.

Moreover, they revealed many of his typical stylistic traits, including the use of exceedingly apt, highly connotative and emotionally intense language, as well as the constant use of balanced sentences.

Roosevelt's speaking was highly consistent. It was consistent both in thematic content and in rhetorical practice. His speaking on civic virtue reflected Roosevelt's consistency. It revealed him using the basic topoi of his rhetoric of militant decency in addressing his concerns about the responsibilities of citizens in a democracy. Moreover, it revealed him utilizing many of the same rhetorical strategies to address those concerns that we have observed him using in speaking about other topics such as foreign policy, and that we find him utilizing consistently throughout his career.

NOTES

1. Theodore Roosevelt, <u>Presidential Addresses and State</u> <u>Papers; European Addresses</u> (New York: The Review of Reviews Company, 1910) 1, 210.

2. This and all subsequent quotations are drawn from the speech text found elsewhere in this volume and drawn from Theodore Roosevelt, <u>The Works of Theodore Roosevelt: National</u> <u>Edition</u> (New York: Charles Scribner's and Sons, 1926), 13, 281-96.

3. Roosevelt used the phrase "the great day of my life" in a letter to Herman Hagedorn in 1917. See Edmund Morris, <u>The Rise of Theodore Roosevelt</u> (New York: Coward, McCann and Geoghegan, Inc., 1979), 650. "The Most Famous Man in America" is the title Morris uses for chapter 26 of his biography, which details Roosevelt's return from Cuba and his election as governor.

4. The quotations in this paragraph and all subsequent quotations from this speech are taken from the text found elsewhere in this volume and taken from Theodore Roosevelt, <u>The Works of Theodore Roosevelt</u> (New York: Charles Scribner's Sons, 1926), 13, 319-31.

5. David H. Burton, <u>Theodore Roosevelt: Confident</u> <u>Imperialist</u> (Philadelphia: University of Pennsylvania Press, 1968), 68-69, finds that the essence of this speech was Roosevelt evangelization of the manly vigor as a fundamental American principle for both the nation and the individual. Burton finds that Roosevelt used the foreign policy challenges of the day as a means of illustrating his point, just as he used the challenge of disunion faced by an earlier generation to also make his point.

6. Theodore Roosevelt, <u>An Autobiography</u> (New York: Charles Scribner's Sons, 1926), 53. This edition of Roosevelt's autobiography serves as volume twenty of Scribner's 1926 national edition of his works.

7.   In both examples used in this paragraph the emphasis is added. However, Roosevelt commonly refer to his speaking as preaching, and his addresses as sermons. Moreover, contemporary commentators frequently did the same.

8.   See The New Roget's Thesaurus, edited by Norman Lewis, (Garden City, N.J.: Garden City Books, 1961), 466 for a list of basic synonyms for "strenuous."

5

The Rhetoric
of Militant Decency
and Progressive Reform

Theodore Roosevelt is frequently credited with having initiated the rhetorical presidency. Under Roosevelt, popular rhetoric became a major tool of presidential governance. Roosevelt's use of the White House as a "bully pulpit" allowed him to speak directly to the people, going over the heads of Congress, and creating and marshalling public support for legislation he sought. Roosevelt helped to define the modern presidency by illustrating its rhetorical potential. He did so on behalf of a body of social and economic reforms commonly called progressivism.[1]

Speaking at a Lincoln Day dinner in New York City on February 12, 1913, Roosevelt defined the objectives of the Progressive movement.

> It is a manifestation of the eternal forces of human growth, a manifestation of the God-given impulse implanted in mankind to make a better race and a better earth. Its purpose is to establish in this world the rights of man, the right not only to religious and political but to economic freedom; and to make these rights real and living.

The Progressive movement advocated a variety of political and economic reforms. Among the reforms associated with the movement were direct primaries, initiative, referendum, recall of judicial decisions, increased federal regulation of big business, minimum wages for women, workmen's compensation, increased conservation, women's suffrage and the prohibition of child labor.[2]

It is characteristic of Roosevelt that he would, as the statement above illustrates, view the movement in highly moralistic terms. Though Roosevelt did not concur with every reform advocated under the banner of progressivism, by 1912 he was its best known spokesman. In that year the Republican party renominated President William Howard Taft in a bitter convention, after a divisive series of primaries. The progressive wing bolted the Republican party to form the nucleus of a new third party, the Progressive party. After nominating Theodore Roosevelt for the presidency, the party was dubbed the Bull Moose Party, because Roosevelt declared himself fit as a bull moose to wage the campaign. With characteristic religious overtones, in 1912 Roosevelt claimed that he and his supporters "stand at Armageddon, and we battle for the Lord."[3]

The 1912 election marked the high tide of Roosevelt's Progressive oratory. But few, if any, of the campaign addresses he gave that year have proven as enduring as two major addresses dealing with progressive reform that Roosevelt gave earlier. Those addresses, "The Man with the Muck-rake," given in 1906, and "The New Nationalism," given in 1910, are among the most significant speeches of Roosevelt's long career. Often selected as the most representative of all of his speeches, "The Man with the Muck-rake" first signaled Roosevelt's movement toward progressivism. It evidences a clear break from Roosevelt's conservative policies and signaled his growing acceptance of the need for economic and political reform. Roosevelt's address at Osawatomie, Kansas, delivered on August 31, 1910 was in effect, his first speech of his 1912 Progressive presidential campaign. It was called "a turning point both in Roosevelt's career and in the history of the nation,"[4] in it Roosevelt codified the progressive proposals he had come to advocate. He aptly gave his philosophy the title of "The New Nationalism." This address clearly signaled the growing schism within the Republican party, marking Roosevelt as the principal spokesman for the liberal branch.

THE MAN WITH THE MUCK-RAKE

On a bright, sunny Saturday, April 14, 1906, President Theodore Roosevelt delivered the major address of the cornerstone laying-ceremonies for the new three-million-dollar House of Representatives office building. Roosevelt had let it be known in advance that he anticipated using this occasion for a major address with national implications. On St. Patrick's Day almost a month earlier, he had previously expressed some of his ideas in an off-the-record impromptu speech at the Washington Gridiron Club. Now, after thoroughly thinking through his ideas and devoting considerable time to preparing his speech, with members of Congress, the Supreme Court, the diplomatic corps, and an expectant press corps listening,

Roosevelt launched into one of the most remarkable speeches of his career.[5]

After quickly acknowledging that Washington was the first American president to lay the cornerstone of a significant government building, Roosevelt observed that "under altered external form we war with the same tendencies toward evil that were evident in Washington's time, and are helped by the same tendencies for good. It is about these that I wish to say a word to-day."[6] Having thus set the stage for a speech dealing with good and evil, Roosevelt took as his text a work of John Bunyan's.

> In Bunyan's "Pilgrim's Progress" you may recall the description of the Man with the Muck-rake, the man who could look no way but downward, with the muck-rake in his hand; who was offered a celestial crown for his muck-rake, but who would neither look up nor regard the crown he was offered, but continued to rake to himself the filth of the floor.

Having focused his audience's attention on the image of the man with the muck-rake, Roosevelt then expanded on that image by presenting his thesis.

> Now, it is very necessary that we should not flinch from seeing what is vile and debasing. There is filth on the floor, and it must be scraped up with the muck-rake;   and there are times and places where this service is the most needed of all the services that can be performed. But the man who never does anything else, who never thinks, or speaks or writes, save of his feats with the muck-rake, speedily becomes not a help to society, not an incitement to good, but one of the most potent forces for evil.

Roosevelt's text and thesis reflected one of the two topoi of militant decency that undergirds this speech; character. The man who focused entirely on the negative, failing to acknowledge the positive, lacked character. For Roosevelt, anything carried to excess, anything done without common sense and moderation, could create evil. Thus, journalists who speak or write only of the negative aspects of society, whose work is marked by exaggeration and excess rather than accuracy and moderation, are not people of character contributing to the social good. Rather, they lack character and hence are "potent forces for evil."

In the body of his speech Roosevelt argued four major points.   The first major point was a carefully qualified amplification of the thesis. The muckrakers, Roosevelt suggested, created problems when their criticism was excessive.

However, Roosevelt prudently observed that "to denounce mud-slinging does not mean the endorsement of whitewashing." Roosevelt well recognized that the muckrakers had exposed many fundamental problems with American life. He assiduously attempted to distinguish between legitimate criticism of the American political, economic, and social system, and excessive criticisms:

> To assail the great and admitted evils of our political and industrial life with such crude and sweeping generalizations as to include decent men in the general condemnation means the searing of the public conscience. There results a general attitude either of cynical belief in and indifference to public corruption or else of a distrustful inability to discriminate between the good and the bad. Either attitude is fraught with untold damage to the country as a whole. The fool who has not sense to discriminate between what is good and what is bad is well-nigh as dangerous as the man who does discriminate and yet chooses the bad. . . . Hysterical sensationalism is the very poorest weapon wherewith to fight for lasting righteousness. The men who with stern sobriety and truth assail the many evils of our time, whether in the public press, or in magazines, or in books, are the leaders and allies of all engaged in the work for social and political betterment. But if they give good reason for distrust of what they say, if they chill the ardor of those who demand truth as a primary virtue, they thereby betray the good cause, and play right into the hands of the very men against whom they are nominally at war.

This condemnation of the excesses of the muckrakers is consistent with remarks Roosevelt had been making as early as 1901. Ultimately, as a variety of Roosevelt scholars have illustrated, Roosevelt's concern was that the muckrakers were stirring up class feelings.' In so doing, he feared that they might well be laying the grounds for the disruption of American society by class warfare. Roosevelt expresses these thoughts in the second major point of his address.

> At this moment we are passing through a period of great unrest-social, political, and industrial unrest. It is of the utmost importance for our future that this should prove to be not the unrest of mere rebelliousness against life, of mere dissatisfaction with the inevitable inequality of conditions, but the unrest of a resolute and eager

ambition to secure the betterment of the individual and the nation. So far as this movement of agitation throughout the country takes the form of a fierce discontent with evil, of a determination to punish the authors of evil, whether in industry or politics, the feeling is to be heartily welcomed as a sign of healthy life. If, on the other hand, it turns into a mere crusade of appetite against appetite, of a contest between the brutal greed of the "have-nots" and the brutal greed of the "haves" then it has no significance for good, but only for evil. If it seeks to establish a line of cleavage, not along the line which divides good men from bad, but along that other line, running at right angles thereto, which divides those who are well off from those who are less well off, then it will be fraught with immeasurable harm to the body politic.

Thus, Roosevelt's second major point was that inherent in the exposures of the muckrakers was the potential to disrupt the very fabric of United States society by creating class conflict. Roosevelt, as we have seen, consistently linked order to justice and equality. Without justice and equality, order was sure to perish. Hence, as the muckrakers illustrated the lack of justice and equality in the United States, Roosevelt grew to believe that responsible citizens and leaders should strive to implement reforms that would restore justice and equality to life in the United States. Failing to do so might well result in the disruption of our social order. Only through reform that redressed the legitimate evils exposed by the muckrakers could our social order be preserved. Thus, the second basic theme of militant decency supporting this speech is Roosevelt's desire for order, a social order based on justice and equality.

Acknowledging the merit of much of the muckrakers criticism of American life, Roosevelt introduced his third and fourth major points by claiming that it is important for the United States "to grapple with the problems connected with the amassing of enormous fortunes and the use of those fortunes, both corporate and individual, in business." He then presented two suggestions for better enabling the United States to grapple with these problems.

Roosevelt's third major point was that one way of treating enormous fortunes was to consider the adoption of a progressive inheritance tax. Roosevelt mentioned this idea but did not amplify it beyond noting that such a tax should be aimed "merely at the inheritance or transmission in their entirety of those fortunes swollen beyond all healthy limits."

Nevertheless, it represents one response to the economic injustices exposed by the muckrakers.

Roosevelt's final major point was that an additional way of treating enormous fortunes would be for the national government to "in some form exercise supervision over corporations engaged in interstate business." Roosevelt observed that virtually all larger corporations are so engaged, and that his administration had already begun to take the first steps in this direction.

Roosevelt recognized that this would require public servants of unquestioned integrity and character.

> The eighth commandment reads: "Thou shall not steal." It does not read: "Thou shalt not steal from the rich man." It does not read: "Thou shalt not steal from the poor man." It reads simply and plainly: "Thou shalt not steal." No good whatever will come from that warped and mock morality which denounces the misdeeds of men of wealth and forgets the misdeeds practiced at their expense; which denounces bribery, but blinds itself to blackmail; which foams with rage if a corporation secures favors by improper methods, and merely leers with hideous mirth if the corporation is itself wronged. The only public servant who can be trusted honestly to protect the rights of the public against the misdeed of the corporation is that public man who will just as surely protect the corporation itself from wrongful aggression.

Roosevelt's two proposals to ensure an equitable and just economic order rested largely on his belief in character. If men of character could be found to equitably legislate and manage taxation and regulation programs, the nation's problems could be successfully resolved. Similarly, the topoi of character also permeates the conclusion of this speech.

Roosevelt concludes this address with a two-paragraph discussion of the need for character. If men had sympathy for one another and attempted to help one another, rather than attempting to improve themselves by pulling down others, Roosevelt was confident that the nation's problems could be managed. "The foundation-stone of national life," Roosevelt concluded, "is, and ever must be, the high individual character of the average citizen."

As Stephen Lucas has claimed, this speech "was a milestone" along Roosevelt's movement to the left, a "movement which would continue through the remainder of his second administration and ultimately bring him to the Bull Moose campaign of 1912." Reaction to the speech was predictable.

Conservatives lauded Roosevelt's denunciation of the muckrakers, but they attacked his proposals for taxation and regulation. Liberals were disturbed by his denunciation of the muckrakers, although they lauded his proposals for taxation and regulation.[8]

Roosevelt scholars have found this speech somewhat peculiar because of the perceived incongruity of Roosevelt's linking his attack on the muckrakers with his proposals for taxation and regulation. Yet for Roosevelt this linking was logically grounded in his lifelong rhetoric of militant decency. His attack on the muckrakers was prompted by his growing concern that many of their exposures of social, political and economic corruption had gone to far and were no longer grounded in fact.[9] Hence he questioned the character of those who were given to excess. Roosevelt's attack on the character of those muckrakers given to excess would help to maintain order by reminding his audience of the need to distinguish between the legitimate and illegitimate attacks made by the muckrakers. It would maintain order by defusing many of the more notorious claims of the muckrakers. Yet Roosevelt recognized that not all of the muckrakers were given to excess. Many had often been accurate and their revelations had the potential to create class conflict and disrupt American life. Hence, he offered two proposals to help ameliorate the economic conditions being exposed by the muckrakers. Roosevelt's proposals for inheritance taxes and increased government regulation of business would help maintain order by illustrating that the nation had an orderly means of handling the legitimate problems exposed by the muckrakers. Undergirding the entire speech, and giving it unity, is a crucial component of Roosevelt's topoi system, his belief in an orderly society.

This speech clearly illustrates many of the rhetorical tactics that Roosevelt used throughout his life. First, it is clearly homiletic in nature. Like a preacher, Roosevelt opened with a text, explained his text, and amplified it by applying it to contemporary problems. Like a preacher, Roosevelt spoke of good and evil throughout this address. Like a preacher, Roosevelt quoted Scripture.

Second, as in many of his other addresses, Roosevelt made relatively little use of evidence in this speech. He did draw on "Pilgrim's Progress," the work of an Elizabethan cleric, and Scripture. Nevertheless the vast majority of the speech consisted of Roosevelt's assertions.

Third, while this speech made use of both analogy and causal reasoning, ultimately, like much of Roosevelt's speaking, its persuasive force rested on either/or reasoning. Either Americans followed his advice, first recognizing that much of what the muckrakers had said is excessive, and second, acting prudently to curb the evils that the muckrakers had legitimately exposed, or the United States may be faced with a conflict that "divides those who are well off from those who are less well off." Such a class conflict, Roosevelt concluded, would be "fraught with immeasurable harm to the body politic."

Finally, more than most of his speeches, this speech revealed Roosevelt as a wordsmith. With this speech Roosevelt coined the term "muckraker" and made it a part of the language. He used highly connotative language throughout the speech. Roosevelt's characteristic invective was rarely more evident than in this address. The muckraker who abused his position was a "liar," "thief," "the despair of honest men," and "a wild preacher of unrest," who suffered from "moral color-blindness." His writing was "hysterical sensationalism," "lurid," and "untruthful." Moreover, wherever Roosevelt found muckrakers, he found evil lurking nearby. Muckrakers were "potent forces for evil," who produced, "tendencies toward evil," and "a sodden acquiescence in evil."

Important as Roosevelt's highly connotative language was to this speech, his characteristic use of balanced sentences was even more so. Roosevelt deliberately choose not to name specific muckrakers in this speech.[10] Hence, it was through the skillful use of balanced sentences that Roosevelt drew the crucial distinction between "good" and "bad" muckrakers.

    * I hail as a benefactor every writer or speaker,
    every man who, on the platform, or in book,
    magazine, or newspaper, with merciless severity
    makes such attack, provided always that he in
    his turn remembers that the attack is of use only
    if it is absolutely truthful.

    * It is because I feel that there should be no
    rest in the endless war against the forces of evil
    that I ask that the war be conducted with sanity
    as well as with resolution.

    * The men with the muck-rakes are often
    indispensable to the well-being of society; but
    only if they know when to stop raking the muck,
    and to look upward to the celestial crown above
    them, to the crown of worthy endeavor.

Roosevelt's characteristic use of balanced sentences allowed him to draw the distinction between "good" and "bad" muckrakers, so necessary in this address.

"The Man with the Muck-rake" is deservedly among Roosevelt's best known speeches. Two of the basic components of his topoi system, his beliefs in order and character, are reflected in the ideas he expresses. They give unity and coherence to a speech that at first glance seems to involve highly disparate topics.

Moreover, it was an artistically sound speech, reflecting Roosevelt's homiletic approach to speechmaking, his reliance on his own assertions and ethos, his use of either/or reasoning, and his exceptional ability as a wordsmith.

THE NEW NATIONALISM

In the years following Roosevelt's 1906 "Man with the Muck-rake" speech, the reform element of the Republican party grew stronger, and Theodore Roosevelt grew more sympathetic. Shortly after leaving office in 1909, Roosevelt read Herbert Croly's The Promise of American Life. Croly's book, and his subsequent discussions with Roosevelt, helped Roosevelt clarify his ideas about political and economic reform. By 1910 the hopes of the Republican progressives centered around Theodore Roosevelt. The Boston Traveler described the political situation that Roosevelt confronted in early 1910.

> A new party is arising in the United States as steadily and inevitably as the water rises in the marshes when the tide comes in. It is more significant than the Liberal movement of 1872 or the Mugwump revolt of 1884. It represents the almost universal demand for the "square deal" for morality in politics and business, for the recognition of HUMAN rights as PROPERTY rights have been recognized in the past, for eliminating crookedness and making straight the ways of government. The progressives, or insurgents, represent this movement and Theodore Roosevelt is its chief spokesman. He typifies an epoch. Roosevelt is not merely a MAN he is a MOVEMENT.[11]

With insurgent Republicans looking to him for leadership, in the late summer of 1910 the ex-president set out on a major speaking tour. Accompanied initially by seventeen journalists, Roosevelt traveled 5,500 miles, delivering fourteen prepared speeches and hundreds of impromptu speeches to often tumultuous crowds. The original seventeen journalists soon swelled in number until it took three full railroad cars to carry all of the press that was reporting on Roosevelt's speaking.

On August 31, in Osawatomie, Kansas, at the dedication of the John Brown battlefield, with thousands of Civil War veterans in an audience estimated at 15,000, the governor of Kansas quieted an expectant audience: "Citizens of Kansas, be still for a minute and I will introduce the greatest man in the

world."   Roosevelt stepped to the podium and delivered "The
New Nationalism" speech. This speech was quickly recognized
as an explicit statement of his beliefs that widened the gap
between Roosevelt and the conservative wing of the Republican
party, making Roosevelt the primary spokesman of the
progressive wing and a likely candidate for the 1912
nomination.[12]

Roosevelt   opened   this   address   with   a   long
acknowledgment of his audience of Civil War veterans and their
contribution to the achievements of "the high purpose of
Abraham Lincoln."   This lengthy introduction culminated in
Roosevelt's observation that Lincoln "forecast our present
struggle and saw the way out." Roosevelt then took as his text
three statements from Lincoln.   Lincoln said, observed
Roosevelt,

> "I hold that while man exists it is his duty to
> improve not only his own condition, but to assist
> in ameliorating mankind." And again, "Labor is
> prior to, and independent of, capital. Capital is
> only the fruit of labor, and could never have
> existed if labor had not first existed. Labor is the
> superior of capital, and deserves much the higher
> consideration."
>
> If that remark was original with me, I
> should be even more strongly denounced as a
> communist agitator than I shall be anyhow. It is
> Lincoln's. I am only quoting it; and that is one
> side; that is the side the capitalist should hear.
> Now let the working man hear his side.
>
> "Capital has its rights, which are as
> worthy of protection as any other rights. . . .
> Nor should this lead to a war upon the owners
> of property.   Property is the fruit of labor; . .
> . property is desirable; is a positive good in the
> world."   And then comes a thoroughly Lincoln-
> like sentence: "Let not him who is houseless pull
> down the house of another, but let him work
> diligently and build one for himself, thus by
> example assuring that his own shall be safe from
> violence when built."

Roosevelt then expanded on his text to present his
thesis. Claiming that Lincoln "took substantially the attitude
that we ought to take," toward the conflict between capital and
labor, Roosevelt claimed that by 1910 this conflict appeared

> as the struggle of freemen to gain and hold the
> right of self-government as against the special
> interests, who twist the methods of free
> government into machinery for defeating the

popular will.   At every stage, and under all circumstances, the essence of the struggle is to equalize opportunity, destroy privilege, and give to the life and citizenship of every individual the highest possible value both to himself and to the commonwealth.

Roosevelt's belief in social responsibility underlies his thesis. By 1910, he argued, socially responsible reform was necessary to equate opportunity, destroy privilege and allow all Americans to develop to their fullest potential, hence benefiting both themselves and the nation.

In the body of this address Roosevelt presented six general goals for the United States.   However, unlike many of his addresses, in this speech he generated specific recommendations for implementing most of his general goals. In so doing, Roosevelt was in effect presenting his interpretation of progressivism.   Moreover, he was also previewing the platform upon which he would campaign in 1912.

The first, and most extensively developed goal that Roosevelt presented was the very essence of the Progressive movement, and a logical consequence of Roosevelt's thesis. "The citizens of the United States," proclaimed Roosevelt, "must effectively control the mighty commercial forces which they have Ist themselves called into being."   To this end, Roosevelt presented a wide variety of proposals. Among them were:

* Prohibiting "the use of corporate funds directly or indirectly for political purposes."

* Supervising "the capitalization of not only public- service corporations, including , particularly, railways, but of all corporations doing an interstate business."

* Regulating in a "thoroughgoing and effective" manner businesses engaged in interstate commerce.

* Limiting the duration of grants to public-service corporation franchises, and "never without proper provision for compensation to the public."

* Extending the concept of public-service corporation franchises "to combinations which control necessaries of life, such as meat, oil, and coal."

* Holding the officers, especially the directors, "personally responsible when any corporation breaks the law."

* Establishing "an expert tariff commission, wholly removed from the possibility of political pressure or of improper business influence."

If adopted, as many of them ultimately were, Roosevelt's specific reforms to "control the mighty commercial forces" would forever change the face of the United States economy.

Roosevelt's proposed reforms were based on two themes that pervaded his thinking and speaking-his concerns for order and social responsibility. Reforms such as those he presented, Roosevelt believed, would help provide all people with equal economic opportunity. Hence by eliminating the perception that some elements of society had unfair advantages, these reforms would contribute to maintaining social order. Moreover, they were socially responsible reforms. Roosevelt believed that they would allow both individuals and society to develop to their maximum potential, and that they demonstrated belief in tolerance and equality.

Roosevelt's second major goal also involved the nation's economic life. "The absence of effective State, and especially, national, restraint upon unfair money-getting," Roosevelt claimed, "has tended to create a small class of enormously wealthy and economically powerful men, whose chief object is to hold and increase their power." Roosevelt carefully pointed out that "we grudge no man a fortune in civil life," but only if it was gained fairly, "without doing damage to the community," and if it was used for the general welfare and benefit of the community. Speaking specifically of his goal to put restraints on the acquisition and use of large fortunes, Roosevelt attempted to prepare his audience for his next recommendations.

> This, I know, implies a policy of a far more active governmental interference with social and economic conditions in this country than we have yet had, but I think we have got to face the fact that such an increase in governmental control is now necessary. . . . the really big fortune, the swollen fortune, by the mere fact of its size acquires qualities which differentiate it in kind as well as in degree from what is possessed by men of relatively small means.

Roosevelt offered two specific proposals to limit large fortunes. First, he advocated "a graduated income tax on big fortunes." Second, he advocated "another tax which is far more easily collected and far more effective-a graduated inheritance

2~1

tax on big fortunes, properly safeguarded against evasion and increasing rapidly in amount with the size of the estate."

Roosevelt's efforts to limit large fortunes reflect his beliefs in order, social responsibility, and work, three of the basic topoi of his belief system. Taxes, particularly graduated taxes, would help ensure that those with fortunes contributed their fair share to the public good. In so doing, they would help ameliorate growing class consciousness and division, which Roosevelt felt could ultimately disrupt the social order. For Roosevelt, taxing large fortunes was a socially responsible way of handling the problem. It guaranteed that a portion of those fortunes would be put to public use.

Finally, Roosevelt's penchant for inheritance taxes, evidenced both in this address and in his earlier "The Man with the Muck-rake" address, reflected his belief in the gospel of work. Inherited money is acquired largely without work. Yet, said Roosevelt in this address, "No man should receive a dollar unless that dollar has been fairly earned." Inheritance taxes, perhaps more than many types of taxes, may have been perceived by Roosevelt as fostering the work ethic.

Roosevelt presented his third and fourth goals without recommending how to achieve them. "It is hardly necessary for me to repeat," he observed as he introduced his third goal, "that I believe in an efficient army and navy large enough to secure for us abroad that respect which is the surest guaranty of peace." Observing that he would speak about his fourth national goal "at length elsewhere," in this speech Roosevelt treated the conservation issue briefly in several sentences. Roosevelt stated that his goal was to allow use of our natural resources while preventing their waste.

Roosevelt's fifth national goal was to enable farmers "to get for themselves and their wives and children not only the benefits of better farming, but also those of better business methods and better conditions of life on the farm." He offered several specific suggestions to help farmers. First, he recommended that those government agencies involved with farmers, such as the federal and state departments of agriculture, as well as state agricultural colleges and experimental stations, "extend their work to cover all phases of farm life, instead of limiting themselves, as they have far too often limited themselves in the past, solely to the question of the production of crops." Second, in "a special word to the farmer," Roosevelt urged the farmer to remember "that the improvement goes on indoors as well as out; let him remember that the farmer's wife should have her share of thought and attention just as much as the farmer himself."

Roosevelt's fifth goal of enabling farmers to improve themselves, although treated somewhat more extensively than the two goals that preceded it, is not well developed. Presented in one long paragraph, Roosevelt's suggestions are somewhat vague.   However, they reflect an awareness that the nation's farmers needed to enter the age of big business, by concerning themselves not only with crop production, but also with business methods. Moreover, his suggestions to farmers reveal his high regard for women and family life. This section of the address is based on Roosevelt's belief in work.   The burden of improving themselves, Roosevelt noted, "will fall, as it should, mainly upon the great organizations of the farmers themselves." Government can help farmers become more efficient, improving their production and business methods, but ultimately the farmer must work to improve himself.

Roosevelt introduced his sixth goal by claiming that "the right to regulate the use of wealth in the public interest is universally admitted.   Let us admit also the right to regulate the terms and conditions of labor, which is the chief element of wealth, directly in the interest of the common good."   Given these admissions, Roosevelt's sixth goal, improving the conditions of the American laborer, followed logically. (+1

Roosevelt presented a variety of specific proposals to improve working conditions.   They included a comprehensive workmen's compensation act, state and national laws to regulate child labor, regulation of work for women, increased vocational training in the public schools, better sanitary conditions for United States workers, and increasing the use of safety equipment in industry and commerce.   Though Roosevelt was ready to make significant reforms on behalf of the worker, he tempered his advocacy of reforms on behalf of the workers by declaring that

> in the interest of the working man himself we
> need to set our faces like flint against mob-
> violence, just as against corporate greed; against
> violence and injustice and lawlessness by wage-
> workers just as much as against lawlessness,
> cunning and greed and selfish arrogance of
> employers. If I could ask but one thing of my
> fellow countrymen, my request would be that,
> whenever they go in for reform, they remember
> the two sides, and that they always exact justice
> from one side as much as from the other.

Roosevelt's goal of improving working conditions, and the specific proposals he advocated to achieve it, reflect his beliefs in social responsibility and character. Employers of character, socially responsible employers, should provide their workers with agreeable working conditions. If they did not, then it was clearly the responsibility of the government to enforce such conditions. This section of the speech also reveals

Roosevelt's concern for order.   Recognizing that he was advocating an extensive group of reforms on behalf of United States labor, Roosevelt pointed out that labor had the responsibility to avoid resorting to violence and lawlessness.

Roosevelt's conclusion is substantially longer than the conclusions of most of his addresses. Essentially it is a three-page restatement of the concerns he expressed in his introduction about property rights and human rights.

> I believe in shaping the ends of government to protect property as well as human welfare. Normally, and in the long run, the ends are the same; but whenever the alternative must be faced, I am for men and not for property, as you were in the Civil War.   I am far from underestimating the importance of dividends; but I rank dividends below human character.

Roosevelt's conclusion is notable for two additional reasons. First, it is here that he appropriated Herbert Croly's phrase to label his program "The New Nationalism." Second, he used the conclusion to add one final idea to this speech. It was an idea with which those who frequently listened to Roosevelt speak were most familiar, because in his conclusion, Roosevelt comments on the importance of individual character. "In the last analysis," Roosevelt claimed,

> the most important elements in any man's career must be the sum of those qualities which, in the aggregate, we speak of as character. If he has not got it, then no law that the wit of man can devise, no administration of the law by the boldest and strongest executive, will avail to help him. You must have the right kind of character."

With a citizenry of character, and the progressive reforms of "The New Nationalism," the United States would overcome it's current problems.

Every key element or topoi of Roosevelt's rhetoric of militant decency manifests itself in this speech. The major problems that Roosevelt addressed in this speech involved the relationships between property rights and human rights, and the implications of those relationships for the government's role in the conduct of the nation's business. Hence, the topoi of social responsibility, work, and order undergird substantial portions of this address.   Roosevelt also acknowledged the importance of power when he discussed his goals for the nation, and concluded by affirming the centrality of character to national development. "The New Nationalism" previewed and summarized Roosevelt's speaking on domestic issues for the remaining eight and one-half years of his life, clearly reflecting the five key themes of Roosevelt's rhetoric of militant decency.

In addition to illustrating much of Roosevelt's thought, this speech also illustrates many of the rhetorical techniques that he commonly employed. The characteristics that mark many of the speeches heretofore examined clearly affect this speech. It is homiletic in nature. The support material Roosevelt used is limited. He relied primarily on his own assertions, although he did make limited use of historical examples. As in many of his other addresses, Roosevelt used either/or and deductive reasoning. Finally, Roosevelt frequently uses intense, highly conative language and balanced sentences.

Roosevelt used this speech to preach a moralistic lesson to his congregants, the American people. Taking his text from Lincoln, Roosevelt preached that human rights must supercede property rights. He then amplified this text, applying it to contemporary problems. Hence, like much of Roosevelt's speaking, the homiletic nature of this speech was evident in both content and form.

Roosevelt advocated a host of reforms in this persuasive address. Yet, unlike the typical speech of persuasion on public policy issues, but consistent with the entire body of his own speaking, Roosevelt made very little use of evidence. The evidence that Roosevelt does use is in the form of historical example. Roosevelt, adapting in part to his audience of Civil War veterans, made four references to the Union armies. Two of them are hypothetical, but so typical that no doubt both his immediate audience and the larger national audience had no trouble accepting them. He made passing references to the successes of several existing federal regulatory agencies, implying that they serve as examples of what might be done more extensively. In his brief discussion of conservation, Roosevelt cited early federal policies for the sale of land as a precedent for his own ideas. Nevertheless, these are relatively isolated pieces of evidence in a lengthy speech that is supported primarily by the assertions of the speaker.

Roosevelt made frequent use of deductive reasoning in this address. Each of Roosevelt's goals for the nation was a broad general statement that served as a general premise in a deductive syllogism. The minor premises were often not stated, as is frequently the case in the oral presentation of syllogistic reasoning. Roosevelt's specific recommendations served as the conclusions.[13] For example, Roosevelt developed his first point as follows:

General Premise (Goal): The citizens of the United States must effectively control the mighty commercial forces that they have themselves called into being.

Minor Premise (Unstated):   Prohibiting the use of corporate funds for political purposes helps control commercial forces.

Conclusion: Therefore, corporations should be prohibited from using their funds for political purposes.
In this fashion, moving from broad general goals to specific policy recommendations, Roosevelt deductively developed much of this speech.

Nevertheless, the ultimate persuasive effectiveness of this speech rests primarily on Roosevelt's characteristic use of either/or reasoning. Throughout this speech Roosevelt observed that either his goals would be attained and his recommendations adopted, or the nation faced disaster. Unless the commercial forces and large fortunes were controlled, economic disaster and the specter of class warfare confronted the United States. Either we maintained a strong military as "the surest guaranty of peace," or we faced the inability to exert our will overseas and an increased likelihood of war. Either we conserved our national resources, or we robbed, "by wasteful use, the generations that come after us." Either farms adopted business methods, or they faced increasing hardships. Either we regulated "the terms and conditions of labor" or "we keep countless men from being good citizens by the conditions of life with which we surround them," and we face the specter of class warfare. In sum, much of Roosevelt's persuasiveness in this address is derived from his use of either/or reasoning to posit his recommendations against unacceptable alternatives.

Roosevelt's use of language in this address is consistent with his other speaking. Although Herbert Croly used the phrase earlier, Roosevelt first used the phrase "The New Nationalism" in this speech. It was an apt description of his program and it quickly became popular. Throughout the speech he used strong, forceful language. Moreover, he consistently made use of balanced sentences to appear reasonable, thoughtful, and impartial.

 * I have small use for the public servant who can always see and denounce the corruption of the capitalist, but who cannot persuade himself, especially before election, to say a word about lawless-mob-violence.

 * I do not ask for overcentralization; but I do ask that we work in a spirit of broad and far-reaching nationalism when we work for what concerns our people as a whole.

> *   I recognize the right and duty of this
> generation to develop and use the natural
> resources of our land; but I do not recognize the
> right to waste them, or to rob, by wasteful use,
> the generations that come after us.

Roosevelt's use of balanced sentences in this speech seems designed to help contribute to his image as a just and impartial former president seeking the best for his nation. Roosevelt was aware that this speech would be controversial, and was no doubt especially concerned about conservative reaction.   Controversial it was.   George Mowry, one of the foremost historians of the Progressive movement has claimed that "when Roosevelt finished at Osawatomie he had probably delivered the most radical speech ever given by an ex-president."   Even conservatives who were close to Roosevelt, such as Henry Cabot Lodge, had reservations about this address.   In some of Roosevelt's speaking his use of balanced sentences often seems almost platitudinous.   However, in this speech Roosevelt's balanced sentences frequently seem to attempt to satisfy not only the progressives but also the conservatives.[14]

CONCLUSIONS

It is impossible to think of the Progressive movement without thinking of Theodore Roosevelt.   Mowry provides an excellent synopsis of the relationship between the man and the movement.

> In the days of its infancy he had lent the
> Progressive movement the prestige of his great
> name.   Without his support of varying intensity
> many progressive proposals would not have been
> written into statutes between 1901 and 1909. .
> .   . Roosevelt's New Nationalism and the
> Progressive platform of 1912 were in themselves
> major steps in the development of progressive
> principles.

Theodore Roosevelt's rhetoric of militant decency reflects many of the same concerns of the Progressive movement.   Hence, it is not surprising to find that few speeches were more important to the evolution of the Progressive movement than Roosevelt's 1906 muckraker address that portended his sympathy to progressive reform, and his 1910 address in which he presented his New Nationalism program of progressive reform.[15]

NOTES

1.   Among the first to use the term were James W. Ceaser, Glen E. Thurow, Jeffrey Tulis, and Joseph M. Bessette, "The Rise of the Rhetorical Presidency," Presidential Studies Quarterly (Spring 1981): 158-71.   For an explanation of Roosevelt's role in expanding the importance of presidential rhetoric see Jeffrey K. Tulis, The Rhetorical Presidency (Princeton, N.J.: Princeton University Press, 1987), 4-19; 95-116. For a succinct analysis of the relationship of rhetoric to other presidential powers in the United States see Theodore Windt, Presidential Rhetoric: The Imperial Age 1961-1974 (Dubuque, Iowa: Kendall Hunt Publishing Company, 1978), 1-5.

2. Theodore Roosevelt, "The Heirs of Abraham Lincoln," in Theodore Roosevelt, The Works of Theodore Roosevelt: National Edition (New York: Charles Scribner's and Sons, 1926), 16, 359. Any competent history that treats the United States in the early 20th century will detail the reforms of the Progressive movement.   See, for example, David Shannon, Twentieth Century America: The United States Since the 1890's (Chicago, Rand McNally Co., 1963), 23-46; John A. Garraty, The American Nation: A History of the United States (New York: Harper and Row, 1971), 739-68.

3.   Theodore Roosevelt, "The Case Against The Reactionaries," in The Works of Theodore Roosevelt: National Edition (New York: Charles Scribner's Sons, 1926), 17, 231.

4.   Richard N. Current, John A. Garraty, Julius Weinberg, Words that Made American History (Boston: Little, Brown and Company, 1972), 2, 315.

5.   For background on the immediate rhetorical situation and Roosevelt's speech preparation see Lynda Beltz, "Theodore Roosevelt's 'Man with the Muck-rake'," Central States Speech Journal (Summer 1969): 97-103; John E. Semonche, "Theodore Roosevelt's 'Muck-rake' Speech: A Reassessment," Mid-America (April 1964): 114-25; and Stephen E. Lucas "Theodore Roosevelt's 'The Man with the Muck-rake': A Reinterpretation," Quarterly Journal of Speech (December 1973): 452-62.

6. This and all references to the speech are taken from the version found elsewhere in this volume and drawn from The Works of Theodore Roosevelt: National Edition, (New York: Charles Scribner's Sons, 1926), 16, 415-24.

7.   See Semonche, "Theodore Roosevelt's 'Muck-rake'" Speech," 114-19 for a concise analysis of the evolution of Roosevelt's attitudes towards the muckrakers. Also see William Henry Harbaugh, The Life and Times of Theodore Roosevelt (New York: Collier Books, 1963), 253-59. Two days before his Gridiron Club remarks and a month before this speech Roosevelt wrote to William Howard Taft observing that some of the muckrakers were socialists, others "merely lurid sensationalists, but they are all building up a revolutionary feeling." Though he went on to observe that these feelings would probably manifest themselves in the form of a political campaign, clearly Roosevelt recognized the potential for disruptive class conflict being created by the muckrakers. See Elting E. Morison, ed., The Letters of Theodore Roosevelt, Vol. V: The Big Stick (Cambridge, Mass.: Harvard University Press, 1952), 184.

8.   Lucas, "Theodore Roosevelt's 'The Man with the Muck-rake': A Reinterpretation," 459.   For summaries of reaction to this speech see Harbaugh, The Life and Times of Theodore Roosevelt, 257-259 and Arthur Weinberg and Lila Weinberg, The Muckrakers (New York: G. P. Putnam's Sons, 1964), 57.

9.   Roosevelt was widely reported to be especially disturbed by the "yellow " journalism of the Hearst newspapers. Perhaps the straw that broke his back was the series of articles by David Graham Phillips, "The Treason of the Senate" which first appeared in Cosmopolitan in March 1906.   Shortly after delivering "The Man with the Muck-rake," Roosevelt wrote George Lorimer, editor of the Saturday Evening Post that "I do not believe that the articles that Mr. Phillips has written, and notably these articles on the Senate, do anything but harm. They contain so much more falsehood than truth that they give no accurate guide for those who are really anxious to war against corruption, and they do excite a hysterical and ignorant feeling against everything existing, good or bad."   Roosevelt added that work such as Phillips's created an atmosphere that made genuine reform difficult because it caused confusion between the need for reform and the need for destruction. See Morrison, The Letters of Theodore Roosevelt, Vol. V: The Big Stick, 269.

10.   See Beltz, "Theodore Roosevelt's 'Man With The Muckrake," 99, for an explanation of this decision.

11. Virtually every biographer acknowledges that Croly, if not altering Roosevelt's thought, helped to clarify it. See, for examples, G. Wallace Chessman, Theodore Roosevelt and the Politics of Power (Boston: Little Brown and Company, 1969), 168-69 and Henry F. Pringle, Theodore Roosevelt: A Biography (New York: Harcourt Brace, Janovich, 1956), 379-80. The Boston Traveler statement is quoted in "A Review of the World," Current Literature, (October 1910): 350.

12. Many of the details in this and the preceding paragraph are drawn from the excellent account of Roosevelt's speaking tour, and the reaction to that tour, found in "A Review of the World," Current Literature, 350-62. Also see Ernest Hamlin Abbott's introduction to Theodore Roosevelt, The New Nationalism, (New York: The Outlook Company, 1910), vi-xxi. The day after this speech, "Roosevelt in 1912" was heard constantly on Roosevelt's train. Later that day, in Kansas City, Roosevelt was greeted with a song calling for his return to the presidency. See Joseph L. Gardner, Departing Glory: Theodore Roosevelt as Ex-President, (New York: Charles Scribner's Sons, 1973), 190-91.

13. Most public speaking textbooks will discuss deductive reasoning. See for example, Stephen E. Lucas, The Art of Public Speaking (New York: Random House, 1989), 327-29.

14. For a contemporary account of the controversy generated by this speech see "A Review of the World," 356-59. For a historical perspective on the controversy, including Lodge's reaction, see George Mowry, Theodore Roosevelt and the Progressive Movement (New York: Hill and Wang, 1960), 145-47.

15. Mowry, Theodore Roosevelt and the Progressive Movement, 380.

Epilogue

The end came quickly for Theodore Roosevelt. Although he suffered at times from a variety of ailments, including inflammatory rheumatism, to the public he no doubt seemed active throughout 1918, when he made two speaking tours on behalf of the war effort. Yet, particularly as the year closed, he was in and out of the hospital and spent much of the day bedridden. By his sixtieth year, the physical resources of the man who had exemplified the strenuous life were wearing down. After a quiet day that included time spent writing, at four o'clock on the morning of January 6, 1919, Roosevelt was stricken with an embolism, or blood clot in the coronary artery. He never awoke from his sleep.[1]

He left behind a unique rhetorical legacy. Roosevelt was not simply the preacher militant. Nor was he the typical political orator. Rather, though he spoke on the political issues of his day, he did so utilizing many of the moral imperatives and the rhetorical forms more commonly associated with the pulpit than with political hustings.

Both Roosevelt and his audiences recognized the religious nature of his political pronouncements. Roosevelt himself used the phrase "bully pulpit" to describe the presidency. Jane Addams called him "a veritable preacher of social righteousness with the irresistible eloquence of faith sanctified by work." Gifford Pinchot, Roosevelt's associate in many of the battles he waged on behalf of conservation, called Roosevelt "the greatest preacher of righteousness in modern times," adding that "there was no man beyond the reach of his preaching and example."[2]

Roosevelt's rhetoric, by every reasonable standard, was effective. Traditionally, communication scholars have critiqued speeches and speakers utilizing four criteria: effectiveness, artistic merit, validity, and motivation. Applying those criteria to Roosevelt, we must ask, first, did Roosevelt accomplished what he wished? Did he secure results?[3]

While it is impossible to measure the precise effect of Roosevelt's speaking, all of the existing evidence suggests that the vast majority of the time he secured the results he wished. Although he twice lost elections involving three or more major candidates (the 1886 New York City mayoralty race and the 1912 Presidential election), he won every other election in which he campaigned, including those to the state legislature, the governorship, the vice presidency and the presidency. His advocacy on behalf of the Hepburn Act is considered to be virtually the first example of a president securing legislation by going over the heads of Congress and speaking directly to the people. His campaign on behalf of this act, and much of his conduct as president, helped expose the rhetorical potential of the presidency. The Progressive movement had many additional spokesman, but Roosevelt's calls for reform helped give early credibility to the movement, and subsequently contributed to the enactment of much of the legislation advocated by the movement, including that which first made the government an active force in directing the nation's economy. His speaking on behalf of a two-ocean navy and preparedness contributed to the strong United States military posture which enabled the United States to participate in world affairs from a position of strength during the closing years of the nineteenth century and the opening decades of the twentieth century. Judging by results, Roosevelt normally got what he wanted.

Second, we must ask if Roosevelt's speeches had artistic merit. Did Roosevelt make use of appropriate principles of communication? Were his rhetorical strategies sound? As the foregoing chapters have illustrated, the answer to these questions is yes. Roosevelt typically adapted well to both his audience and the occasion. His speeches were easy to follow, due in part to the homiletic nature of his organization frequently involving the use of a text in the opening minutes of the speech, an elaboration of the text into a thesis appropriate for his audience and the occasion, and then the application of that text and thesis to current problems. Roosevelt's topical organization might have benefited from greater use of clear early statements of the topics he anticipated covering in the body of his speeches. Nevertheless, on balance they are not difficult for an audience to follow.

Roosevelt made limited use of evidence. However, the evidence that he did use, primarily in the form of examples, was used well. Roosevelt relied mostly on his own assertions and experiences to support his contentions. Most speakers might have difficulty relying so heavily on their own credibility or ethos. However, Roosevelt's unquestioned integrity and the diversity of his background combined to make his word acceptable to most audiences.

Roosevelt's use of language and his delivery were both exceptional. Earlier chapters have noted that he coined many terms still in use. He made use of highly picturesque language. Moreover, he delivered his speeches in a vigorous forthright style that constantly won him the praise of his contemporaries.[4] Through the use of eye contact, constant gesturing, and frequent variation in the volume of his voice, Roosevelt projected an animation that contributed appreciably to his overall effectiveness. Although the critic can certainly find weaknesses in Roosevelt's speaking, on balance it evidences considerable artistic merit.

Third, we must ask whether Roosevelt was presenting valid ideas. Do his ideas have merit, even with the passage of time? Was he, as some critics would ask, speaking truth? The answer to all of these questions is yes. The moral imperatives of Roosevelt's rhetoric of militant decency remain as valid today as they were when he spoke. The five topoi that animated his speaking: power, order, work, social responsibility, and character, as well as his application of those themes to the problems of his day, remain compelling today.   Roosevelt's positions on most of the domestic issues he dealt with, most notably those of the Progressive movement, have been largely implemented, and the merit of his policies has been largely proven.   Though some critics have claimed that his foreign policy speaking and actions were jingoistic and unnecessarily aggressive, even those criticisms seem pallid when contrasted to the record of his foreign policy successes.[5]   Although Roosevelt has been critized for mouthing platitudes, many of his ideas, as we have seen, were far-reaching and controversial. Roosevelt's basic ideas and his application of them to the problems of his day remain remarkably convincing.

Fourth, we must ask of Roosevelt's motives. Did he speak for the general welfare, or did he speak to advance himself and his associates? Were his motives honorable? Was he, as Quintilian would ask, a good man? Mind reading is difficult, especially when the subject has been dead for over seventy years. However, given our understanding of Roosevelt, he seems to have spoken out of a sincere belief that his policies would improve the general welfare. His motives were honorable. He was a good man.

As was observed earlier, it was unusual for a man of Roosevelt's class to even enter public life.   But Roosevelt entered, in part because he felt he could bring something of value to public service. He constantly spoke of the need for character among our public servants. He sincerely believed that his policies would prove best for the nation. He advocated a two-ocean navy and preparedness as policies that would preserve peace and avoid war. He clearly would benefit in winning the elections he campaigned in, but certainly he had additional motives.   By 1912, for example, he advocated domestic reform, in part, to avoid economic and class warfare that he felt would be inevitable if the balance between capitalist and laborer was not more equitable.   In sum, although no man's motives can ever be fully understood, much less a man as complex as Theodore Roosevelt, he seems to warrant Quintilian's highest praise as much as any pubic man. Actuated in part by the five moral imperatives of his rhetoric of militant decency, Theodore Roosevelt was a man of good intentions, an honorable man, a good man.

Judging by any of the commonly accepted standards-the results he attained, the artistic merit he exhibited, the validity of his ideas, or the righteousness of his motives-Theodore Roosevelt was an effective speaker. He has too often been readily dismissed as a jingoistic, belligerent, pompous leader, frequently given to uttering platitudes. Such judgments grotesquely underestimate the man. Roosevelt was a complex man who played a major role in his own day, leaving an enduring legacy for those who followed. Driven from an early age to value power, order, work, social responsibility, and character, Theodore Roosevelt utilized the rhetoric of militant decency to help fashion the United States in the twentieth century.

NOTES

1.   For details on Roosevelt's final days, see Joseph L. Gardner, Departing Glory: Theodore Roosevelt as Ex-President (New York: Charles Scribner's Sons, 1973), 395-400.

2.   Roosevelt's remark was reported in Lyman Abbott, Silhouettes of My Contemporaries (New York: Doubleday, Page and Company, 1921), 310 and widely repeated. See Christian F. Reisner, Roosevelt's Religion (New York: Abington Press, 1922), 205, for the remarks of Addams and Pinchot.

3.   For a highly readable explanation of the five broad bases discussed in this and the following paragraphs, see Bert E. Bradley, Fundamentals of Speech Communication (Dubuque, Iowa: Wm. C. Brown Company, 1978), 371-78.

4.   One of the most remarkable critiques of a speaker's delivery that this author has ever read is John Lee Whitingale, "Theodore   Roosevelt-His   Face,"   Metropolitan   Magazine,

(December 1902): 627. Whitingale claims that while Roosevelt makes excellent use of the traditional aspects of delivery, such as voice and gesture, the key to his successful delivery is his expressive face. "There is nothing more impressive in his presence," claims Whitingale, "than the character which asserts itself in his countenance."

5. The historical community's judgment on Roosevelt's foreign policy ideas is in the throes of revision. Once simplistically dismissed as being jingoistically militaristic, Roosevelt's policies have won growing admiration, particularly since the 1979 publication of Frederick W, Mark's <u>Velvet on Iron: The Diplomacy of Theodore Roosevelt.</u>

II
COLLECTED SPEECHES

The Duties
of American Citizenship

Buffalo, New York, January 26, 1983

Of course, in one sense, the first essential for a man's being a good citizen is his possession of the home virtues of which we think when we call a man by the emphatic adjective of manly. No man can be a good citizen who is not a good husband and a good father, who is not honest in his dealings with other men and women, faithful to his friends and fearless in the presence of his foes, who has not got a sound heart, a sound mind, and a sound body; exactly as no amount of attention to civil duties will save a nation if the domestic life is undermined, or there is lack of the rude military virtues which alone can assure a country's position in the world. In a free republic the ideal citizen must be one willing and able to take arms for the defense of the flag, exactly as the ideal citizen must be the father of many healthy children. A race must be strong and vigorous; it must be a race of good fighters and good breeders, else its wisdom will come to naught and its virtue be ineffective; and no sweetness and delicacy, no love for and appreciation of beauty in art or literature, no capacity for building up material prosperity, can possibly atone for the lack of the great virile virtues.

But this is aside from my subject, for what I wish to talk of is the attitude of the American citizen in civic life. It ought to be axiomatic in this country that every man must devote a reasonable share of his time to doing his duty in the political life of the community. No man has a right to shirk his political duties under whatever plea of pleasure or business; and while such shirking may be pardoned in those of small means, it is entirely unpardonable in those among whom it is most common--in the people whose circumstances give them freedom in the struggle for life. In so far as the community grows to think rightly, it will likewise grow to regard the young man of means who shirks his duty to the State in time of peace as being only one degree worse than the man who thus shirks it in time of war. A great many of our men in business, or of our young men who are bent on enjoying life (as they have a perfect right to do if only they do not sacrifice other things to enjoyment), rather plume themselves upon being good citizens if they even vote; yet voting is the very least of their duties. Nothing worth gaining is ever gained without effort. You can no more have freedom without striving and suffering for it than you can win success as a banker or a lawyer without labor and effort, without self-denial in youth and the display of a ready and alert intelligence in middle age. The people who say that they have not time to attend to politics are simply saying that they are unfit to live in a free community. Their place is under a despotism; or if they are content to do nothing but vote, you can take despotism tempered by an occasional plebescite, like that of the second Napoleon. In one of Lowell's magnificent stanzas about the Civil War he speaks of the fact which his countrymen were then learning, that freedom is not a gift that tarries long in the hands of cowards: nor yet does it tarry long in the hands of the sluggard and the idler, in the hands of the man so much absorbed in the pursuit of pleasure or in the pursuit of gain, or so much wrapped up in his own easy home life as to be unable to take his part in the rough struggle with his fellow men for political supremacy. If freedom is worth having, if the right of self-government is a valuable right, then the one and the other must be retained exactly as our forefathers acquired them, by labor, and especially by labor in organization; that is in combination with our fellows who have the same interests and the same principles. We should not accept the excuse of the business man who attributed his failure to the fact that his social duties were so pleasant and engrossing that he had no time left for work in his office; nor would we pay much heed to his further statement that he did not like business anyhow because he thought the morals of the business community by no means what they should be, and saw that the great successes were most often won by men of the Jay Gould stamp. It is just the same way with politics. It makes one feel half angry and half amused, and wholly contemptuous, to find men of high business or social standing in the community saying that they really have not got time to go to ward meetings, to organize political clubs, and to take a personal share in all the important details of practical politics; men who further urge against their going the fact that they think the condition of political morality low, and are afraid that they may be required to do what is not right if they go into politics.

The first duty of an American citizen, then, is that he shall work in politics; his second duty is that he shall do that work in a practical manner; and his third is that it shall be done in accord with the highest principles of honor and justice. Of course, it is not possible to define rigidly just the way in which the work shall be made practical. Each man's individual temper and convictions must be taken into account. To a certain extent his work must be done in accordance with his individual beliefs and theories of right and wrong. To a yet greater extent it must be done in combination with others, he yielding or modifying certain of his own theories and beliefs so as to enable him to stand on a common ground with his fellows, who have likewise yielded or modified certain of their theories and beliefs. There is no need of dogmatizing about independence on the one hand or party allegiance on the other. There are occasions when it may be the highest duty of any man to act outside of parties and against the one with which he has himself been hitherto identified; and there may be many more occasions when his highest duty is to sacrifice some of his own cherished opinions for the sake of the success of the party which he on the whole believes to be right. I do not think that the average citizen, at least in one of our great cities, can very well manage to support his own party all the time on every issue, local and otherwise; at any rate if he can do so he has been more fortunately placed than I have been. On the other hand, I am fully convinced that to do the best work people must be organized; and of course an organization is really a party, whether it be a great organization covering the whole nation and numbering its millions of adherents, or an association of citizens in a particular locality, banded together to win a certain specific victory, as, for instance, that of municipal reform. Somebody has said that a racing-yacht, like a good rifle, is a bundle of incompatibilities; that you must get the utmost possible sail power without sacrificing some other quality if you really do get the utmost sail power; that, in short, you have got to make more or less of a compromise on each in order to acquire the dozen things needful; but, of course, in making this compromise you must be very careful for the sake of something unimportant not to sacrifice any of the great principles of successful naval architecture. Well, it is about so with a man's political work. He has got to preserve his independence on the one hand; and on the other, unless he wishes to be a wholly ineffective crank, he has got to have some sense of party allegiance and party responsibility, and he has got to realize that in any given exigency it may be a matter of duty to sacrifice one quality, or it may be a matter of duty to sacrifice the other.

If it is difficult to lay down any fixed rules for party action in the abstract; it would, of course, be wholly impossible to lay them down for party action in the concrete, with reference to the organizations of the present day. I think that we ought to be broad-minded enough to recognize the fact that a good citizen, striving with fearlessness, honesty, and common sense to do his best for the nation, can render service to it in many different ways, and by connection with many different organizations. It is well for a man if he is able conscientiously to feel that his views on the great questions of the day, on such questions as the tariff, finance, immigration, the regulation of the liquor traffic, and others like them, are such as to put him in accord with the bulk of those of his fellow citizens who compose one of the greatest parties: but it is perfectly supposable that he may feel so strongly for or against certain principles held by one party, or certain principles held by the other, that he is unable to give his full adherence to either. In such a case I feel that he has no right to plead this lack of agreement with either party as an excuse for refraining from active political work prior to election. It will, of course, bar him from the primaries of the two leading parties, and preclude him from doing his share in organizing their management; but, unless he is very unfortunate, he can surely find a number of men who are in the same position as himself and who agree with him on some specific piece of political work, and they can turn in practically and effectively long before election to try to do this new piece of work in a practical manner.

One seemingly very necessary caution to utter is, that a man who goes into politics should not expect to reform everything right off, with a jump. I know many excellent young men who, when awakened to the fact that they have neglected their political duties, feel an immediate impulse to form themselves into an organization which shall forthwith purify politics everywhere, national, State, and city alike; and I know of a man who having gone round once to a primary, and having, of course, been unable to accomplish anything in a place where he knew no one and could not combine with anyone, returned saying it was quite useless for a good citizen to try to accomplish anything in such a manner. To these too hopeful or too easily discouraged people I always feel like reading Artemus Ward's article upon the people of his town who came together in a meeting to resolve that the town should support the Union and the Civil War, but were unwilling to take any part in putting down the rebellion unless they could go as brigadier-generals. After the battle of Bull Run there were a good many hundreds of thousands of young men in the North who felt it to be their duty to enter the Northern armies; but no one of them who possessed much intelligence expected to take high place at the outset, or anticipated that individual action would be of decisive importance in any given campaign. He went in as private or sergeant, lieutenant or captain, as the case might be, and did his duty in his company, in his regiment, after a while in his brigade. When Ball's Bluff and Bull Run succeeded the utter failure of the Peninsular campaign, when the terrible defeat of Fredericksburg was followed by the scarcely less disastrous day at Chancellorsville, he did not announce (if he had any pluck or manliness about him) that he considered it quite useless for any self-respecting citizen to enter the Army of the Potomac, because he really was not of much weight in its councils, and did not approve of its management; he simply gritted his teeth and went doggedly on with his duty, grieving over, but not disheartened at the innumerable shortcomings and follies committed by those who helped to guide the destinies of the army, recognizing also the bravery, the patience, intelligence, and resolution with which other men in high places offset the follies and shortcomings, and persevering with equal mind through triumph and defeat, until finally he saw the tide of failure turn at Gettysburg and the full flood of victory come with Appomattox.

I do wish that more of our good citizens would go into politics, and would do it in the same spirit with which their fathers went into the Federal armies. Begin with the little thing, and do not expect to accomplish anything without an effort. Of course, if you go to a primary just once, never having taken the trouble to know any of the other people who go there, you will find yourself wholly out of place; but if you keep on attending and try to form associations with other men whom you meet at the political gatherings, or whom you can persuade to attend them, you will very soon find yourself a weight. In the same way, if a man feels that the politics of his city, for instance, are very corrupt and wants to reform them, it would be an excellent idea for him to begin with his district. If he joins with other people, who think as he does, to form a club where abstract political virtue will be discussed he may do a great deal of good. We need such clubs; but he must also get to know his own ward or his own district, put himself in communication with the decent people in that district, of whom we may rest assured there will be many, willing and able to do something practical for the procurance of better government. Let him set to work to procure a better assemblyman or better alderman before he tries his hand at making a mayor, a governor, or a president. If he begins at the top he may make a brilliant temporary success, but the chances are a thousand to one that he will only be defeated eventually; and in no event will the good he does stand on the same broad and permanent foundation as if he had begun at the bottom. Of course, one or two of his efforts may be failures; but if he has the right stuff in him he will go ahead and do his duty irrespective of whether he meets with success or defeat. It is perfectly right to consider the question of failure while shaping one's efforts to succeed in the struggle for the right; but there should be no consideration of it whatsoever when the question is as to whether one should or should not make a struggle for the right. When once a band of one hundred and fifty or two hundred honest, intelligent men, who mean business and know their business, is found in any district, whether in one of the regular organizations or outside, you can guarantee that the local politicians of that district will begin to treat it with a combination of fear, hatred, and respect, and that its influence will be felt; and that while sometimes men will be elected to office in direct defiance of its wishes, more often the successful candidates will feel that they have to pay some regard to its demands for public decency and honesty.

But in advising you to be practical and to work hard, I must not for one moment be understood as advising you to abandon one iota of your self-respect and devotion to principle. It is a bad sign for the country to see one class of our citizens sneer at practical politicians, and another at Sunday-school politics. No man can do both effective and decent work in public life unless he is a practical politician on the one hand, and a sturdy believer in Sunday-school politics on the other. He must always strive manfully for the best, and yet, like Abraham Lincoln, must often resign himself to accept the best possible. Of course when a man verges on to the higher ground of statesmanship, when he becomes a leader, he must very often consult with others and defer to their opinion, and must be continually settling in his mind how far he can go in just deference to the wishes and prejudices of others while yet adhering to his own moral standards: but I speak not so much of men of this stamp as I do of the ordinary citizen, who wants to do his duty as a member of the commonwealth in its civic life; and for this man I feel that the one quality which he ought always to hold most essential is that of disinterestedness. If he once begins to feel that he wants office himself, with a willingness to get it at the cost of his convictions, or to keep it when gotten, at the cost of his convictions, his usefulness is gone. Let him make up his mind to do his duty in politics without regard to holding office at all, and let him know that often the men in this country who have done the best work for our public life have not been the men in office. If, on the other hand, he attains public position, let him not strive to plan out for himself a career. I do not think that any man should let himself regard his political career as a means of livelihood, or as his sole occupation in life; for if he does he immediately becomes most seriously handicapped. The moment that he begins to think how such and such an act will affect the voters in his district, or will affect some great political leader who will have an influence over his destiny, he is hampered and his hands are bound. Not only may it be his duty often to disregard the wishes of politicians, but it may be his clear duty at times to disregard the wishes of the people. The voice of the people is not always the voice of God; and when it happens to be the voice of the devil, then it is a man's clear duty to defy its behests. Different political conditions breed different dangers. The demagogue is as unlovely a creature as the courtier, though one is fostered under republican and the other under monarchical institutions. There is every reason why a man should have an honorable ambition to enter public life, and an honorable ambition to stay there when he is in; but he ought to make up his mind that he cares for it only as long as he can stay in it on his own terms, without sacrifice of his own principles; and if he does thus make up his mind he can really accomplish twice as much for the nation, and can reflect a hundredfold greater honor upon himself, in a short term of service, than can the man who grows gray in the public employment at the cost of sacrificing what he believes to be true and honest. And moreover, when a public servant has definitely made up his mind that he will pay no heed to his own future, but will do what he honestly deems best for the community, without regard to how his actions may affect his prospects, not only does he become infinitely more useful as a public servant, but he has a far better time. He is freed from the harassing care which is inevitably the portion of him who is trying to shape his sails to catch every gust of the wind of political favor.

But let me reiterate, that in being virtuous he must not become ineffective, and that he must not excuse himself for shirking his duties by any false plea that he cannot do his duties and retain his self-respect. This is nonsense, he can; and when he urges such a plea it is a mark of mere laziness and self-indulgence. And again, he should beware how he becomes a critic of the actions of others, rather than a doer of deeds himself; and in so far as he does act as a critic (and of course the critic has a great and necessary function) he must beware of indiscriminate censure even more than of indiscriminate praise. The screaming vulgarity of the foolish spread-eagle orator who is continually yelling defiance at Europe, praising everything American, good and bad, and resenting the introduction of any reform because it has previously been tried successfully abroad, is offensive and contemptible to the last degree; but after all it is scarcely as harmful as the peevish, fretful, sneering, and continual faultfinding of the refined, well-educated man, who is always attacking good and bad alike, who genuinely distrusts America, and in the true spirit of servile colonialism considers us inferior to the people across the water. It may be taken for granted that the man who is always sneering at our public life and our public men is a thoroughly bad citizen, and that what little influence he wields in the community is wielded for evil. The public speaker or the editorial writer who teaches men of education that their proper attitude toward American politics should be one of dislike or indifference is doing all he can to perpetuate and aggravate the very evils of which he is ostensibly complaining. Exactly as it is generally the case that when a man bewails the decadence of our civilization he is himself physically, mentally, and morally a first-class type of the decadent, so it is usually the case that when a man is perpetually sneering at American politicians, whether worthy or unworthy, he himself is a poor citizen and a friend of the very forces of evil against which he professes to contend. Too often these men seem to care less for attacking bad men, than for ruining the characters of good men with whom they disagree on some pubic question; and while their influence against the bad is almost nil, they are sometimes able to weaken the hands of the good by withdrawing from them support to which they are entitled; and they thus count in the sum total of forces that work for evil. They answer to the political prohibitionist, who, in a close contest between a temperance man and a liquor-seller, diverts enough votes from the former to elect the liquor-seller. Occasionally it is necessary to beat a pretty good man, who is not quite good enough, even at the cost of electing a bad one; but it should be thoroughly recognized that this can be necessary only occasionally and indeed, I may say, only in very exceptional cases, and that as a rule where it is done the effect is thoroughly unwholesome in every way, and those taking part in it deserve the severest censure from all honest men.

Moreover, the very need of denouncing evil makes it all the more wicked to weaken the effect of such denunciations by denouncing also the good. It is the duty of all citizens, irrespective of party, to denounce, and, so far as may be, to punish crimes against the public on the part of politicians or officials. But exactly as the public man who commits a crime against the public is one of the worst of criminals, so, close on his heels in the race for iniquitous distinction, comes the man who falsely charges the public servant with outrageous wrongdoing; whether it is done with foul-mouthed and foolish directness in the vulgar and violent party organ, or with sarcasm, innuendo, and the half-truths that are worse than lies, in some professed organ of independence. Not only should criticism be honest, but it should be intelligent, in order to be effective. I recently read in a religious paper an article railing at the corruption of our public life, in which it stated incidentally that the lobby was recognized as all-powerful in Washington. This is untrue. There was a day when the lobby was very important at Washington, but its influence in Congress is now very small indeed; and from a pretty intimate acquaintance with several Congresses I am entirely satisfied that there is among the members a very small proportion indeed who are corruptible, in the sense that they will let their action be influenced by money or its equivalent. Congressmen are very often demagogues; they are very often blind partisans; they are often exceedingly short-sighted, narrow-minded, and bigoted; but they are not usually corrupt; and to accuse a narrow-minded demagogue of corruption when he is perfectly honest, is merely to set him more firmly in his evil course and to help him with his constituents, who recognize that the charge is entirely unjust, and in repelling it lose sight of the man's real shortcomings. I have known more than one State legislature, more than one board of aldermen against which the charge of corruption could perfectly legitimately be brought, but it cannot be brought against Congress. Moreover these sweeping charges really do very little good. When I was in the New York legislature, one of the things that I used to mind most was the fact that at the close of every session the papers that affect morality invariably said that particular legislature was the worst legislature since the days of Tweed. The statement was not true as a rule; and, in any event, to lump all the members, good and bad, in sweeping condemnation simply hurt the good and helped the bad. Criticism should be fearless, but I again reiterate that it should be honest and should be discriminating. When it is sweeping and unintelligent, and directed against good and bad alike, or against the good and bad qualities of any man alike, it is very harmful. It tends steadily to deteriorate the character of our public men; and it tends to produce a very unwholesome spirit among young men of education, and especially among the young men in our colleges.

Against nothing is fearless and specific criticism more urgently needed than against the "spoils system," which is the degradation of American politics. And nothing is more effective in thwarting the purposes of the spoilsmen than the civil-service reform. To be sure, practical politicians sneer at it. One of them even went so far as to say that civil-service reform is asking a man irrelevant questions. What more irrelevant question could there be than that of the practical politician who asks the aspirant for his political favor-"Whom did you vote for in the last election?"   There is certainly nothing more interesting, from a humorous point of view, than the heads of departments urging changes to be made in their underlings, "on the score of increased efficiency" they say; when as the result of such a change the old incumbent often spends six months teaching the new incumbent how to do the work almost as well as he did himself!   Occasionally the civil-service reform has been abused, but not often.   Certainly the reform is needed when you contemplate the spectacle of a New York City treasurer who acknowledges his annual fees to be eighty-five thousand dollars, and who pays a deputy one thousand five hundred dollars to do his work-when you note the corruptions in the New York legislature, where one man says he has a horror of the Constitution because it prevents active benevolence, and another says that you should never allow the Constitution to come between friends!   All these corruptions and vices are what every good American citizen must fight against.

Finally, the man who wishes to do his duty as a citizen in our country must be imbued through and through with the spirit of Americanism.   I am not saying this as a matter of spread-eagle rhetoric: I am saying it quite soberly as a piece of matter-of-fact, common-sense advice, derived from my own experience of others.   Of course, the question of Americanism has several sides.   If a man is an educated man, he must show his Americanism by not getting misled into following out and trying to apply all the theories of the political thinkers of other countries, such as Germany and France, to our own entirely different conditions.   He must not get a fad, for instance, about responsible government; and above all things he must not, merely because he is intelligent, or a college professor well read in political literature, try to discuss our institutions when he has had no practical knowledge of how they are worked.   Again, if he is a wealthy man, a man of means and standing, he must really feel, not merely affect to feel, that no social differences obtain save such as a man can in some way himself make by his own actions.   People sometimes ask me if there is not a prejudice against a man of wealth and education in ward politics.   I do not think that there is, unless the man in turn shows that he regards the facts of his having wealth and education as giving him a claim to superiority aside from the merit he is able to prove himself to have in actual service.   Of course, if he feels that he ought to have a little better treatment than a carpenter, a plumber, or a butcher, who happens to stand beside him, he is going to be thrown out of the race very quickly, and probably quite roughly; and if he starts in to patronize and elaborately condescend to these men he will find that they resent this attitude even more.   Do not let him think about the matter at all.   Let him go into the political contest with no more thought of such matters than a college boy gives to the social standing of the members of his own and rival teams in a hotly contested football-match.   As soon as he begins to take an interest in politics (and he will speedily not only get interested for the sake of politics, but also take a good healthy interest in playing the game itself-an interest which is perfectly normal and praise-worthy, and to which only a prig would object), he will begin to work up the organization in the way that will be most effective, and he won't care a rap about who is put to work with him, save in so far as he is a good fellow and an efficient worker.   There was one time that a number of men who think as we do here to-night (one of the number being myself) got hold of one of the assembly districts of New York, and ran it in really an ideal way, better than any other assembly district has ever been run before or since by either party.   We did it by hard work and good organization; by working practically, and yet by being honest and square in motive and method: especially did we do it by all turning in as straight-out Americans without any regard to distinctions of race origin.   Among the many men who did a great deal in organizing our victories was the son of a Presbyterian clergyman, the nephew of a Hebrew rabbi, and two well-known Catholic gentlemen.   We also had a Columbia College professor (the stroke-oar of a university crew), a noted retail butcher, and the editor of a local German paper, various brokers, bankers, lawyers, bricklayers and a stone-mason who was particularly useful to us, although on questions of theoretic rather than applied politics he had a decidedly socialistic turn of mind.

Again, questions of race origin, like questions of creed, must not be considered: we wish to do good work, and we are all Americans, pure and simple.   In the New York legislature, when it fell to my lot to choose a committee--which I always esteemed my most important duty at Albany--no less than three out of the four men I chose were of Irish birth or parentage; and three abler and more fearless and disinterested men never sat in a legislative body; while among my especial political and personal friends in that body was a gentleman from the southern tier of counties, who was, I incidentally found out, a German by birth, but who was just as straight United States as if his ancestors had come over here in the <u>Mayflower</u> or in Henry Hudson's yacht.   Of course, none of these men of Irish or German birth would have been worth their salt had they continued to act after coming here as Irishmen or Germans, or as anything but plain straight-out Americans.   We have not any room here for a divided allegiance.   A man has got to be an American and nothing else; and he has no business to be mixing us up with questions of foreign politics, British or Irish,

German or French, and no business to try to perpetuate their language and customs in the land of complete religious toleration and equality. If, however, he does become honestly and in good faith an American, then he is entitled to stand precisely as all other Americans stand, and it is the height of un-Americanism to discriminate against him in any way because of creed or birthplace.   No spirit can be more thoroughly alien to American institutions, than the spirit of the Know-Nothings.

In facing the future and in striving, each according to the measure of his individual capacity, to work out the salvation of our land, we should be neither timid pessimists nor foolish optimists. We should recognize the dangers that exist and that threaten us: we should neither overestimate them nor shrink from them, but steadily fronting them should set to work to overcome and beat them down. Grave perils are yet to be encountered in the stormy course of the Republic-perils from political corruption, perils from individual laziness, indolence and timidity, perils springing from the greed of the unscrupulous rich, and from the anarchic violence of the thriftless and turbulent poor. There is every reason why we should recognize them, but there is no reason why we should fear them or doubt our capacity to overcome them, if only each will, according to the measure of his ability, do his full duty, and endeavor so to live as to deserve the high praise of being called a good American citizen.

Washington's Forgotten Maxim

Newport, Rhode Island, June 2, 1897

A century has passed since Washington wrote "To be prepared for war is the most effectual means to promote peace." We pay to this maxim the lip loyalty we so often pay to Washington's words; but it has never sunk deep into our hearts. Indeed of late years many persons have refused it even the poor tribute of lip loyalty, and prate about the iniquity of war as if somehow that was a justification for refusing to take the steps which can alone in the long run prevent war or avert the dreadful disasters it brings in its train. The truth of the maxim is so obvious to every man of really far-sighted patriotism that its mere statement seems trite and useless; and it is not over-creditable to either our intelligence or our love of country that there should be, as there is, need to dwell upon and amplify such a truism.

In this country there is not the slightest danger of an overdevelopment of warlike spirit, and there never has been any such danger. In all our history there has never been a time when preparedness for war was any menace to peace. On the contrary, again and again we have owed peace to the fact that we were prepared for war; and in the only contest which we have had with a European power since the Revolution, the War of 1812, the struggle and all its attendant disasters were due solely to the fact that we were not prepared to face, and were not ready instantly to resent, an attack upon our honor and interest; while the glorious triumphs at sea which redeemed that war were due to the few preparations which we had actually made. We are a great peaceful nation; a nation of merchants and manufacturers, of farmers and mechanics; a nation of workingmen, who labor incessantly with head or hand.

It is idle to talk of such a nation ever being led into a course of wanton aggression or conflict with military powers by the possession of a sufficient navy.

The danger is of precisely the opposite character. If we forget that in the last resort we can only secure peace by being ready and willing to fight for it, we may some day have bitter cause to realize that a rich nation which is slothful, timid, or unwieldy is an easy prey for any people which still retains those most valuable of all qualities, the soldierly virtues. We but keep to the traditions of Washington, to the traditions of all the great Americans who struggled for the real greatness of America, when we strive to build up those fighting qualities for the lack of which is a nation, as in an individual, no refinement, no culture, no wealth, no material prosperity, can atone.

Preparation for war is the surest guaranty for peace. Arbitration is an excellent thing, but ultimately those who wish to see this country at peace with foreign nations will be wise if they place reliance upon a first-class fleet of first-class battleships rather than on any arbitration treaty which the wit of man can devise. Nelson said that the British fleet was the best negotiator in Europe, and there was much truth in the saying. Moreover, while we are sincere and earnest in our advocacy of peace, we must not forget that an ignoble peace is worse than any war. We should engrave in our legislative halls those splendid lines of Lowell:

"Come, Peace! not like a mourner bowed
For honor lost and dear ones wasted,
But proud, to meet a people proud,
With eyes that tell to triumph tasted!"

Peace is a goddess only when she comes with sword girt on thigh. The ship of state can be steered safely only when it is always possible to bring her against any foe with "her leashed thunders gathering for the leap." A really great people, proud and high-spirited, would face all the disasters of war rather than purchase that base prosperity which is bought at the price of national honor. All the great masterful races have been fighting races and the minute that a race loses the hard fighting virtues, then, no matter what else it may retain, no matter how skilled in commerce and finance, in science or art, it has lost its proud right to stand as the equal of the best. Cowardice in a race, as in an individual, is the unpardonable sin, and a wilful failure to prepare for danger may in its effects be as bad a cowardice. The timid man who cannot fight, and the selfish, short-sighted, or foolish man who will not take the steps that will enable him to fight, stand on almost the same plane.

It is not only true that a peace may be so ignoble and degrading as to be worse than any war; it is also true that it may be fraught with more bloodshed than most wars. Of this there has been melancholy proof during the last two years. Thanks largely to the very unhealthy influence of the men whose business it is to speculate in the money market, and who approach every subject from the financial standpoint, purely; and thanks quite as much to the cold-blooded brutality and calculating timidity of many European rulers and statesmen, the peace of Europe has been preserved, while the Turk has been allowed to butcher the Armenians with hideous and unmentionable barbarity, and has actually been helped to keep Crete in slavery. War has been averted at the cost of bloodshed and infinitely more suffering and degradation to wretched women and children than have occurred in any European struggle since the days of Waterloo. No war of recent years, no matter how wanton, has been so productive of horrible misery as the peace which the powers have maintained during the continuance of the Armenian butcheries. The men who would preach this peace, and indeed the men who have preached universal peace in terms that have prepared the way for such a peace as this, have inflicted a wrong on humanity greater than could be inflicted by the most reckless and war-loving despot. Better a thousand times err on the side of over-readiness to fight, than to err on the side of tame submission to injury, or cold-blooded indifference to the misery of the oppressed.

Popular sentiment is just when it selects as popular heroes the men who have led in the struggle against malice domestic or foreign levy. No triumph of peace is quite so great as the supreme triumphs of war. The courage of the soldier, the courage of the statesman who has to meet storms which can be quelled only by soldierly qualities-this stands higher than any quality called out merely in time of peace. It is by no means necessary that we should have war to develop soldierly attributes and soldierly qualities; but if the peace we enjoy is of such kind that it causes their loss, then it is far too dearly purchased, no matter what may be its attendant benefits. It may be that some time in the dim future of the race the need for war will vanish; but that time is yet ages distant. As yet no nation can hold its place in the world, or can do any work really worth doing, unless it stands ready to guard its rights with an armed hand. That orderly liberty which is both the foundation and the capstone of our civilization can be gained and kept only by men who are willing to fight for an ideal; who hold high the love of honor, love of faith, love of flag, and love of country. It is true that no nation can be really great unless it is great in peace; in industry, integrity, honesty. Skilled intelligence in civic affairs and industrial enterprises alike; the special ability of the artist, the man of letters, the man of science, and the man of business; the rigid determination to wrong no man, and to stand for righteousness-all these are necessary in a great nation. But it is also necessary that the nation should have physical no less than moral courage; the capacity to do and dare and die at need, and that grim and steadfast resolution which alone will carry a great people through a great peril. The occasion may come at any instant when

'Tis man's perdition to be safe
When for the truth he ought to die.

All great nations have shown these qualities. The Dutch held but a little corner of Europe. Their industry, thrift, and enterprise in the pursuits of peace and their cultivation of the arts helped to render them great; but these qualities would have been barren had they not been backed by those sterner qualities which rendered them able to wrest their freedom from the cruel strength of Spain, and to guard it against the banded might of England and of France. The merchants and the artists of Holland did much for her; but even more was done by the famished burghers who fought to the death on the walls of Harlem and Leyden, and the great admirals who led their fleets to victory on the broad and narrow seas.

England's history is rich in splendid names and splendid deeds. Her literature is even greater than that of Greece. In commerce she has stood in the modern world as more than ever Carthage was when civilization clustered in a fringe around the Mediterranean. But she has risen far higher than ever Greece of Carthage rose, because she possesses also the great, masterful qualities which were possessed by the Romans who overthrew them both. England has been fertile in soldiers and administrators; in men who triumphed by sea and by land; in adventurers and explorers who won for her the world's waste spaces; and it is because of this that the English-speaking race now shares with the Slav the fate of the coming years.

We of the United States have passed most of our few years of national life in peace. We honor the architects of our wonderful material prosperity; we appreciate the necessity of thrift, energy, and business enterprise, and we know that even these are of no avail without the civic and social virtues. But we feel, after all, that the men who have dared greatly in war, or the work which is akin to war, are those who deserve best of the country. The men of Bunker Hill and Trenton, Saratoga and Yorktown, the men of New Orleans and Mobile Bay, Gettysburg and Appomattox are those to whom we owe most. None of our heroes of peace, save a few great constructive statesmen, can rank with our heroes of war. The Americans who stand highest on the list of the world's worthies are Washington, who fought to found the country which he afterward governed, and Lincoln, who saved it through the blood of the best and bravest in the land; Washington, the soldier and statesman, the man of cool head, dauntless heart, and iron will, the greatest of good men and the best of great men; and Lincoln, sad, patient, kindly Lincoln, who for four years toiled and suffered for the people, and when his work was done laid down his life that the flag which had been rent in sunder might once more be made whole and without a seam.

It is on men such as these, and not on the advocates of peace at any price, or upon those so short-sighted that they refuse to take into account the possibility of war, that we must rely in every crisis which deeply touches the true greatness and true honor of the Republic. The United States has never once in the course of its history suffered harm because of preparation for war, or because of entering into war. But we have suffered incalculable harm, again and again, from a foolish failure to prepare for war or from reluctance to fight when to fight was proper. The men who to-day protest against a navy, and protest also against every movement to carry out the traditional policy of the country in foreign affairs, and to uphold the honor of the flag, are themselves but following in the course of those who protested against the acquisition of the great West, and who failed to make proper preparations for the War of 1812, or refused to support it after it had been made. They are own brothers to the men whose short-sightedness and supine indifference prevented any reorganization of the personnel of the navy during the middle of the century, so that we entered upon the Civil War with captains seventy years old. They are close kin to the men who, when the Southern States seceded, wished to let the Union be disrupted in peace rather than restored through the grim agony of armed conflict.

I do not believe that any considerable number of our citizens are stamped with this timid lack of patriotism. There are some doctrinaires whose eyes are so firmly fixed on the golden vision of universal peace that they cannot see the grim facts of real life until they stumble over them, to their own hurt, and, what is much worse, to the possible undoing of their fellows. There are some educated men in whom education merely serves to soften the fiber and to eliminate the higher, sterner qualities which tell for national greatness; and these men prate about love for mankind, or for another country, as being in some hidden way a substitute for love of their own country. What is of more weight, there are not a few men of means who have made the till their fatherland, and who are always ready to balance a temporary interruption of moneymaking, or a temporary financial and commercial disaster, against the self-sacrifice necessary in upholding the honor of the nation and the glory of the flag.

But after all these people, though often noisy, form but a small minority of the whole. They would be swept like chaff before the gust of popular fury which would surely come if ever the nation really saw and felt a danger or an insult. The real trouble is that in such a case this gust of popular fury would come too late. Unreadiness for war is merely rendered more disastrous by readiness to bluster; to talk defiance and advocate a vigorous policy in words, while refusing to back up these words by deeds, is cause for humiliation. It has always been true, and in this age it is more than ever true, that it is too late to prepare for war when the time for peace has passed. The short-sightedness of many people, the goodhumored indifference to facts of others, the sheer ignorance of a vast number, and the selfish reluctance to insure against future danger by present sacrifice among yet others-these are the chief obstacles to building up a proper navy and carrying out a proper foreign policy.

The men who opposed the War of 1812, and preferred to have the nation humiliated by unresented insult from a foreign power rather than see her suffer the losses of an honorable conflict, occupied a position little short of contemptible; but it was not much worse than that of the men who brought on the war and yet deliberately refused to make the preparations necessary to carry it to a successful conclusion. The visionary schemes for defending the country by gunboats, instead of by a fleet of seagoing battle-ships; the refusal to increase the navy to a proper size; the determination to place reliance upon militia instead of upon regularly trained troops; and the disasters which followed upon each and every one of these determinations should be studied in every school-book in the land so as to enforce in the minds of all our citizens the truth of Washington's adage, that in time of peace it is necessary to prepare for war.

All this applied in 1812 but it applies with tenfold greater force now. Then, as now, it was the navy upon which the country had to depend in the event of war with a foreign power; and then, as now, one of the chief tasks of a wise and far-seeing statesmanship should have been the upbuilding of a formidable fighting navy. In 1812 untold evils followed from the failure to provide such a fighting navy; for the splendid feats of our few cruisers merely showed what could have been done if we had a great fleet of battle-ships. But ships, guns, and men were much more easily provided in time of emergency at the beginning of this century than at the end. It takes months to build guns and ships now, where it then took days, or at the most, weeks; and it takes far longer now to train men to the management of the vast and complicated engines with which war is waged. Therefore preparation is much more difficult, and requires a much longer time; and yet wars are so much quicker, they last so comparatively short a period, and can be begun so instantaneously that there is very much less time than formerly in which to make preparations.

No battle-ship can be built inside of two years under no matter what stress of circumstances, for we have not in this country the plant to enable us to work faster. Cruisers would take almost as long. Even torpedo boats, the smallest of all, could not be put in first-class form under ninety days. Guns available for use against a hostile invader would require two or three months; and in the case of the larger guns, the only ones really available for the actual shock of battle, could not be made under eight months. Rifles and military munitions of every kind would require a corresponding length of time for preparation; in most cases we should have to build, not merely the weapons we need, but the plant with which to make them in any large quantity. Even if the enemy did not interfere with our efforts, which they undoubtedly would, it would, therefore, take from three to six months after the outbreak of a war, for which we were unprepared, before we could in the slightest degree remedy our unreadiness. During this six months it would be impossible to overestimate the damage that could be done by a resolute and powerful antagonist. Even at the end of that time we would only be beginning to prepare to parry his attack, for it would be two years before we could attempt to return it. Since the change in military conditions in modern times there has never been an instance in which a war between two nations has lasted more than about two years. In most recent wars the operations of the first ninety days have decided the result of the conflict. All that followed has been a mere vain effort to strive against the stars in their courses by doing at the twelfth hour what it was useless to do after the eleventh.

We must therefore make up our minds once for all to the fact that it is too late to make ready for war when the fight has once begun. The preparation must come before that. In the case of the Civil War none of these conditions applied. In 1861 we had a good fleet, and the Southern Confederacy had not a ship. We were able to blockade the Southern ports at once, and we could improvise engines of war more than sufficient to put against those of any enemy who also had to improvise them. and who labored under even more serious disadvantages. The <u>Monitor</u> was got ready in the nick of time to meet the <u>Merrimac</u>, because the Confederates had to plan and build the latter while we were planning and building the former; but if ever we have to go to war with a modern military power we shall find its <u>Merrimacs</u> already built, and it will then be altogether too late to try to build <u>Monitors</u> to meet them.

If this point needs any emphasis surely the history of the War of 1812 applies to it. For twelve years before that war broke out even the blindest could see that we were almost certain to be drawn into hostilities with one or the other of the pair of combatants whose battle royal ended at Waterloo. Yet we made not the slightest preparation for war. The authorities at Washington contented themselves with trying to build a flotilla of gunboats which could defend our own harbors without making it necessary to take the offensive ourselves. We already possessed a dozen first-class cruisers, but not a battle-ship of any kind. With almost incredible folly the very Congress that declared war voted down the bill to increase the navy by twenty battle-ships; though it was probably too late then, anyhow, for even under the simpler conditions of that day such a fleet could not have been built and put into first-class order in less than a couple of years. Bitterly did the nation pay for its want of foresight and forethought. Our cruisers won a number of striking victories, heartening and giving hope to the nation in the face of disaster; but they were powerless to do material harm to the gigantic naval strength of Great Britain. Efforts were made to increase our little navy, but in the face of a hostile enemy already possessing command of the seas this was impossible. Two or three small cruisers were built; but practically almost all the fighting on the ocean was done by the handful of frigates and sloops which we possessed when the war broke out. Not a battle-ship was able to put to sea until after peace was restored. Meanwhile our coast was blockaded from one end to the other and was harried at will by the hostile squadrons. Our capital city was burned, and the ceaseless pressure of the blockade produced such suffering and irritation as nearly to bring about a civil war among ourselves. If in the first decade of the present century the American people and their rulers had possessed the wisdom to provide an efficient fleet of powerful battle-ships there would probably have been no War of 1812; and even if war had come, the immense loss to, and destruction of, trade and commerce by the blockade would have been prevented. Merely from the monetary standpoint the saving would have been incalculable; and yet this would haven been the smallest part of the gain.

It can therefore be taken for granted that there must be adequate preparation for conflict, if conflict is not to mean disaster. Furthermore, this preparation must take the shape of an efficient fighting navy. We have no foe able to conquer or overrun our territory. Our small army should always be kept in first-class condition, and every attention should be paid to the National Guard; but neither on the North nor on the South have we neighbors capable of menacing us with invasion or long resisting a serious effort on our part to invade them. The enemies we may have to face will come from over sea; they may come from Europe, or they may come from Asia. Events move fast in the West; but this generation has been forced to see that they move even faster in the oldest East. Our interests are as great in the Pacific as in the Atlantic, in the Hawaiian Islands as in the West Indies. Merely for the protection of our own shores we need a great navy; and what is more, we need it to protect our interests in the islands from which it is possible to command our shores and to protect our commerce on the high seas.

In building this navy, we must remember two things: First, that our ships and guns should be the very best of their kind; and second, that no matter how good they are, they will be useless unless the man in the conning tower and the man behind the guns are also the best of their kind. It is mere folly to send men to perish because they have arms with which they cannot win. With poor ships, were an Admiral Nelson and Farragut rolled in one, he might be beaten by any first-class fleet; and he surely would be beaten if his opponents were in any degree his equals in skill and courage; but without this skill and courage no perfection of material can avail, and with them very grave short-comings in equipment may be overcome. The men who command our ships must have as perfect weapons ready to their hands as can be found in the civilized world, and they must be trained to the highest point in using them. They must have skill in handling the ships, skill in tactics, skill in strategy, for ignorant courage cannot avail; but without courage neither will skill avail. They must have in them the dogged ability to bear punishment, the power and desire to inflict it, the daring, the resolution, the willingness to take risks and incur responsibility which have been possessed by the great captains of all ages, and without which no man can ever hope to stand in the front rank of fighting man.

Tame submission to foreign aggression of any kind is a mean and unworthy thing; but it is even meaner and more unworthy to bluster first, and then either submit or else refuse to make those preparations which can alone obviate the necessity for submission. I believe with all my heart in the Monroe Doctrine, and, I believe also the great mass of the American people are loyal to it; but it is worse than idle to announce our adherence to this doctrine and yet to decline to take measures to show that ours is not mere lip loyalty. We had far better submit to interference by foreign powers with the affairs of this continent than to announce that we will not tolerate such interference, and yet refuse to make ready the means by which alone we can prevent it. In public as in private life, a bold front tends to insure peace and not strife. If we possess a formidable navy, small is the chance indeed that we shall ever be dragged into a war to uphold the Monroe Doctrine. If we do not possess such a navy, war may be forced on us at any time.

It is certain, then, that we need a first-class navy. It is equally certain that this should not be merely a navy for defense. Our chief harbors should, of course, be fortified and put in condition to resist the attack of any enemy's fleet; and one of our prime needs is an ample force of torpedo boats to use primarily for coast defense. But in war the mere defensive never pays, and can never result in anything but disaster. If is not enough to parry a blow. The surest way to prevent its repetition is to return it. No master of the prize ring ever fought his way to supremacy by mere dexterity in avoiding punishment. He had to win by inflicting punishment. If the enemy is given the choice of time and place to attack, sooner or later he will do irreparable damage, and if he is at any point beaten back, why, after all, it is merely a repulse, and there are no means of following it up and making it a rout. We cannot rely upon coast protection alone. Forts and heavy land guns and torpedo boats are indispensable, and the last, on occasion, may be used for offensive purposes also. But in the present state of naval and military knowledge we must rely mainly, as all great nations always have relied, on the battle-ship, the fighting ship of the line. Gunboats and light cruisers serve an excellent purpose and we could not do without them. In time of peace they are the police of the seas; in time of war they would do some harrying of commerce, and a great deal of scouting and skirmishing; but our main reliance must be on the great armored battle-ships with their heavy guns and shot-proof vitals. In the last resort we must trust to the ships whose business is to fight and not to run, and who can themselves go to sea and strike at the enemy when they choose, instead of waiting peacefully to receive his blow when and where he deems it best to deliver it. If in the event of war our fleet of battle-ships can destroy the hostile fleet, then our coasts are safe from the menace of serious attack; even a fight that ruined our fleet would probably so shatter the hostile fleet as to do away with all chance of invasion; but if we have no fleet wherewith to meet the enemy on the high seas, or to anticipate his stroke by our own, then every city within reach of the tides must spend men and money in preparation for an attack that may not come, but which would cause crushing and irredeemable disaster if it did come.

Still more is it necessary to have a fleet of great battle-ships if we intend to live up to the Monroe Doctrine, and to insist upon its observance in the two Americas and the islands on either side of them. If a foreign power, whether in Europe or Asia, should determine to assert its position in those lands wherein we feel that our influence should be supreme, there is but one way in which we can effectively interfere. Diplomacy is utterly useless where there is not force behind it; the diplomat is the servant, not the master, of the soldier. The prosperity of peace, commercial and material prosperity, gives no weight whatever when the clash of arms comes. Even great naked strength is useless if there is no immediate means through which that strength can manifest itself. If we mean to protect the people of the lands who look to us for protection from tyranny and aggression; if we mean to uphold our interests in the teeth of the formidable Old World powers, we can only do it by being ready at any time, if the provocation is sufficient to meet them on the seas, where the battle for supremacy must be fought. Unless we are prepared so to meet them. let us abandon all talk of devotion to the Monroe Doctrine or to the honor of the American name.

This nation cannot stand still if it is to retain its self-respect, and to keep undimmed the honorable traditions inherited from the men who with the sword founded it and by the sword preserved it. We ask that the work of upbuilding the navy, and of putting the United States where it should be put among maritime powers, go forward without a break. We ask this not in the interest of war, but in the interest of peace. No nation should ever wage war wantonly, but no nation should ever avoid it at the cost of the loss of national honor. A nation should never fight unless forced to; but it should always be ready to fight. The mere fact that it is ready will generally spare it the necessity of fighting. If this country now had a fleet of twenty battle-ships their existence would make it all the more likely that we should not have war. It is very important that we should, as a race, keep the virile fighting qualities and should be ready to use them at need; but it is not at all important to use them unless there is need. One of the surest ways to attain these qualities is to keep our navy in first-class trim. There never is, and never has been, on our part a desire to use a weapon because of its being well tempered. There is not the least danger that the possession of a good navy will render this country overbearing toward its neighbors. The direct contrary is the truth.

An unmanly desire to avoid a quarrel is often the surest way to precipitate one; and utter unreadiness to fight is even surer. If at the time of our trouble with Chile, six years ago, we had not already possessed the nucleus of the new navy we should almost certainly have been forced into fighting, and even as it was trouble was only averted because of the resolute stand then taken by the president and by the officers of the navy who were on the spot. If at that time the Chileans had been able to get ready the battle-ship which was building for them, a war would almost certainly have followed, for we had no battle-ship to put against it.

If in the future we have war, it will almost certainly come because of some action, or lack of action, on our part in the way of refusing to accept responsibilities at the proper time, or failing to prepare for war when war does not threaten. An ignoble peace is even worse than an unsuccessful war; but an unsuccessful war would leave behind it a legacy of bitter memories which would hurt our national development for a generation to come. It is true that no nation could actually conquer us, owing to our isolated position; but we would be seriously harmed, even materially, by disasters that stopped far short of conquest; and in these matters, which are are more important than things material, we could readily be damaged beyond repair. No material loss can begin to compensate for the loss of national self-respect. The damage to our commercial interests by the destruction of one of our coast cities would be as nothing compared to the humiliation which would be felt by every American worthy of the name if we had to submit to such an injury without amply avenging it. It has been finely said that "a gentleman is one who is willing to lay down his life for little things"; that is for those things which seem little to the man who cares only whether shares rise or fall in value, and to the timid doctrinaire who preaches timid peace from his cloistered study.

Much of that which is best and highest in national character is made up of glorious memories and traditions. The fight well fought, the life honorably lived, the death bravely met-those count for more in building a high and fine type of temper in a nation than any possible success in the stock market, than any possible prosperity in commerce or manufactures. A rich banker may be a valuable and useful citizen, but not a thousand rich bankers can leave to the country such a heritage as Farragut left, when, lashed in the rigging of the <u>Hartford</u>, he forged past the forts and over the unseen death below, to try his wooden stem against the ironclad hull of the great Confederate ram. The people of some given section of our country may be better off because a shrewd and wealthy man has built up therein a great manufacturing business, or has extended a line of railroad past its doors; but the whole nation is better, the whole nation is braver, because Cushing pushed his little torpedoboat through the darkness to sink beside the sinking <u>Albemarle</u>.

Every feat of heroism makes us forever indebted to the man who performed it. All daring and courage, all iron endurance of misfortune, all devotion to the ideal of honor and the glory of the flag, make for a fine and nobler type of manhood. It is not only those who do and dare and endure that are benefited; but also the countless thousands who are not themselves called upon to face the peril, to show the strength, or to win the reward. All of us lift our heads higher because those of our countrymen whose trade it is to meet danger have met it well and bravely. All of us are poorer for every base or ignoble deed done by an American, for every instance of selfishness or weakness or folly on the part of the people as a whole. We are all worse off when any of us fails at any point in his duty toward the State in time of peace, or his duty toward the State in time of war. If ever we had to submit tamely to wrong or insult, every man among us worthy of the name of American would feel dishonored and debased. On the other hand, the memory of every triumph won by Americans, by just so much helps to make each American nobler and better. Every man among us is more fit to meet the duties and responsibilities of citizenship because of the perils over which, in the past, the nation has triumphed; because of the blood and sweat and tears, the labor and the anguish, through which, in the days that have gone, our forefathers moved on to triumph. There are higher things in this life than the soft and easy enjoyment of material comfort. It is through strife, or the readiness for strife, that a nation must win greatness. We ask for a great navy, partly because we think that the possession of such a navy is the surest guaranty of peace, and partly because we feel that no national life is worth having if the nation is not willing, when the need shall arise, to stake everything on the supreme arbitrament of war, and to pour out its blood, its treasure, and its tears like water, rather than submit to the loss of honor and renown.

In closing, let me repeat that we ask for a great navy, we ask for an armament fit for the nation's needs, not primarily to fight, but to avert fighting. Preparedness deters the foe, and maintains right by the show of ready might without the use of violence. Peace, like freedom, is not a gift that tarries long in the hands of cowards, or of those too feeble or too-short-sighted to deserve it; and we ask to be given the means to insure that honorable peace which alone is worth having.

The Strenuous Life

Chicago, Illinois, April 10, 1899

In speaking to you, men of the greatest city of the West, men of the State which gave to the country Lincoln and Grant, men who preeminently and distinctly embody all that is most American in the American character, I wish to preach, not the doctrine of ignoble ease, but the doctrine of the strenuous life, the life of toil and effort, of labor and strife; to preach that highest form of success which comes, not to the man who desires mere easy peace, but to the man who does not shrink from danger, from hardship, or from bitter toil, and who out of these wins the splendid ultimate triumph.

A life of slothful ease, a life of that peace which springs merely from lack either of desire or of power to strive after great things, is as little worthy of a nation as of an individual. I ask only that what every self-respecting American demands from himself and from his sons shall be demanded of the American nation as a whole. Who among you would teach your boys that ease, that peace, is to be the first consideration in their eyes--to be the ultimate goal after which they strive? You men of Chicago have made this city great, you men of Illinois have done your share, and more than your share, in making America great, because you neither preach nor practice such a doctrine. You work yourselves, and you bring up your sons to work. If you are rich and are worth you salt, you will teach your sons that though they may have leisure, it is not to be spent in idleness; for wisely used leisure merely means that those who possess it, being free from the necessity of working for their livelihood, are all the more bound to carry on some kind of non-remunerative work in science, in letters, in art, in exploration, in historical research--work of the type we most need in this country, the successful carrying out of which reflects most honor upon the nation. We do not admire the man of timid peace. We admire the man who embodies victorious effort; the man who never wrongs his neighbor, who is prompt to help a friend, but who has those virile qualities necessary to win in the stern strife of actual life. It is hard to fail, but it is worse never to have tried to succeed. In this life we get nothing save by effort. Freedom from effort in the present merely means that there has been stored up effort in the past. A man can be freed from the necessity of work only by the fact that he or his fathers before him have worked to good purpose. If the freedom thus purchased is used aright, and the man still does actual work though of a different kind, whether as a writer or a general, whether in the field of politics or in the field of exploration and adventure, he shows he deserves his good fortune. But if he treats this period of freedom from the need of actual labor as a period, not of preparation, but of mere enjoyment, even though perhaps not of vicious enjoyment, he shows that he is simply a cumberer of the earth's surface, and he surely unfits himself to hold his own with his fellows if the need to do so should again arise. A mere life of ease is not in the end a very satisfactory life, and, above all, it is a life which ultimately unfits those who follow it for serious work in the world.

In the last analysis a healthy state can exist only when the men and women who make it up lead clean, vigorous, healthy lives; when the children are so trained that they shall endeavor, not to shirk difficulties, but to overcome them; not to seek ease, but to know how to wrest triumph from toil and risk. The man must be glad to do a man's work, to dare and endure and to labor; to keep himself, and to keep those dependent upon him. The woman must be the housewife, the helpmeet of the homemaker, the wise and fearless mother of many healthy children. In one of Daudet's powerful and melancholy books he speaks of "the fear of maternity, the haunting terror of the young wife of the present day." When such words can be truthfully written of a nation, that nation is rotten to the heart's core. When men fear work or fear righteous war, when women fear motherhood, they tremble on the brink of doom; and well it is that they should vanish from the earth, where they are fit subjects for the scorn of all men and women who are themselves strong and brave and highminded.

As it is with the individual, so it is with the nation. It is a base untruth to say that happy is the nation that has no history. Thrice happy is the nation that has a glorious history. Far better it is to dare mighty things, to win glorious triumphs, even though checkered by failure, than to take rank with those poor spirits who neither enjoy much nor suffer much, because they live in the gray twilight that knows not victory nor defeat. If in 1861 the men who loved the Union had believed that peace was the end of all things, and war and strife the worst of all things, and had acted up to their belief, we would have saved hundreds of thousands of lives, we would have saved hundreds of millions of dollars. Moreover, besides saving all the blood and treasure we then lavished, we would have prevented the heartbreak of many women, the dissolution of many homes, and we would have spared the country those months of gloom and shame when it seemed as if our armies marched only to defeat. We could have avoided all this suffering simply by shrinking from strife. And if we had thus avoided it, we would have shown that we were weaklings, and that we were unfit to stand among the great nations of the earth. Thank God for the iron in the blood of our fathers, the men who upheld the wisdom of Lincoln, and bore sword or rifle in the armies of Grant! Let us, the children of the men who proved themselves equal to the mighty days, let us, the children of the men who carried the great Civil War to a triumphant conclusion, praise the God of our fathers that the ignoble counsels of peace were rejected; that the suffering and loss, the blackness of sorrow and despair, were unflinchingly faced and the years of strife endured; for in the end the slave was freed, the Union restored, and mighty American republic placed once more as a helmeted queen among nations.

We of this generation do not have to face a task such as that our fathers faced, but we have our tasks, and woe to us if we fail to perform them! We cannot, if we would, play the part of China, and be content to rot by inches in ignoble ease within our borders, taking no interest in what goes on beyond them, sunk in a scrambling commercialism; heedless of the higher life, the life of aspiration, of toil and risk, busying ourselves only with the wants of our bodies for the day until suddenly we should find, beyond a shadow of question, what China has already found, that in this world the nation that has trained itself to a career of unwarlike and isolated ease is bound, in the end, to go down before other nations which have not lost the manly and adventurous qualities. If we are to be a really great people, we must strive in good faith to play a great part in the world. We cannot avoid meeting great issues. All that we can determine for ourselves is whether we shall meet them well or ill. In 1898 we could not help being brought face to face with the problem of war with Spain. All we could decide was whether we should shrink like cowards from the contest, or enter into it as beseemed a brave and high-spirited people; and, once in, whether failure or success should crown our banners. So it is now. We cannot avoid the responsibilities that confront us in Hawaii, Cuba, Porto Rico, and the Philippines. All we can decide is whether we shall meet them in a way that will redound to the national credit, or whether we shall make of our dealings with these new problems a dark and shameful page in our history. To refuse to deal with them at all merely amounts to dealing with them badly. We have a given problem to solve. If we undertake the solution, there is, of course, always danger that we may not solve it aright; but to refuse to undertake the solution simply renders it certain that we cannot possibly solve it aright. The timid man, the lazy man, the man who distrusts his country, the over-civilized man, who has lost the great fighting, masterful virtues, the ignorant man, the man of dull mind, whose soul is incapable of feeling the mighty lift that thrills "stern men with empires in their brains"--all these, of course, shrink from seeing the nation undertake its new duties; shrink from seeing us build a navy and an army adequate to our needs; shrink from seeing us do our share of the world's work, by bringing order out of chaos in the great, fair tropic islands from which the valor of our soldiers and sailors has driven the Spanish flag. These are the men who fear the strenuous life, who fear the only national life which is really worth leading. They believe in that cloistered life which saps the hardy virtues in a nation, as it saps them in the individual; or else they are wedded to that base spirit of gain and greed which recognizes in commercialism the be-all and end-all of national life, instead of realizing that, though an indispensable element, it is, after all, but one of the many elements that go to make up true national greatness. No country can long endure if its foundations are not laid deep in the material prosperity which comes from thrift, from business energy and enterprise, from hard unsparing effort in the fields of industrial activity; but neither was any nation ever yet truly great if it relied upon material prosperity alone. All honor must be paid to the architects of our material prosperity, to the great captains of industry who have built our factories and our railroads, to the strong men who toil for wealth with brain or hand; for great is the debt of the nation to these and their kind. But our debt is yet greater to the men whose highest type is to be found in a statesman like Lincoln, a soldier like Grant. They showed by their lives that they recognized the law of work, the law of strife; they toiled to win a competence for themselves and those dependent upon them; but they recognized that there were yet other and even loftier duties-- duties to the nation and duties to the race.

We cannot sit huddled within our own borders and avow ourselves merely an assemblage of well-to-do hucksters who care nothing for what happens beyond. Such a policy would defeat even its own end; for as the nations grow to have ever wider and wider interests, and are brought into closer and closer contact, if we are to hold our own in the struggle for naval and commercial supremacy, we must build up our power without our borders. We must build the isthmian canal, and we must grasp the points of vantage which will enable us to have our say in deciding the destiny of the oceans of the East and the West.

So much for the commercial side. From the standpoint of international honor the argument is even stronger. The guns that thundered off Manila and Santiago left us echoes of glory, but that also left us a legacy of duty. If we drove out a medieval tyranny only to make room for savage anarchy, we had better not have begun the task at all. It is worse than idle to say that we have no duty to perform, and can leave to their fates the islands we have conquered. Such a course would be the course of infamy. It would be followed at once by utter chaos in the wretched islands themselves. Some stronger, manlier power would have to step in and do the work, and we would have shown ourselves weaklings, unable to carry to successful completion the labors that great and high-spirited nations are eager to undertake.

The work must de done; we cannot escape our responsibility; and if we are worth our salt, we shall be glad of the chance to do the work--glad of the chance to show ourselves equal to one of the great tasks set modern civilization. But let us not deceive ourselves as to the importance of the task. Let us not be misled by vainglory into underestimating the strain it will put on our powers. Above all, let us, as we value our own self-respect, face the responsibilities with proper seriousness, courage, and high resolve. We must demand the highest order of integrity and ability in our public men who are to grapple with these new problems. We must hold to a rigid accountability those public servants who show unfaithfulness to the interest of the nation or inability to rise to the high level of the new demands upon our strength and our resources.

Of course we must remember not to judge any public servant by any one act, and especially should we beware of attacking the men who are merely the occasions and not the causes of disaster. Let me illustrate what I mean by the army and the navy. If twenty years ago we had gone to war, we should have found the navy as absolutely unprepared as the army. At that time our ships could not have encountered with success the fleets of Spain any more than nowadays we can put untrained soldiers, no matter how brave, who are armed with archaic black-powder weapons, against well-drilled regulars armed with the highest type of modern repeating rifle. But in the early eighties the attention of the nation became directed to our naval needs. Congress most wisely made a series of appropriations to build a new navy, and under a succession of able and patriotic secretaries, of both political parties, the navy was gradually built up, until its material became equal to its splendid personnel, with the result that in the summer of 1898 it leaped to its proper place as one of the most brilliant and formidable fighting navies in the entire world. We rightly pay all honor to the men controlling the navy at the time it won these great deeds, honor to Secretary Long and Admiral Dewey, to the captains who handled the ships in action, to the daring lieutenants who braved death in the smaller craft, and to the heads of bureaus at Washington who saw that the ships were so commanded, so armed, so equipped, so well engined, as to insure the best results. But let us also keep ever in mind that all of this would not have availed if it had not been for the wisdom of the men who during the preceding fifteen years had built up the navy. Keep in mind the secretaries of the navy during those years; keep in mind the senators and congressmen who by their votes gave the money necessary to build and to armor the ships, to construct the great guns, and to train the crews; remember also those who actually did build the ships, the armor, and the guns; and remember the admirals and captains who handled battle-ship, cruiser, and torpedoboat on the high seas, alone and in squadrons, developing the seamanship, the gunnery, and the power of acting together, which their successors utilized so gloriously at Manila and off Santiago.   And, gentlemen, remember the converse too. Remember that justice has two sides. Be just to those who built up the navy, and, for the sake of the future of the country, keep in mind those who opposed its building up. Read the Congressional Record. Find out the senators and congressmen who opposed the grants for building the new ships; who opposed the purchase of armor, without which the ships were worthless; who opposed any adequate maintenance for the Navy Department, and strove to cut down the number of men necessary to man our fleets. The men who did these things were one and all working to bring disaster on the country. They have no cause to feel proud of the valor of our sea-captains, of the renown of our flag. Their motives may or may not have been good, but their acts were heavily fraught with evil. They did ill for the national honor, and we won in spite of their sinister opposition.

Now apply all this to our public men of to-day. Our army has never been built up as it should be built up. I shall not discuss with an audience like this the puerile suggestion that a nation of seventy millions of freemen is in danger of losing its liberties from the existence of an army of one hundred thousand men, three-fourths of whom will be employed in certain foreign islands, in certain coast fortresses, and on

Indian reservations. No man of good sense and stout heart can take such a proposition seriously. If we are such weaklings as the proposition implies, then we are unworthy of freedom in any event. To no body of men in the United States is the country so much indebted as to the splendid officers and enlisted men of the regular army and navy. There is no body from which the country has less to fear, and none of which it should be prouder, none which it should be more anxious to upbuild.

Our army needs complete reorganization-not merely enlarging-and the reorganization can only come as the result of legislation. A proper general staff should be established, and the positions of ordnance, commissary, and quartermaster officers should be filled by detail from the line. Above all, the army must be given the chance to exercise in large bodies. Never again should we see, as we saw in the Spanish war, major-generals in command of divisions who had never before commanded three companies together in the field.   Yet, incredible to relate, Congress has shown a queer inability to learn some of the lessons of the war.   There were large bodies of men in both branches who opposed the declaration of war, who opposed the ratification of peace, who opposed the upbuilding of the army, and who even opposed the purchase of armor at a reasonable price for the battle-ships and cruisers, thereby putting an absolute stop to the building of any new fighting ships for the navy. If, during the years to come, any disaster should befall our arms, afloat or ashore, and thereby any shame come to the United States, remember that the blame will lie upon the men whose names appear upon the roll-calls of Congress on the wrong side of these great questions.   On them will lie the burden of any loss of our soldiers and sailors, of any dishonor to the flag; and upon you and the people of this country will lie the blame if you do not repudiate, in no unmistakable way, what these men have done. The blame will not rest upon the untrained commander of untried troops, upon the civil officers of a department the organization of which has been left utterly inadequate, or upon the admiral with an insufficient number of ships; but upon the public men who have so lamentably failed in forethought as to refuse to remedy these evils long in advance, and upon the nation that stands behind those public men.

So, at the present hour, no small share of the responsibility for the blood shed in the Philippines, the blood of our brothers, and the blood of their wild and ignorant foes, lies at the thresholds of those who so long delayed the adoption of the treaty of peace, and of those who by their worse than foolish words deliberately invited a savage people to plunge into a war fraught with sure disaster for them-a war, too, in which our own brave men who follow the flag must pay with their blood for the silly, mock humanitarianism of the prattlers who sit at home in peace.

The army and the navy are the sword and the shield which this nation must carry if she is to do her duty among the nations of the earth--if she is not to stand merely as the China of the western hemisphere. Our proper conduct toward the tropic islands we have wrested from Spain is merely the form which our duty has taken at the moment. Of course we are bound to handle the affairs of our own household well. We must see that there is civic honesty, civic cleanliness, civic good sense in our home administration of city, State, and nation. We must strive for honesty in office, for honesty toward the creditors of the nation and of the individual; for the widest freedom of individual initiative where possible, and for the wisest control of individual initiative where it is hostile to the welfare of many. But because we set our own household in order we are not thereby excused from playing our part in the great affairs of the world. A man's first duty is to his own home, but he is not thereby excused from doing his duty to the State; for if he fails in this second duty it is under the penalty of ceasing to be a free-man. In the same way, while a nation's first duty is within its own borders, it is not thereby absolved from facing its duties in the world as a whole; and if it refuses to do so, it merely forfeits its right to struggle for a place among the peoples that shape the destiny of mankind.

In the West Indies and the Philippines alike we are confronted by most difficult problems. It is cowardly to shrink from solving them in the proper way; for solved they must be, if not by us, then by some stronger and more manful race. If we are too weak, too selfish, or too foolish to solve them, some bolder and abler people must undertake the solution. Personally, I am far too firm a believer in the greatness of my country and the power of my countrymen to admit for one moment that we shall ever be driven to the ignoble alternative.

The problems are different for the different islands. Porto Rico is not large enough to stand alone. We must govern it wisely and well, primarily in the interest of its own people. Cuba is, in my judgement, entitled ultimately to settle for itself whether it shall be an independent state or an integral portion of the mightiest of republics. But until order and stable liberty are secured, we must remain in the island to insure them, and infinite tact, judgment, moderation, and courage must be shown by our military and civil representatives in keeping the island pacified, in relentlessly stamping out brigandage, in protecting all alike, and yet in showing proper recognition to the men who have fought for Cuban liberty. The Philippines offer a yet graver problem. Their population includes halfcaste and native Christians, warlike Moslems, and wild pagans. Many of their people are utterly unfit for self-government, and show no signs of becoming fit. Others may in time become fit but at present can only take part in self-government under wise supervision, at once firm and beneficent. We have driven Spanish tyranny from the islands. If we now let it be replaced by savage anarchy, our work has been for harm and not for good. I have scant patience with those who fear to undertake the task of governing the Philippines, and who openly avow that they do fear to undertake it, or that they shrink from it because of the expense and trouble; but I have even scantier patience with those who make a pretense of humanitarianism to hide and cover their timidity, and who cant about "liberty" and the "consent of the governed," in order to excuse themselves for their unwillingness to play the part of men. Their doctrines, if carried out, would make it incumbent upon us to leave the Apaches of Arizona to work out their salvation, and to decline to interfere in a single Indian reservation. Their doctrines condemn your forefathers and mine for ever having settled in these United States.

England's rule in India and Egypt has been of great benefit to England, for it has trained up generations of men accustomed to look at the larger and loftier side of public life. It has been of even greater benefit to India and Egypt. And finally, and most of all, it has advanced the cause of civilization. So, if we do our duty aright in the Philippines, we will add to that national renown which is the highest and finest part of national life, will greatly benefit the people of the Philippine Islands, and, above all, we will play our part well in the great work of uplifting mankind. But to do this work, keep in mind that we must show in a very high degree the qualities of courage, of honesty, and of good judgment. Resistance must be stamped out. The first and all-important work to be done is to establish the supremacy of our flag. We must put down armed resistance before we can accomplish anything else, and there should be no parleying, no faltering, in dealing with our foe. As for those in our own country who encourage the foe, we can afford contemptuously to disregard them; but it must be remembered that their utterances are not saved from being treasonable merely by the fact that they are despicable.

When once we have put down armed resistance, when once our rule is acknowledged, then an even more difficult task will begin, for then we must see to it that the islands are administered with absolute honesty and with good judgement. If we let the public service of the islands be turned into the prey of the spoils politician, we shall have begun to tread the path which Spain trod to her own destruction. We must send out there only good and able men, chosen for their fitness, and not because of their partisan service, and these men must not only administer impartial justice to the natives and serve their own government with honesty and fidelity, but must show the utmost tact and firmness, remembering that, with such people as those with whom we are to deal, weakness is the greatest of crimes, and that next to weakness comes lack of consideration for their principles and prejudices.

I preach to you, then, my countrymen, that our country calls not for the life of ease but for the life of strenuous endeavor. The twentieth century looms before us big with the fate of many nations. If we stand idly by, if we seek merely swollen, slothful ease and ignoble peace, if we shrink from the hard contests where men must win at hazard of their lives and at the risk of all they hold dear, then the bolder and stronger peoples will pass us by, and will win for themselves the domination of the world. Let us therefore boldly face the life of strife, resolute to do our duty well and manfully; resolute to uphold righteousness by deed and by word; resolute to be both honest and brave, to serve high ideals, yet to use practical methods. Above all, let us shrink from no strife, moral or physical, within or without the nation, provided we are certain that the strife is justified, for it is only through strife, through hard and dangerous endeavor, that we shall ultimately win the goal of true national greatness.

The Man
with the Muck-rake

Washington D.C., April 14, 1906

Over a century ago Washington laid the corner-stone of the
Capitol in what was then little more than a tract of wooded
wilderness here beside the Potomac. We now find it necessary
to provide by great additional buildings for the business of the
government. This growth in the need for the housing of the
government is but a proof and example of the way in which the
nation has grown and the sphere of action of the national
government has grown. We now administer the affairs of a
nation in which the extraordinary growth of population has
been outstripped by the growth of wealth and the growth in
complex interests. The material problems that face us to-day
are not such as they were in Washington's time, but the
underlying facts of human nature are the same now as they
were then. Under altered external form we war with the same
tendencies toward evil that were evident in Washington's time,
and are helped by the same tendencies for good. It is about
some of these that I wish to say a word to-day.

In Bunyan's "Pilgrim's Progress" you may recall the
description of the Man with the Muck-rake, the man who could
look no way but downward, with the muck-rake in his hand;
who was offered a celestial crown for his muck-rake, but who
would neither look up nor regard the crown he was offered, but
continued to rake to himself the filth of the floor.

In "Pilgrim's Progress" the Man with the Muck-rake is set
forth as the example of him whose vision is fixed on carnal
instead of on spiritual things. Yet he also typifies the man who
in this life consistently refuses to see aught that is lofty, and
fixes his eyes with solemn intentness only on that which is vile
and debasing. Now, it is very necessary that we should not

flinch from seeing what is vile and debasing. There is filth on the floor, and it must be scraped up with the muck-rake; and there are times and places where this service is the most needed of all the services that can be performed. But the man who never does anything else, who never thinks or speaks or writes, save of his feats with the muck-rake, speedily becomes, not a help to society, not an incitement to good, but one of the most potent forces for evil.

There are, in the body politic, economic and social, many and grave evils, and there is urgent necessity for the sternest war upon them. There should be relentless exposure of and attack upon every evil man whether politician or business man, every evil practice, whether in politics, in business, or in social life. I hail as a benefactor every writer or speaker, every man who, on the platform, or in book, magazine, or newspaper, with merciless severity makes such attack, provided always that he in his turn remembers that the attack is of use only if it is absolutely truthful. The liar is no whit better than the thief, and if his mendacity takes the form of slander, he may be worse than most thieves. It puts a premium upon knavery untruthfully to attack an honest man, or even with hysterical exaggeration to assail a bad man with untruth. An epidemic of indiscriminate assault upon character does not good, but very great harm. The soul of every scoundrel is gladdened whenever an honest man is assailed, or even when a scoundrel is untruthfully assailed.

Now, it is easy to twist out of shape what I have just said, easy to affect to misunderstand it, and, if it is slurred over in repetition, not difficult really to misunderstand it. Some persons are sincerely incapable of understanding that to denounce mud-slinging does not mean the indorsement of whitewashing; and both the interested individuals who need whitewashing, and those others who practice mud-slinging, like to encourage such confusion of ideas. One of the chief counts against those who make indiscriminate assault upon men in business or men in public life, is that they invite a reaction which is sure to tell powerfully in favor of the unscrupulous scoundrel who really ought to be attacked, who ought to be exposed, who ought, if possible, to be put in the penitentiary. If Aristides is praised overmuch as just, people get tired of hearing it; and overcensure of the unjust finally and from similar reasons results in their favor.

Any excess is almost sure to invite a reaction; and, unfortunately, the reaction, instead of taking the form of punishment of those guilty of the excess, is very apt to take the form either of punishment of the unoffending or of giving immunity, and even strength, to offenders. The effort to make financial or political profit out of the destruction of character can only result in public calamity. Gross and reckless assaults on character, whether on the stump or in newspaper, magazine, or book, create a morbid and vicious public sentiment, and at the same time act as a profound deterrent to able men of normal sensitiveness and tend to prevent them from entering the public service at any price. As an instance in point, I may mention that one serious difficulty encountered in getting the right type of men to dig the Panama Canal is the certainty that they will be exposed, both without, and I am sorry to say, sometimes within, Congress, to utterly reckless assaults on their character and capacity.

At the risk of repetition let me say again that my plea is, not for immunity to but for the most unsparing exposure of the politician who betrays his trust, of the big business man who makes or spends his fortune in illegitimate or corrupt ways. There should be a resolute effort to hunt every such man out of the position he has disgraced. Expose the crime, and hunt down the criminal; but remember that even in the case of crime, if it is attacked in sensational, lurid, and untruthful fashion, the attack may do more damage to the public mind than the crime itself. It is because I feel that there should be no rest in the endless war against the forces of evil that I ask that the war be conducted with sanity as well as with resolution. The men with the muck-rakes are often indispensable to the well-being of society; but only if they know when to stop raking the muck, and to look upward to the celestial crown above them, to the crown of worthy endeavor. There are beautiful things above and round about them; and if they gradually grow to feel that the whole world is nothing but muck, their power of usefulness is gone. If the whole picture is painted black there remains no hue whereby to single out the rascals for distinction from their fellows. Such painting finally induces a kind of moral color-blindness; and people affected by it come to the conclusion that no man is really black, and no man really white, but they are all gray. In other words, they neither believe in the truth of the attack, nor in the honesty of the man who is attacked; they grow as suspicious of the accusation as of the offense; it becomes well-nigh hopeless to stir them either to wrath against wrong-doing or to enthusiasm for what is right; and such a mental attitude in the public gives hope to every knave, and is the despair of honest men.

To assail the great and admitted evils of our political and industrial life with such crude and sweeping generalizations as to include decent men in the general condemnation means the searing of the public conscience. There results a general attitude either of cynical belief in and indifference to public corruption or else of a distrustful inability to discriminate between the good and the bad. Either attitude is fraught with untold damage to the country as a whole. The fool who has not sense to discriminate between what is good and what is bad is well-nigh as dangerous as the man who does discriminate and yet chooses the bad. There is nothing more distressing to every good patriot, to every good American, than the hard, scoffing spirit which treats the allegation of dishonesty in a public man as a cause for laughter. Such laughter is worse than the crackling of thorns under a pot, for it denotes not merely the vacant mind, but the heart in which high emotions have been choked before they could grow to fruition.

There is any amount of good in the world, and there never was a time when loftier and more disinterested work for the betterment of mankind was being done than now. The forces that tend for evil are great and terrible, but the forces of truth and love and courage and honesty and generosity and sympathy are also stronger than ever before. It is a foolish and timid, no less than a wicked, thing to blink the fact that the forces of evil are strong, but it is even worse to fail to take into account the strength of the forces that tell for good. Hysterical sensationalism is the very poorest weapon wherewith to fight for lasting righteousness. The men who with stern sobriety and truth assail the many evils of our time, whether in the public press, or in magazines, or in books, are the leaders and allies of all engaged in the work for social and political betterment. But if they give good reason for distrust of what they say, if they chill the ardor of those who demand truth as a primary virtue, they thereby betray the good cause, and play into the hands of the very men against whom they are nominally at war.

In his "Ecclesiastical Polity" that fine old Elizabethan divine, Bishop Hooker, wrote:

He that goeth about to persuade a multitude that they are not so well governed as they ought to be, shall never want attentive and favorable hearers; because they know the manifold defects whereunto every kind of regimen is subject, but the secret lets and difficulties, which in public proceedings are innumerable and inevitable, they have not ordinarily the judgement to consider.

This truth should be kept constantly in mind by every free people desiring to preserve the sanity and poise indispensable to the permanent success of self-government. Yet, on the other hand, it is vital not to permit this spirit of sanity and self-command to degenerate into mere mental stagnation. Bad though a state of hysterical excitement is, and evil though the results are which come from the violent oscillations such excitement invariably produces, yet a sodden acquiescence in evil is even worse. At this moment we are passing through a period of great unrest--social, political, and industrial unrest. It is of the utmost importance for our future that this should prove to be not the unrest of mere rebelliousness against life, of mere dissatisfaction with the inevitable inequality of conditions, but the unrest of a resolute and eager ambition to secure the betterment of the individual and the nation. So far as this movement of agitation throughout the country takes the form of a fierce discontent with evil, of a determination to punish the authors of evil, whether in industry or politics, the feeling is to be heartily welcomed as a sign of healthy life.

If, on the other hand, it turns into a mere crusade of appetite against appetite, of a contest between the brutal greed of the "have-nots" and the brutal greed of the "haves," then it has no significance for good, but only for evil. If it seeks to establish a line of cleavage, not along the line which divides good men from bad, but along that other line, running a right angle thereto, which divides those who are well off from those who are less well off, then it will be fraught with immeasurable harm to the body politic.

We can not more and no less afford to condone evil in the man of capital than evil in the man of not capital. The wealthy man who exults because there is a failure of justice in the effort to bring some trust magnate to an account for his misdeeds is as bad as, and no worse than, the so-called labor leader who clamorously strives to excite a foul class feeling on behalf of some other labor leader who is implicated in murder. One attitude is as bad as the other, and no worse; in each case the accused is entitled to exact justice; and in neither case is there need of action by others which can be construed into an expression of sympathy for crime.

It is a prime necessity that if the present unrest is to result in permanent good the emotion shall be translated into action, and that the action shall be marked by honesty, sanity, and self-restraint. There is mighty little good in a mere spasm of reform. The reform that counts is that which comes through steady, continuous growth; violent emotionalism leads to exhaustion.

It is important to this people to grapple with the problems connected with the amassing of enormous fortunes, and the use of those fortunes, both corporate and individual, in business. We should discriminate in the sharpest way between fortunes well-won and fortunes ill-won; between those gained as an incident to performing great services to the community as a whole, and those gained in evil fashion by keeping just within the limits of mere law-honesty. Of course no amount of charity in spending such fortunes in any way compensates for misconduct in making them. As a matter of personal conviction, and without pretending to discuss the details or formulate the system, I feel that we shall ultimately have to consider the adoption of some such scheme as that of a progressive tax on all fortunes, beyond a certain amount either given in life or devised or bequeathed upon death to any individual--a tax so framed as to put it out of the power of the owner of one of these enormous fortunes to hand on more than a certain amount to any one individual; the tax, of course, to be imposed by the National and not the State Government. Such taxation should, of course, be aimed merely at the inheritance or transmission in their entirety of those fortunes swollen beyond all healthy limits.

Again, the National Government must in some form exercise supervision over corporations engaged in interstate business--and all large corporations are engaged in interstate business--whether by license or otherwise, so as to permit us to deal with the far-reaching evils of overcapitalization. This year we are making a beginning in the direction of serious effort to settle some of these economic problems by the railway-rate legislation. Such legislation, if so framed, as I am sure it well be, as to secure definite and tangible results, will amount to something of itself; and it will amount to a great deal more in so far as it is taken as a first step in the direction of a policy of superintendence and control over corporate wealth engaged in interstate commerce, this superintendence and control not to be exercised in a spirit of malevolence toward the men who have created the wealth, but with the firm purpose both to do justice to them and to see that they in their turn do justice to the public at large.

The first requisite in the public servants who are to deal in this shape with corporations, whether as legislators or as executives, is honesty. This honesty can be no respecter of persons. There can be no such thing as unilateral honesty. The danger is not really from corrupt corporations; it springs from the corruption itself, whether exercised for or against corporations.

The eighth commandment reads: "Thou shalt not steal." It does not read: "Thou shalt not steal from the rich man." It does not read: "Thou shalt not steal from the poor man." It reads simply and plainly: "Thou shalt not steal." No good whatever will come from that warped and mock morality which denounces the misdeeds of men of wealth and forgets the misdeeds practiced at their expense; which denounces bribery, but blinds itself to blackmail; which foams with rage if a corporation secures favors by improper methods, and merely leers with hideous mirth if the corporation is itself wronged. The only public servant who can be trusted honestly to protect the rights of the public against the misdeed of a corporations is that public man who will just as surely protect the corporation itself from wrongful aggression. If a public man is willing to yield to popular clamor and do wrong to the men of wealth or to rich corporations, it may be set down as certain that if the opportunity comes he will secretly and furtively do wrong to the public in the interest of a corporation.

But, in addition to honesty, we need sanity. No honesty will make a public man useful if that man is timid or foolish, if he is a hot-headed zealot or an impracticable visionary. As we strive for reform we find that it is not at all merely the case of a long up-hill pull. On the contrary, there is almost as much of breeching work as of collar work; to depend only on traces means that there will soon be a runaway and an upset. The men of wealth who to-day are trying to prevent the regulation and control of their business in the interest of the public by the proper government authorities will not succeed, in my judgement, in checking the progress of the movement. But if they did succeed they would find that they had sown the wind and would surely reap the whirlwind, for they would ultimately provoke the violent excesses which accompany a reform coming by convulsion instead of by steady and natural growth.

On the other hand, the wild preachers of unrest and discontent, the wild agitators against the entire existing order, the men who act crookedly, whether because of sinister design or from mere puzzle-headedness, the men who preach destruction without proposing any substitute for what they intend to destroy, or who propose a substitute which would be far worse than the existing evils--all these men are the most dangerous opponents of real reform. If they get their way they will lead the people into a deeper pit than any into which they could fall under the present system. If they fail to get their way they will still do incalculable harm by provoking the kind of reaction which, in its revolt against the senseless evil of their teaching, would enthrone more securely than ever the very evils which their misguided followers believe they are attacking.

More important than aught else is the development of the broadest sympathy of man for man. The welfare of the wageworker, the welfare of the tiller of the soil, upon these depend the welfare of the entire country; their good is not to be sought in pulling down others; but their good must be the prime object of all our statesmanship.

Materially we must strive to secure a broader economic opportunity for all men, so that each shall have a better chance to show the stuff of which he is made. Spiritually and ethically we must strive to bring about clean living and right thinking. We appreciate the things of the body are important; but we appreciate also the things of the soul are immeasurably more important. The foundation-stone of national life is, and ever must be, the high individual character of the average citizen.

The New Nationalism

Osawatomie, Kansas, August 31, 1910

We come here to-day to commemorate one of the epochmaking events of the long struggle for the rights of man--the long struggle for the uplift of humanity. Our country--this great Republic--means nothing unless it means the triumph of a real democracy, the triumph of popular government, and, in the long run, of an economic system under which each man shall be guaranteed the opportunity to show the best that there is in him. That is why the history of America is now the central feature of the history of the world; for the world has set its face hopefully toward our democracy; and, O my fellow citizens, each one of you carries on your shoulders not only the burden of doing well for the sake of your own country, but the burden of doing well and of seeing that this nation does well for the sake of mankind.

There have been two great crises in our country's history: first, when it was formed, and then, again, when it was perpetuated; and, in the second of these great crises--in the time of stress and strain which culminated in the Civil War, on the outcome of which depended the justification of what had been done earlier, you men of the Grand Army, you men who fought through the Civil War, not only did you justify your generation, not only did you render life worth living for our generation, but you justified the wisdom of Washington and Washington's colleagues. If this Republic had been founded by them only to be split asunder into fragments when the strain came, then the judgment of the world would have been that Washington's work was not worth doing. It was you who crowned Washington's work, as you carried to achievement the high purpose of Abraham Lincoln.

Now, with this second period of our history the name of John Brown will be forever associated; and Kansas was the theater upon which the first act of the second of our great national life dramas was played.   It was the result of the struggle in Kansas which determined that our country should be in deed as well as in name devoted to both union and freedom; that the great experiment of democratic government on a national scale should succeed and not fail.   In name we had the Declaration of Independence in 1776; but we gave the lie by our acts to the words of the Declaration of Independence until 1865; and words count for nothing except in so far as they represent acts.   This is true everywhere; but, O my friends, it should be truest of all in political life.   A broken promise is bad enough in private life.   It is worse in the field of politics. No man is worth his salt in public life who makes on the stump a pledge which he does not keep after election; and, if he makes such a pledge and does not keep it, hunt him out of public life.   I care for the great deeds of the past chiefly as spurs to drive us onward in the present.   I speak of the men of the past partly that they may be honored by our praise of them, but more that they may serve as examples for the future.

It was a heroic struggle; and, as is inevitable with all such struggles, it had also a dark and terrible side.   Very much was done of good, and much also of evil; and, as was inevitable in such a period of revolution, often the same man did both good and evil.   For our great good fortune as a nation, we, the people of the United States as a whole, can now afford to forget the evil, or, at least, to remember it without bitterness, and to fix our eyes with pride only on the good that was accomplished. Even in ordinary times there are very few of us who do not see the problems of life as through a glass, darkly; and when the glass is clouded by the murk of furious popular passion, the vision of the best and the bravest is dimmed.   Looking back, we are all of us now able to do justice to the valor and the disinterestedness and the love of the right, as to each it was given to see the right, shown both by the men of the North and the men of the South in that contest which was finally decided by the attitude of the West.   We can admire the heroic valor, the sincerity, the self-devotion shown alike by the men who wore the blue and the men who wore the gray; and our sadness that such men should have had to fight one another is tempered by the glad knowledge that ever hereafter their descendants shall be found fighting side by side, struggling in peace as well as in war for the uplift of their common country, all alike resolute to raise to the highest pitch of honor and usefulness the nation to which they all belong.   As for the veterans of the Grand Army of the Republic, they deserve honor and recognition such as is paid to no other citizens of the

Republic; for to them the republic owes its all; for to them it owes its very existence.   It is because of what you and your comrades did in the dark years that we of to-day walk, each of us, head erect, and proud that we belong, not to one of a dozen little squabbling contemptible commonwealths, but to the mightiest nation upon which the sun shines.

I do not speak of this struggle of the past merely from the historic standpoint.   Our interest is primarily in the application to-day of the lessons taught by the contest of half a century ago.   It is of little use for us to pay lip-loyalty to the mighty men of the past unless we sincerely endeavor to apply to the problems of the present precisely the qualities which in other crises enable the men of that day to meet those crises. It is half melancholy and half amusing to see the way in which well-meaning people gather to do honor to the man who, in company with John Brown, and under the lead of Abraham Lincoln, faced and solved the great problems of the nineteenth century, while, at the same time, these same good people nervously shrink from, or frantically denounce, those who are trying to meet the problems of the twentieth century in the spirit which was accountable for the successful solution of the problems of Lincoln's time.

Of that generation of men to whom we owe so much, the man to whom we owe most is, of course, Lincoln.   Part of our debt to him is because he forecast our present struggle and saw the way out.   He said:

"I hold that while man exists it is his duty to improve not only his own condition, but to assist in ameliorating mankind."

And again:

"Labor is prior to, and independent of, capital.   Capital is only the fruit of labor, and could never have existed if labor had not first existed.   Labor is the superior of capital, and deserves much the higher consideration."

If that remark was original with me, I should be even more strongly denounced as a Communist agitator than I shall be anyhow.   It is Lincoln's.   I am only quoting it; and that is one side; that is the side the capitalist should hear.   Now, let the working man hear his side.

"Capital has its rights, which are as worthy of protection as any other rights. . . . Nor should this lead to a war upon the owners of property.   Property is the fruit of labor; . . . property is desirable; is a positive good in the world."

And then comes a thoroughly Lincolnlike sentence:

"Let not him who is houseless pull down the house of another, but let him work diligently and build one for himself, thus by example assuring that his own shall be safe from violence when built."

It seems to me that, in these words, Lincoln took substantially the attitude that we ought to take; he showed the proper sense of proportion in his relative estimates of capital and labor, of human rights and property rights. Above all, in this speech, as in many others, he taught a lesson in wise kindliness and charity; an indispensable lesson to us of to-day. But this wise kindliness and charity never weakened his arm or numbed his heart. We cannot afford weakly to blind ourselves to the actual conflict which faces us to-day. The issue is joined, and we must fight or fail.

In every wise struggle for human betterment one of the main objects, and often the only object, has been to achieve in large measure equality of opportunity. In the struggle for this great end, nations rise from barbarism to civilization, and through it people press forward from one stage of enlightenment to the next. One of the chief factors in progress is the destruction of special privilege. The essence of any struggle for healthy liberty has always been, and must always be, to take from some one man or class of men the right to enjoy power, or wealth, or position, or immunity, which has not been earned by service to his or their fellows. That is what you fought for in the Civil War, and that is what we strive for now.

At many stages in the advance of humanity, this conflict between the men who possess more than they have earned and the men who have earned more than they possess is the central condition of progress. In our day it appears as the struggle of freemen to gain and hold the right of self-government as against the special interests, who twist the methods of free government into machinery for defeating the popular will. At every stage, and under all circumstances, the essence of the struggle is to equalize opportunity, destroy privilege, and give to the life and citizenship of every individual the highest possible value both to himself and to the commonwealth. That is nothing new. All I ask in civil life is what you fought for in the Civil War. I ask that civil life be carried on according to the spirit in which the army was carried on. You never get perfect justice, but the effort in handling the army was to bring to the front the men who could do the job. Nobody grudged promotion to Grant, or Sherman, or Thomas, or Sheridan, because they earned it. The only complaint was when a man got promotion which he did not earn.

Practical equality of opportunity for all citizens, when we achieve it, will have two great results. First, every man will have a fair chance to make of himself all that in him lies; to reach the highest point to which his capacities, unassisted by special privilege of his own and unhampered by the special privilege of others, can carry him, and to get for himself and his family substantially what he has earned. Second, equality of opportunity means that the commonwealth will get from every citizen the highest service of which he is capable.   No man who carries the burden of the special privileges of another can give to the commonwealth that service to which it is fairly entitled.

I stand for the square deal.   But when I say that I am for the square deal, I mean not merely that I stand for fair play under the present rules of the games, but that I stand for having those rules changed so as to work for a more substantial equality of opportunity and of reward for equally good service.   One word of warning, which, I think, is hardly necessary in Kansas.   When I say I want a square deal for the poor man, I do not mean that I want a square deal for the man who remains poor because he has not got the energy to work for himself.   If a man who has had a chance will not make good, then he has got to quit.   And you men of the Grand Army, you want justice for the brave man who fought, and punishment for the coward who shirked his work.   Is not that so?

Now, this means that our government, national and State, must be freed from the sinister influence or control of special interests.   Exactly as the special interests of cotton and slavery threatened our political integrity before the Civil War, so now the great special business interests too often control and corrupt the men and methods of government for their own profit.   We must drive the special interests out of politics.   That is one of our tasks to-day.   Every special interest is entitled to justice--full, fair, and complete--and, now, mind you, if there were any attempt by mob-violence to plunder and work harm to the special interest, whatever it may be, and I most dislike, and the wealthy man, whomsoever he may be, for whom I have the greatest contempt, I would fight for him, and you would if you were worth your salt.   He should have justice.   For every special interest is entitled to justice, but not one is entitled to a vote in Congress, to a voice on the bench, or to representation in any public office.   The Constitution guarantees protections to property, and we must make that promise good.   But it does not give the right of suffrage to any corporation.

The true friend of property, the true conservative, is he who insists that property shall be the servant and not the master of the commonwealth; who insists that the creature of man's making shall be the servant and not the master of the man who made it.   The citizens of the United States must effectively control the mighty commercial forces which they have themselves called into being.

There can be no effective control of corporations while their political activity remains.   To put an end to it will be neither a short nor an easy task, but it can be done.

We must have complete and effective publicity of corporate affairs, so that people may know beyond peradventure whether the corporations obey the law and whether their management entitles them to the confidence of the public. It is necessary that laws should be passed to prohibit the use of corporate funds directly or indirectly for political purposes; it is still more necessary that such laws should be thoroughly enforced. Corporate expenditures for political purposes, and especially such expenditures by public-service corporations, have supplied one of the principal sources of corruption in our political affairs.

It has become entirely clear that we must have government supervision of the capitalization, not only of public-service corporations, including, particularly, railways, but of all corporations doing an interstate business. I do not wish to see the nation forced into the ownership of the railways if it can possibly be avoided, and the only alternative is thoroughgoing and effective regulation, which shall be based on a full knowledge of all the facts, including a physical valuation of property. This physical valuation is not needed, or, at least, is very rarely needed, for fixing rates; but it is needed as the basis of honest capitalization.

We have come to recognize that franchises should never be granted except for a limited time, and never without proper provision for compensation to the public. It is my personal belief that the same kind and degree of control and supervision which should be exercised over public-service corporations should be extended also to combinations which control necessaries of life, such as meat, oil, and coal, or which deal in them on an important scale. I have not doubt that the ordinary man who has control of them is much like ourselves. I have no doubt he would like to do well, but I want to have enough supervision to help him realize that desire to do well.

I believe that the officers, and, especially, the directors, of corporations should be held personally responsible when any corporation breaks the law.

Combinations in industry are the result of an imperative economic law which cannot be repealed by political legislation. The effort at prohibiting all combination has substantially failed. The way out lies, not in attempting to prevent such combinations, but in completely controlling them in the interest of the public welfare. For that purpose the Federal Bureau of Corporations is an agency of first importance. Its powers, and, therefore, its efficiency, as well as that of the Interstate Commerce Commission, should be largely increased. We have a right to expect from the Bureau of Corporations and from the Interstate Commerce Commission a very high grade of public service. We should be as sure of the proper conduct of the interstate railways and the proper management of interstate business as we are now sure of the conduct and management of the national banks, and we should have as effective supervision in one case as in the other. The Hepburn Act, and the amendment to the act in the shape in which it finally passed Congress at the last session, represent a long step in advance, and we must go yet further.

There is a wide-spread belief among our people that under the methods of making tariffs, which have hitherto obtained, the special interests are too influential. Probably this is true of both the big special interests and the little special interests. These methods have put a premium on selfishness, and, naturally, the selfish big interests have gotten more than their smaller, though equally selfish brothers. The duty of Congress is to provide a method by which the interest of the whole people shall be all that receives consideration. To this end there must be an expert tariff commission, wholly removed from the possibility of political pressure or of improper business influence. Such a commission can find the real difference between cost of production, which is mainly the difference of labor cost here and abroad. As fast as its recommendations are made, I believe in revising one schedule at a time. A general revision of the tariff almost inevitably leads to logrolling and the subordination of the general public interest to local and special interests.

The absence of effective State, and, especially, national, restraint upon unfair money-getting has tended to create a small class of enormously wealthy and economically powerful men, whose chief object is to hold and increase their power. The prime need is to change the conditions which enable these men to accumulate power which is not for the general welfare that they should hold or exercise. We grudge no man a fortune which represents his own power and sagacity, when exercised with entire regard to the welfare of his fellows.   Again, comrades over there, take the lesson from your own experience. Not only did you not grudge, but you gloried in the promotion of the great generals who gained their promotion by leading the army to victory. So it is with us. We grudge no man a fortune in civil life if it is honorably obtained and well used. It is not even enough that it should have gained without doing damage to the community. We should permit it to be gained only so long as the gaining represents benefit to the community. This, I know, implies a policy of a far more active governmental interference with social and economic conditions in this country than we have yet had, but I think we have got to face the fact that such an increase in governmental control is now necessary.

No man should receive a dollar unless that dollar has been fairly earned. Every dollar received should represent a dollar's worth of service rendered--not gambling in stocks, but service rendered. The really big fortune, the swollen fortune, by the mere fact of its size acquires qualities which differentiate it in kind as well as in degree from what is possessed by men of relatively small means. Therefore, I believe in a graduated income tax on big fortunes, and in another tax which is far more easily collected and far more effective--a graduated inheritance tax on big fortunes, properly safeguarded against evasion and increasing rapidly in amount with the size of the estate.

The people of the United States suffer from periodical financial panics to a degree substantially unknown among the other nations which approach us in financial strength. There is no reason why we should suffer what they escape. It is of profound importance that our financial system should be promptly investigated, and so thoroughly and effectively revised as to make it certain that hereafter our currency will no longer fail at critical times to meet our needs.

It is hardly necessary for me to repeat that I believe in an efficient army and a navy large enough to secure for us abroad that respect which is the surest guaranty of peace. A word of special warning to my fellow citizens who are as progressive as I hope I am. I want them to keep up their interest in our internal affairs; and I want them also continually to remember Uncle Sam's interest abroad. Justice and fair dealing among nations rest upon principles identical with those which control justice and fair dealing among the individuals of which nations are composed, with the vital exception that each nation must do its own part in international police work. If you get into trouble here, you can call for the police; but if Uncle Sam gets into trouble, he has got to be his own policeman, and I want to see him strong enough to encourage the peaceful aspirations of other peoples in connection with us. I believe in national friendships and heartiest good-will to all nations; but national friendships, like those between men, must be founded on respect as well as on liking, on forbearance as well as upon trust. I should be heartily ashamed of any American who did not try to make the American Government act as justly toward the other nations in international relations as he himself would act toward any individual in private relations. I should be heartily ashamed to see us wrong a weaker power, and I should hang my head forever if we tamely suffered wrong from a stronger power.

Of conservation I shall speak more at length elsewhere. Conservation means development as much as it does protection. I recognize the right and duty of this generation to develop and use the natural resources of our land; but I do not recognize the right to waste them, or to rob, by wasteful use, the generations that come after us. I ask nothing of the nation except that it so behave as each farmer here behaves with reference to his own children. That farmer is a poor creature who skins the land and leaves it worthless to his children. The farmer is a good farmer who, having enabled the land to support himself and to provide for the education of his children, leaves it to them a little better than he found it himself.   I believe the same thing of a nation.

Moreover, I believe that the natural resources must be used for the benefit of all our people, and not monopolized for the benefit of the few, and here again is another case in which I am accused of taking a revolutionary attitude. People forget now that one hundred years ago there were public men of good character who advocated the nation selling its public lands in great quantities, so that the nation could get the most money out of it, and giving it to the men who could cultivate it for their own uses. We took the proper democratic ground that the land should be granted in small sections to the men who were actually to till it and live on it.   Now, with the water-power, with the forests, with the mines, we are brought face to face with the fact that there are many people who will go with us in conserving the resources only if they are to be allowed to exploit them for their benefit. That is one of the fundamental reasons why the special interest should be driven out of politics. Of all the questions which can come before this nation, short of the actual preservation of its existence in a great war, there is none which compares in importance with the great central task of leaving this land even a better land for our descendants than it is for us, and training them into a better race to inhabit the land and pass it on. Conservation is a great moral issue for it involves the patriotic duty of insuring the safety and continuance of the nation. Let me add that the health and vitality of our people are at least as well worth conserving as their forests, waters, lands, and minerals, and in this great work the national government must bear a most important part.

I have spoken elsewhere also of the great task which lies before the farmers of the country to get for themselves and their wives and children not only the benefits of better farming, but also those of better business methods and better conditions of life on the farm. The burden of this great task will fall, as it should, mainly upon the great organizations of the farmers themselves. I am glad it will, for I believe they are all able to handle it.   In particular, there are strong reasons why the Departments of Agriculture of the various States, and the United States Department of Agriculture, and the agricultural colleges and experiment stations should extend their work to cover all phases of farm life, instead of limiting themselves, as they have far too often limited themselves in the past, solely to the question of the production of crops. And now a special word to the farmer. I want to see him make the farm as fine a farm as it can be made; and let him remember to see that the improvement goes on indoors as well as out; let him remember that the farmer's wife should have her share of thought and attention just as much as the farmer himself.

Nothing is more true than that excess of every kind is followed by reaction; a fact which should be pondered by reformer and reactionary alike. We are face to face with new conceptions of the relations of property to human welfare, chiefly because certain advocates of the rights of property as against the rights of men have been pushing their claims too far. The man who wrongly holds that every human right is secondary to his profit must now give way to the advocate of human welfare, who rightly maintains that every man holds his property subject to the general right of the community to regulate its use to whatever degree the public welfare may require it.

But I think we may go still further. The right to regulate the use of wealth in the public interest is universally admitted. Let us admit also the right to regulate the terms and conditions of labor, which is the chief element of wealth, directly in the interest of the common good. The fundamental thing to do for every man is to give him a chance to reach a place in which he will make the greatest possible contribution to the public welfare. Understand what I say there. Give him a chance, not push him up if he will not be pushed. Help any man who stumbles; if he lies down, it is a poor job to try to carry him; but if he is a worthy man, try your best to see that he gets a chance to show the worth that is in him. No man can be a good citizen unless he has a wage more than sufficient to cover the bare cost of living, and hours of labor short enough so that after his day's work is done he will have time and energy to bear his share in the management of the community, to help in carrying the general load. We keep countless men from being good citizens by the conditions of life with which we surround them. We need comprehensive workmen's compensation acts, both State and national laws to regulate child labor and work for women, and, especially, we need in our common schools not merely education in book-learning, but also practical training for daily life and work. We need to enforce better sanitary conditions for our workers and to extend the use of safety appliances for our workers in industry and commerce, both within and between the States. Also, friends, in the interest of the working man himself we need to set our faces like flint against mob-violence just as against corporate greed; against violence and injustice and lawlessness by wage-workers just as much as against lawless

cunning and greed and selfish arrogance of employers.   If I
could ask but one thing of my fellow countrymen, my request
would be that, whenever they go in for reform, they remember
the two sides, and that they always exact justice from one side
as much as from the other.   I have small use for the public
servant who can always see and denounce the corruption of the
capitalist, but who cannot persuade himself, especially before
elections, to say a word about lawless mob-violence.   And I
have equally small use for the man, be he a judge on the
bench, or editor of a great paper, or wealthy and influential
private citizen, who can see clearly enough and denounce the
lawlessness of mob-violence, but whose eyes are closed so that
he is blind when the question is one of corruption in business
on a gigantic scale.   Also remember what I said about excess
in reformer and reactionary alike.   If the reactionary man, who
thinks of nothing but the rights of property, could have his
way, he would bring about a revolution; and one of my chief
fears in connection with progress comes because I do not want
to see our people, for lack of proper leadership, compelled to
follow men whose intentions are excellent, but whose eyes are
a little too wild to make it really safe to trust them.   Here in
Kansas there is one paper which habitually denounces me as
the tool of Wall Street, and at the same time frantically
repudiates the statement that I am a Socialist on the ground
that is an unwarranted slander of the Socialists.

National efficiency has many factors.   It is a necessary
result of the principle of conservation widely applied.   In the
end it will determine our failure or success as a nation.
National efficiency has to do, not only with natural resources
and with men, but is equally concerned with institutions.   The
State must be made efficient for the work which concerns only
the people of the State; and the nation for that which concerns
all the people.   There must remain no neutral ground to serve
as a refuge for lawbreakers, and especially for lawbreakers of
great wealth, who can hire the vulpine legal cunning which will
teach them how to avoid both jurisdictions.   It is a misfortune
when the national legislature fails to do its duty in providing a
national remedy, so that the only national activity is the purely
negative activity of the judiciary in forbidding the State to
exercise power in the premises.

I do not ask for overcentralization; but I do ask that we
work in a spirit of broad and far-reaching nationalism when we
work for what concerns our people as a whole.   We are all
Americans.   Our common interests are as broad as the
continent.   I speak to you here in Kansas exactly as I would
speak in New York or Georgia, for the most vital problems are
those which affect us all alike.   The national government
belongs to the whole American people, and where the whole

American people are interested, that interest can be guarded effectively only by the national government. The betterment which we seek must be accomplished, I believe, mainly through the national government.

The American people are right in demanding that New Nationalism, without which we cannot hope to deal with new problems. The New Nationalism puts the national need before sectional or personal advantage. It is impatient of the utter confusion that results from local legislatures attempting to treat national issues as local issues. It is still more impatient of the impotence which springs from overdivision of governmental powers, the impotence which makes it possible for local selfishness or for legal cunning, hired by wealthy special interests, to bring national activities to a deadlock. This New Nationalism regards the executive power as the steward of the public welfare. It demands of the judiciary that it shall be interested primarily in human welfare rather than in property, just as it demands that the representative body shall represent all the people rather than any one class or section of the people.

I believe in shaping the ends of government to protect property as well as human welfare. Normally, and in the long run, the ends are the same; but whenever the alternative must be faced, I am for men and not for property, as you were in the Civil War. I am far from underestimating the importance of dividends; but I rank dividends below human character. Again, I do not have any sympathy with the reformer who says he does not care for dividends. Of course, economic welfare is necessary, for a man must pull his own weight and be able to support his family. I know well that the reformers must not bring upon the people economic ruin, or the reforms themselves will go down in the ruin. But we must be ready to face temporary disaster, whether or not brought on by those who will war against us to the knife. Those who oppose all reform will do well to remember that ruin in its worst form is inevitable if our national life brings us nothing better than swollen fortunes for the few and the triumph in both politics and business of a sordid and selfish materialism.

If our political institutions were perfect, they would absolutely prevent the political domination of money in any part of our affairs. We need to make our political representatives more quickly and sensitively responsive to the people whose servants they are. More direct action by the people in their own affairs under proper safeguards is vitally necessary. The direct primary is a step in this direction, if it is associated with a corrupt-practices act effective to prevent the advantage of the man willing recklessly and unscrupulously to spend money over his more honest competitor. It is particularly important that all moneys received or expended for campaign purposes should be publicly accounted for, not only after election, but before election as well. Political action must be made simpler, easier, and freer from confusion for every citizen. I believe that the prompt removal of unfaithful or incompetent public servants should be made easy and sure in whatever way experience shall show to be most expedient in any given class of cases.

One of the fundamental necessities in a representative government such as ours is to make certain that the men to whom the people delegate their power shall serve the people by whom they are elected, and not the special interests. I believe that every national officer, elected or appointed, should be forbidden to perform any service or receive any compensation, directly or indirectly, from interstate corporations; and a similar provision could not fail to be useful within the States.

The object of government is the welfare of the people. The material progress and prosperity of a nation are desirable chiefly so far as they lead to the moral and material welfare of all good citizens. Just in proportion as the average man and woman are honest, capable of sound judgement and high ideals, active in public affairs--but, first of all, sound in their home life, and the father and mother of healthy children whom they bring up well--just so far, and no farther, we may count our civilization a success. We must have--I believe we have already--a genuine and permanent moral awakening, without which no wisdom of legislation or administration really means anything; and, on the other hand, we must try to secure the social and economic legislation without which any improvement due to purely moral agitation is necessarily evanescent. Let me again illustrate by a reference to the Grand Army. You could not have won simply as a disorderly and disorganized mob. You needed generals; you needed careful administration of the most advanced type; and a good commissary--the cracker line. You well remember that success was necessary in many different lines in order to bring about general success. You had to have the administration at Washington good, just as you had to have the administration in the field; and you had to have the work of the generals good. You could not have triumphed without that administration and leadership; but it would all have been worthless if the average soldier had not had the right stuff in him. He had to have the right stuff in him, or you could not get it out of him. In the last analysis, therefore, vitally necessary though it was to have the right kind of organization and the right kind of generalship, it was even more vitally necessary that the average soldier should have the fighting edge, the right character. So it is in our civil life. No matter how honest and decent we are in our private lives, if we do not have the right kind of law and the right kind of administration of the law, we cannot go forward as a nation.   That is imperative; but it must be an addition to, and not a substitution for, the qualities that make us good citizens.   In the last analysis, the most important elements in any man's career must be the sum of those qualities which, in the aggregate, we speak of as character.   If he has not got it, then no law that the wit of man can devise, no administration of the law by the boldest and strongest executive, will avail to help him.   We must have the right kind of character--character that makes a man, first of all, a good man in the home, a good father, a good husband--that makes a man a good neighbor. You must have that, and, then, in addition, you must have the kind of law and the kind of administration of the law which will give to those qualities in the private citizen the best possible chance for development.   The prime problem of our nation is to get the right type of good citizenship, and, to get it, we must have progress, and our public men must be genuinely progressive.

This Nation's Needs

Plattsburgh, New York, August 25, 1915

I wish to congratulate all who have been at this Plattsburg camp and at the similar camps throughout the country upon the opportunity they have had to minister to their own self-respect by fitting themselves to serve the country if the need should arise. You have done your duty. In doing it you have added to your value as citizens. You have the right to hold your heads higher because you are fulfilling the prime duty of freemen.

No man is fit to be free unless he is not merely willing but eager to fit himself to fight for his freedom, and no man can fight for his freedom unless he is trained to act in conjunction with his fellows. The worst of all feelings to arouse in others is the feeling of contempt. Those men have mean souls who desire that this nation shall not be fit to defend its own rights and that its sons shall not possess a high and resolute temper. But even men of stout heart need to remember that when the hour for action has struck no courage will avail unless there has been thorough training, thorough preparation in advance.

The greatest need for this country is a first-class navy. Next, we need a thoroughly trained regular or professional army of 200,000 men if we have universal military service; and of at least half a million men if we do not have such universal military service.

At present a single army corps from Germany or Japan (which, if subtracted from the efficient fighting forces of either would not even be felt) could at any time be ferried across the ocean and take New York or San Francisco and destroy them or hold them to ransom with absolutely impunity and the

United States at present would be helpless to do more than blame some scapegoat for what was really the fault of our people as a whole in failing to prepare in advance against the day of disaster.

But the professional navy and the professional army are not enough.   Free citizens should be able to do their own fighting.   The professional pacifist is as much out of place in a democracy as is the poltroon himself; and he is no better citizen than the poltroon.   Probably no body of citizens in the United States during the last five years have wrought so efficient for national decadence and international degradation as the professional pacifists, the peace-at-any-price men, who have tried to teach our people that silly all inclusive arbitration treaties and the utterance of fatuous platitudes at peace congresses are substitute for adequate military preparedness.

These people are seeking to Chinafy this country.   A high Japanese military officer recently remarked to a gentleman of my acquaintance that the future dominion over the seas and lands of the Pacific lay with Japan, because China was asleep and America was falling asleep, and in this world the future lay with the nations of patriotic and soldierly spirit.   If the United States were to follow the lead of the professional pacifists and to permit itself to be Chinafied, this observer's opinion would be quite correct.

It is an abhorrent thing to make a wanton or an unjust war.   It is an abhorrent thing to trespass on the rights of the weak.   But it is an utterly contemptible thing to be unable and unwilling to fight for one's own rights in the first place, and then, if possessed of sufficient loftiness of soul, to fight for the rights of the weak who are wronged.   The greatest service that has ever been rendered mankind has been rendered by the men who have not shrunk from righteous war in order to bring about righteous peace, by soldier-statesmen of the type of Washington, by statesmen of the type of Abraham Lincoln, whose work was done by soldiers.   The men of the Revolution and the men of the civil war and the women who raised these men to be soldiers are the men and women to whom we owe a deathless debt of gratitude.

This means that all our young men should be trained so that at need they can fight.   Under the conditions of modern warfare it is the wildest nonsense to talk of men springing to arms in mass unless they have been taught how to act and how to use the arms to which they spring.

For thirteen months America has played an ignoble part among the nations.   We have tamely submitted to seeing the weak, whom we had covenanted to protect, wronged.   We have seen our own men, women, and children murdered on the high seas without action on our part.   We have treated elocution as a substitute for action. During this time our government has not taken the smallest step in the way of preparedness to defend our own rights. Yet these thirteen months have made evident the lamentable fact that force is more dominant now in the affairs of the world than ever before; that the most powerful of modern military nations is utterly brutal and ruthless in its disregard of international morality, and that righteousness divorced from force is utterly futile. Reliance upon high-sounding words unbacked by deeds is proof of a mind that dwells only in the realm of shadow and sham.

This camp has lasted two months. It has done immense good to you who have been able to come here--although, by the way, you must not think that it has more than marked the beginning of training you to your duties. But you have been able to come because you are either yourself fairly well-to-do or else because you happen to have employers who are both public-spirited and fairly well-to-do, and who give you holidays with pay.

The government has not paid a dollar for this camp. Inasmuch as we as a nation have done nothing whatever for national defense during the last thirteen months, the time when during all our history it was most necessary to prepare for self-defense, it is well that private individuals should have tried, however insufficiently, to provide some kind of substitute for proper governmental action. The army officers and enlisted men have put all good Americans under a fresh debt by what they have done in connection with this camp, and we owe much to the private citizens who have advanced the money without which the camp could not have been held.

But you men have had to buy your own uniforms; you have had to spend money in fifty different ways; in other words, you have had to pay for the privilege of learning how to serve your country. This means that for every one man like yourselves who can afford to come here there are a hundred equally good American citizens, equally patriotic, who would like to come and are unable to. It is undemocratic that the young farmer, that the young hired man on a farm, that the hardworking clerk or mechanic or day laborer, all of whom wish to serve the country as much as you do and are as much entitled to the benefit of this camp as you are, should be unable to attend such a camp.

They cannot attend to it unless the nation does as Switzerland has done and gives the opportunity for every generous and right-thinking American to learn by, say, six month's actual service in one year or two years how to do his duty to the country if the need arises--and the Americans who are not right-thinking should be made to serve anyhow, for a democracy has full rights to the service of its citizens.

Such service would be an immense benefit to the man industrially.   It would not only help the nation, but it would help each individual who undergoes the training.   Switzerland has universal military service, and it is the most democratic and least militaristic of countries, and a much more orderly and less homicidal country than our own.

Camps like this are schools of civic virtue as well as of military efficiency.   They should be universal and obligatory for all our young men.   Every man worth his salt will wish to come to them.

As for the professional pacifists and the poltroons and college sissies who organize peace-at-any-price societies, and the mere money-getters and mere money spenders, they should be made to understand that they have got to render whatever service the country demands.   They must be made to submit to training in doing their duty.   Then if, in the event of war, they prove unfit to fight, at any rate they can be made to dig trenches and kitchen sinks, or do whatever else a debauch of indulgence in professional pacificism has left them fit to do. Both the professional pacifists and the professional hyphenated American need to be taught that it is not for them to decide the conditions under which they will fight.   They will fight whoever the nation decides to fight, and whenever the nation deems a war necessary.   Camps like this are the best possible antidotes to hyphenated Americanism.   The worst thing that could befall this country would be to have the American nation become a tangle of jangling nationalities, a knot of German-Americans, Irish-Americans, English-Americans, and French-Americans.   If divided in such fashion, we shall most certainly fall.   We can stand as a nation only if we are genuinely united.

The events of the past year have shown us that in any crisis the hyphenated American is an active force against America, an active force for wrongdoing.   The effort to hoist two flags on the same flagpole always means that one flag is hoisted underneath, and the hyphenated American invariably hoists the flag of the United States underneath.   We must all be American and nothing else.   You in this camp include men of every creed and every national origin--Jew and Gentile, Catholic and Protestant, men of English and Irish, German and French, Slavonic and Latin and Scandinavian descent.   But you are all Americans, and nothing else.   You have only one nationality. You acknowledge but one country.   You are loyal to only one flag.

There exists no finer body of American citizens in this country than those citizens of German birth or descent who are in good faith Americans and nothing else.   We could create an entire national administration from the president down to the last cabinet officer, every one of whose members would be of

German blood and some of them of German birth, but all of them Americans and nothing else, all of them Americans of such a type that the men who feel as I do could heartily and without reserve support them in all our international relations. But the Americans of German blood who are of this type are not hyphenated Americans. They are not German-Americans. They are just plain Americans like the rest of us.   The professional German-American has shown himself within the last twelve months to be an enemy to this country as well as to humanity. The recent exposures of the way in which these German-Americans have worked together with the emissaries of the German Government--often by direct corruption--against the integrity of American institutions and against America doing its international duty should arouse scornful indignation in every American worth calling such.   The leaders among the professional German-Americans have preached and practiced what comes perilously near to treason against the United States

Under The Hague Convention it was our bounden duty to take whatever action was necessary to prevent and if not to prevent, then to undo, the hideous wrong that was done to Belgium. We have shirked this duty. We have shown a spirit so abject that Germany has deemed it safe to kill our women and children on the high seas. As for the export of munitions of war, it would be a base abandonment of morality to refuse to make these shipments. Such a refusal is proposed only to favor the nation that sank the <u>Lusitania</u> and the <u>Arabic</u> and committed the crime against Belgium, the greatest international crime committed since the close of the Napoleonic contests a century ago. It is not a lofty thing, on the contrary it is an evil thing, to practice a timid and selfish neutrality between right and wrong. It is wrong for an individual. It is still more wrong for a nation. But it is worse in the name of neutrality to favor the nation that has done evil.

As regards the export of munitions of war, the morality of the act depends upon the use to which the munitions are to be put. It was wrong to subjugate Belgium. It is wrong to keep her in subjugation. It is an utterly contemptible thing not to help in every possible way to undo this wrong.   The manufacturers of cannon, rifles, cartridges, automobiles, or saddlery who refuse to ship them for use by the armies that are striving to restore Belgium to its own people should be put on a roll of dishonor.

Exactly the same morality should obtain internationally that obtains nationally. It is right for a private firm to furnish arms to the policeman who puts down the thug, the burglar, the white slaver and the blackhander. It is wrong to furnish the blackhander, the burglar, and the white slaver with weapons to be used against the policeman. The analogy holds true in international life.

Germany has herself been the greatest manufacturer of munitions of war to be supplied to belligerent. She supplied munitions to England to subjugate the Boers and to the Turk to keep the Christians in subjection. Let us furnish munitions to the men who, showing courage which we have not shown, wish to rescue Belgium from subjection and spoliation and degradation. And let us encourage munition makers so that we may be able to hold our own when the hour of peril comes to us in our turn, as assuredly it will come if we show ourselves too "neutral" to speak a word on behalf of the weak who are wronged and too slothful and lazy to prepare to defend ourselves against wrong. Most assuredly it will come to us if we succeed in persuading great military nations that we are too proud to fight, that we are not prepared to undertake defensive war for our own vital interest and national honor.

Therefore, friends, let us shape our conduct as a nation in accordance with the highest rules of international morality. Let us treat others justly and keep the engagements we have made, such as those in The Hague Conventions, to secure just treatment for others. But let us remember that we shall be wholly unable to render service to others and wholly unable to fulfill the prime law of national being, the law of self-preservation, unless we are thoroughly prepared to hold our own. Let us show that a free democracy can defend itself successfully against any organized and aggressive, military despotism. To do so we must prepare as a nation; and the men of this camp and the men responsible for starting this camp have shown our government and our people the path along which we should tread.

Chronology of Speeches

Theodore Roosevelt was clearly among the most prolific speakers in American public life. The following chronology of speeches has been collated from a wide variety of sources. Nevertheless, given the often spontaneous nature of his remarks, especially during his campaigns, it is a virtually impossible task to produce a complete chronology. As indicated earlier in this volume, Roosevelt prepared most of his addresses in advance, typically delivering them from a manuscript, though utilizing that manuscript far less than most manuscript speakers. Consequently, a large number of Roosevelt speeches are available to the researcher.

Three principal sources of Roosevelt's speeches exist. While many anthologies of his speeches were published, clearly the most extensive published speech collection can be found in <u>The Works of Theodore Roosevelt</u>. This is the most readily available comprehensive collection of Roosevelt speeches and includes virtually all of the speeches commonly associated with Roosevelt and extensive samples of his speaking drawn from each major period of his life.

The Roosevelt papers held by the Library of Congress provide the researcher with a wealth of Roosevelt speech material. Significantly, many of the speeches held in the Library of Congress collection also include one or more of the earlier drafts, as well as the final speech manuscript that was delivered. The Library of Congress collection of Roosevelt's speeches are almost all from his presidential years.

The final major collection of Roosevelt speeches can be found among the holdings of the Theodore Roosevelt collection at Harvard University. The heart of this collection is the library of the Roosevelt Memorial Association, which was donated to Harvard and to which Harvard has steadily added. Volume five of the <u>Theodore Roosevelt Collection Dictionary Catalogue and Shelflist</u>, which indexes the entire collection, concludes with a sixty-page listing of the speeches, excerpts from speeches, or references to speeches, found in the collection. Essentially, these are all published works, but many are from campaign documents, rare magazines, newspapers, privately printed documents, and similar difficult-to-obtain material.

SPEECHES

The Election of the Speaker, New York State Assembly, Albany, New York, January 24, 1882.

Investigation of Westbrook, New York State Assembly, Albany, New York, April 6, 1882.

Governor Cleveland's Veto of the Five-cent Fare Bill, New York State Assembly, Albany, New York, March 2, 1883.

The Civil Service Reform Bill, New York State Assembly, Albany, New York, April 9,   1883.

The Convict Labor Bill, New York State Assembly, Albany, New York, April 18, 1883.

Investigation of New York City Departments, New York State Assembly, Albany, New York March 14, 1884.

Address at Faneuil Hall, Boston, Massachusetts, October 20, 1884.

Address to Young Republican Club, New York City, October 19, 1884.

Address to Young Men's Republican Club, New York City, October 22, 1884.

Address at Grand Opera House, New York City, October 19, 1886.

Address at Cooper Union, New York City, October 27, 1886.

Address at People Theatre, Minneapolis, Minnesota, October 12, 1888.

Address at Federal Club, New York City, December 13, 1888.

Address to the Civil Service Reform Association, Baltimore, Maryland, February 23, 1889.

Address at Dedication of George W. Curtis Memorial, New York City, November 14, 1892.

The Duties of American Citizenship, Buffalo, New York, January 26, 1893.

The Northwest in the Nation, State Historical Society Wisconsin, Madison Wisconsin, January 24, 1893.

Address to the Civil Service Association, Boston, Massachusetts, February 20, 1893.

Address at Carnegie Hall, New York City, August 8, 1895.

Address to Sound Money League, New York City, September 11, 1896

Address to American Republican College League, Chicago,

October 15, 1896
Address at Detroit, Michigan, October 17, 1896.
Washington's Forgotten Maxim, Naval War College, Newport
Rhode Island, June 2, 1897.
The Duties of a Great Nation, New York City, October 5, 1898.
Address to the Republican Twenty-Third Assembly District
Meeting, New York City, October 11, 1898.
Address at New York City, October 15, 1898.
Addresses at Nyack, West Nyack, Saugherties, Catskill,
Waterlist, Cohoes, Mechanicsville, Ballstone, Saratoga,
Fort Edward, Cornwall, Haverstraw, Newburg, Kingston,
Woodruff, and Glen Falls, New York, October 17, 1898.
Addresses at Rouse's Point, Norwood, Madrid, Malone, Moore's
Junction, Westport, Ogdenberg, and Plattsburg, New
York, October 18, 1898.
Addresses at Gouverneur, Carthage, Canton, Pottsdam, Lowville
and Boonville, New York, October 19, 1898.
Addresses at Eckford Hall, Arion Hall, Criterion Theatre, and
Academy of Music, Brooklyn, New York, October 19, 1898.
Addresses at Durland's Riding Academy, Metropolitan Bicycle
Academy, and Grand Central Opera House, New York
City, October 20, 1898.
Addresses at Little Falls, Johnstown, Gloversville (2), and
Poughkeepsie, New York, October 21, 1898.
Addresses at Elmira, Suffern, Hillburn, Cortland (3), Port Jarvis,
Hankin, Deposit, and Binghamton, New York, October
24, 1898.
Addresses at Buffalo (3), Corning, Hornellville, Warsaw, Addison,
Canisteo, Cameron, Castile, Attica, and Silver Springs,
New York, October 25, 1898.
Addresses at Middleport, Medina, Albion, Brookport,
Spenderport, Palmyra, Lyons, Fairport, and Rochester
(2), New York, October 26, 1898.
Addresses at Auburn (3), Canandaigua, Shortsville, Phelps,
Clifton Springs, Geneva, and Seneca Falls, New York,
October 27, 1898.
Addresses at Oswego, Pulaski, Watertown, Rome, Richland,
Phoenix, Fulton, and Utica, New York, October 28, 1898.
Addresses at Herkimer, Schenectady, Fonda, St. Johnsville,
Amsterdam, Canajoharie, Fort Plains, and Staten Island,
New York, October 29, 1898.
Addresses at Brooklyn (6), Harlem, and New York City, October
31, 1898.
Addresses at New York City (4), November 1, 1898.
Addresses at Long Island City, Valley Stream, Rockville Center,
Freport, Little Amityville, Babylon, Patchogue, Bay Shore,
Westhampton, Southhampton, Sag Harbor, Greenport,

Mattituck, Riverhead, Farmington, Hicksville, Mineola, Flora Park, and Flushing, New York, November 2, 1898.

Addresses at Albany and Troy, New York, November 3, 1898.

Addresses at Brooklyn (5), and New York City, November 4, 1898.

Addresses at New York City (11), including major address at Cooper Union, November 4, 1898.

Addresses at New York City (2), November 5, 1898.

Addresses at Hornellsville, Andover, Welleville, Belmont, Friendship, Cuba, Olean, Salamanca, Little Valley, Cattarugus, Dayton, Jamestown (2), and Dunkirk (2), New York, November 7, 1898.

Address to the dinner for General Miles, New York City, November 11, 1898.

Address to the Republican Club Dinner, New York City, November 12, 1898.

Address at Lowell Institute, Boston, Massachusetts, November 16, 1898.

Report on Cuban Conditions, to War Department Investigating Committee, New York City, November 22, 1898.

Report on Cuban Conditions, to War Department Investigating Committee (Day two), New York City, November 23, 1898.

Address at Boston, December 10, 1898.

Addresses to the New England Society of the City of New York, and The Children's Aid Society, New York City, December 22, 1898.

Inaugural Address, New York State Assembly, Albany, New York, January 2, 1899.

Address at Banquet in Honor of Rear Admiral Sampson, New York City, January 7, 1899.

Address to National Guard Association, Albany, New York, January 18, 1899.

Address in review of Twenty-Third Regiment, Brooklyn, New York, January 20, 1899.

Address to Alumni Banquet of Golden Jubilee of City College of New York, New York City, January 28, 1899.

Address presenting sword to Commodore J. W. Philip, New York City, February 3, 1899.

Address to New York State YMCA, Albany, New York, February 12, 1899.

America's Part of the World's Work, Republican Club Dinner, New York City, February 13, 1899.

Address to Tenth Annual Banquet of Chamber of Commerce, Syracuse, New York, February 22, 1899.

Address to New York State Republican Editorial Association, Albany, New York, March 2, 1899.

Yale in the War, Yale Alumni Club dinner, New York City, March 3, 1899.

Good Citizenship, West Side Republican Club, New York City, March 10, 1899.

Address at New York City, March 16, 1899.

Address to Citizens Union Club, New York City, March 24, 1899.

Address to the Harvard Club of Chicago, Chicago, April 10, 1899.

The Strenuous Life, Hamilton Club, Chicago, April 10, 1899.

Address at Michigan University, Ann Arbor, Michigan, April 11, 1899.

Address at dinner for Senator Frye, New York City, April 26, 1899

Address at the City Club, New York City, May 9, 1899.

Address to the Independent Club, Buffalo, New York, May 15, 1899.

Address to the City Club, New York City, May 19, 1899.

Address to the Grand Army of the Republic, New York City, May 30, 1899.

Address to the Hungarian Republican Club, New York City, May 31, 1899.

Commencement Address, Columbia University, New York City, June 7, 1899.

Address at the unveiling of Frederick Douglass Monument, Rochester, New York, June 9, 1899.

The Educated Man, Class Day Address, Cornell University, Ithaca, New York, June 20, 1899.

Addresses enroute to Rough Riders Reunion, Chicago, June 22, 1899.

Address to Rough Riders Reunion, Las Vegas, New Mexico, June 24, 1899.

Address at Raton, New Mexico, June 24, 1899.

Address on the presentation of medal from the People of New Mexico to Rough Riders, Las Vegas, New Mexico, June 25, 1899.

Address at Fort Madison and Galesburg, Illinois, June 27, 1899.

Address to the Milwaukee Chamber of Commerce, Milwaukee, Wisconsin, June 28, 1899.

Fourth of July Address, Oyster Bay, New York, July 4, 1899.

Practical Politics and Decent Politics, Summer School of Theology, Ocean Grove, New Jersey, August 3, 1899.

Address to Firemen's Association of New York, Yonkers, New York, August 15, 1899.

Address to Annual Meeting of the Western New York Pioneer's Association, Olcott, New York, August 16, 1899.

Address at Niagera County Pioneer Picnic, Olcott, New York, August 16, 1899.

Address at Pioneer's Association Grounds, Silver Lake, New York, August 18, 1899.

Address at Chautaugua, New York, August 19, 1899.

172 Chronology of Speeches

Address to 26th Regiment of U.S. Volunteers, Plattsburgh, New
York, August 21, 1899.
Address to Catholic University, Cliff Haven, New York, August
21, 1899.
Address at Farmer's Club Fair, Hornellsville, New York, August
30, 1899.
This Nation, Cattaraugus County Fair, Little Valley, New York,
August 31, 1899.
Canals and Their Management, Jefferson County Fair Grounds,
Watertown, New York, September 1, 1899.
Address at Oswegatchie Agricultural Fair, Ogdensburg, New
York, September 5, 1899.
Address at Fulton County Fair Grounds, Johnstown, New York,
September 6, 1899.
Address at Deleware County Fair, Delhi, New York, September
7, 1899.
Address at Chenengo County Fair, Norwich, New York,
September 7, 1899.
Address at New York State Fair, Syracuse, New York, September
8, 1899.
Address at Orange County Fair, Middletown, New York,
September 12, 1899.
Address at Walton, New York, September 13, 1899.
Address at Lewis County Fair, Lowville, New York, September
14, 1899.
Address at Wayne County Fair, Lyons, New York, September 15,
1899.
Address on the anniversary of the Battle of Antietam, Brooklyn,
New York, September 16, 1899.
Address at Suffolk County Fair, Riverhead, New York,
September 19, 1899.
Address at Otsage County Fair, Cooperstown, New York,
September 21, 1899.
Address at the unveiling of Statue of Governor Horatio Seymour,
Utica, New York, September 23, 1899.
Address at the opening of the Republican Campaign, Akron,
Ohio, September 23, 1899.
Address at Queens County Fair, Mineola, New York, September
27, 1899.
Address at laying of cornerstone of new library, Oyster Bay,
New York, October 2, 1899.
Address at Binghamton, New York, October 5, 1899.
Addresses at Frederick Douglass Memorial Day service, Elmira,
and at Waverly, New York, October 6, 1899.
Address to State Assembly of Mothers, Albany, New York,
October 18, 1899.
Address to Republican meeting, New York City, October 19, 1899.
Address on the Philippines, Cincinnati, Ohio, October 21, 1899.

Address at Cincinnati, Ohio, October 22, 1899.
Addresses at Cumberland, Barton, Lonaconing, Frostburg, Handcock, Sherry Run, Williamsport, Hagerstown, Brunswick, Mt. Savage, Maryland, and Piedmont, West Virginia, October 25, 1899.
Addresses at Frederick, Union Bridge, Westminster, Bruceville, and Baltimore, Maryland, October 26, 1899.
Address to annual dinner of the Republican Club, Boston, Massachusets, October 31, 1899.
Address to New York Chamber of Commerce, New York City, November 21, 1899.
Address to University of South Alumni Association, New York City, January 19, 1900.
Address to Union League, New York City, January 20, 1900.
Address to New York State Association of Bankers, New York City, February 6, 1900.
Address to the Dewy Arch Fund Banquet, New York City, February 6, 1900.
Address to Harvard Club, New York City, February 21, 1900.
Address to Press Club Dinner, New York City, February 21, 1900.
Address at Sixty-fifth Regiment Arsenal, Buffalo, New York, February 22, 1900
Address at Saturn Club, Buffalo, New York, February 22, 1900.
Address at Twentieth Century Club, Buffalo, New York, February 22, 1900.
Address to Mother's Council, Newburg, New York, February 28, 1900.
Good Citizenship, Trinity Episcopal Church, Newburg, New York, February 28, 1900.
Address at the Ohio Society Dinner, New York City, March 3, 1900.
Address to West Side Republican Club, New York City, March 9, 1900.
Address to Friends of the State Canal, New York City, March 10, 1900.
Address to Newspapermen, Chicago, April 26, 1900.
Address at Marquette Club, Chicago, April 26, 1900.
Addresses at Grant, Galena, Illinois, April 27, 1900.
Address to New York City Charter Commission Revision Committee, Albany, New York, May 4, 1900.
Address at New School Building cornerstone laying, Oyster Bay, New York, May 15, 1900.
Address to Hungarian Republican Club, New York City, May 16, 1900.
Municipal Finance, Merchant Association, New York City, May 25, 1900.
Address to Children of the First Reformed Church, Brooklyn,

New York, May 25, 1900.
Address at St. Paul's School, Concord, New Hampshire, June 7, 1900.
Promise and Performance, Rochester University, Rochester, New York, June 12, 1900.
Address at the unveiling of Soldier's Monument, Caledonia, New York, June 13, 1900.
Address to Republican National Convention, Philadelphia, Pennsylvania June 21, 1900.
Address to Rough Riders Reunion, Oklahoma City, Oklahoma, July 2, 1900.
Address to Rough Rider's Reunion, Wichita, Kansas, July 2, 1900.
Addresses at Harper, Kingman, and Hutchinson, Kansas, July 4, 1900.
Address at Galesburg, Illinois, July 5, 1900.
Address at Announcement of his Nomination for Vice-President, Oyster Bay, New York, July 12, 1900.
Address at Nassau County Courthouse cornerstone laying, Mineola, New York, July 13, 1900.
Address at St. Paul, Minnesota, July 17, 1900.
Addresses at Chicago, and Milwaukee (2), Wisconsin, July 18, 1900.
Americanism, Jewish Chautaugua, Atlantic City, New Jersey, July 23, 1900.
Address at St. Dominic's Church Fair, Oyster Bay, New York, August 16, 1900.
The Labor Question, Chicago, Illinois September 3, 1900.
Address at New York State Republican Convention, Saratoga, New York, September 5, 1900.
Address at Detroit, Michigan, September 6, 1900.
Address to Trinity Reform Dutch Church, Chicago, September 7, 1900.
Addresses at Grand Rapids (2), Bay City, Owosso, Lansing, and Saginaw, Michigan, September 7, 1900.
Addresses at Holland Michigan, Madison, and South Bend, Indiana, September, 8, 1900.
Address during service, Trinity Reform Dutch Church, Chicago, September 9, 1900.
Address at LaCrosse, Wisconsin, September 10, 1900.
Addresses at Madison, Sioux Falls, Yankton, and Flandreau, South Dakota, September 11, 1900.
Address at Mitchell, South Dakota, September 12, 1900.
Address at Fargo, North Dakota, September 13, 1900.
Address at Jamestown, North Dakota, September 15, 1900.
Address at Miles City, Montana, September 16, 1900.
Addresses at Helena (2), Billings, Columbus, and Big Timber, Montana, September 17, 1900.

Addresses at Clancy and Butte, Montana, September 18, 1900.
Addresses at Rexford, Pocatello, and Blackfoot, Idaho, September 19, 1900.
Address at Logan, Utah, September 20, 1900.
Address at Salt Lake City, Utah, September 21, 1900.
Address at Green River, Wyoming, September 22, 1900.
Address at Cheyenne, Wyoming, September 24, 1900.
Addresses at Denver (3), Greeley, Boulder, Eaton, Loveland, and Longmont, Colorado, September 25, 1900.
Address at Victor, Colorado, September 26, 1900.
Addresses at Leadville and Canyon City, Colorado, September 27, 1900.
Addresses at Hutchinson, Prairie View, Smith Center, Mankato, Belleville, and Saila, Kansas, September 28, 1900.
Addresses at Kansas City and Armourdale, Kansas, September 29, 1900.
Addresses at McCook, Falls City, Beatrice, Tecumsey, Fairmont, Sutton, Alburn, and Lincoln, Nebraska, October 1, 1900.
Addresses at Lincoln, Lexington, and Aurora, Nebraska, October 2, 1900.
Addresses at Valentine, Bassett, O'Neill, and West Point, Nebraska, October 4, 1900.
Addresses at Waterloo, Iowa, and Rock Island, Illinois, October 5, 1900.
Addresses at Chicago (2), October 6, 1900.
Address at St. Louis, Missouri, October 9, 1900.
Addresses at Fort Wayne, Indiana (2), October 10, 1900.
Address at Indianapolis, Indiana, October 11, 1900.
Addresses at Evansville (2), and Plainfield, Indiana, October 12, 1900.
Addresses at Henderson, Madisonville, Earlington, Guthrie, Russellville, Bowling Green, Murfordville, and Louisville, Kentucky, October 13, 1900.
Addresses at Winchester, Lexington, and Covington, Kentucky, October 15, 1900.
Addresses at Dayton and Columbus, Ohio, October 16, 1900.
Addresses at Toledo, Cleveland, and Norwalk, Ohio, October 17, 1900.
Addresses at Martins Ferry, Akron, Canton, Ohio, Wheeling, and Parkersburg, West Virginia, October 18, 1900.
Address at Charleston, West Virginia October 19, 1900.
Address at Baltimore, Maryland, October 20, 1900.
Addresses at Nyack, Kingston, and Newburgh (2), New York, October 22, 1900.
Addresses at Bloomville, Oneonta, Otegao, Unadilla, Sidney, Norwich, Fleischmann, Arkville, Stamford, Roxbury, and Shandaken, New York, October 23, 1900.
Addresses at Earlsville, Cazeenovia, Canastota, Union, Herkimer

Oneida, Rome, Utica, Watertown and Oswego, New York, October 24, 1900.

Addresses at Syracuse (2), Auburn (3), Watertown, Camden, Oswego, New York, October 25, 1900.

Addresses at Schenectady and New York City, October 26, 1900.

Addresses at Middletown, Port Jervis, and Binghamton (5), New York, October 27, 1900.

Addresses at Courtland (2), and Elmira (3), New York, October 29, 1900.

Addresses at Canandaigus, Corning, Bath, Avon, Livonia, Geneva, Penn Yan, and Rochester (2) New York, October 30, 1900.

Addresses at Brockport, Holly, Medina, Albion, Lockport, Niagara Falls and Buffalo (3), New York, October 31, 1900.

Addresses at Batavia, Jamestown, and Dunkirk (3), New York, November 1, 1900.

Addresses at Olean, Cuba, Randolph, Wellerville, Hornellsville, New York, November 2, 1900.

Address at Oyster Bay, New York, October 5, 1900.

Address at banquet in honor of President McKinley, Philadelphia, Pennsylvania, November 24, 1900.

Address to National Civil Service Reform League, New York City, December 14, 1900.

Address at Dedication of Soldiers' and Sailors' Monument, New York City, December 15, 1900.

Address at Sullivan Street School, New York City, December 19, 1900.

Address at Christ Episcopal Church Christmas Festival, Oyster Bay, New York, December 25, 1900.

Christian Citizenship, YMCA, New York City, December 30, 1900.

Our Country, Legal Aid Society, New York City, March 23, 1901

Addresses at Harvard University and Home Market Club, Boston, Massachusetts, April 30, 1901.

The Two Americas, Pan-American Exposition Opening Ceremonies, Buffalo, New York, May 20, 1901.

Address to Citizen's League, Huntington, New York, June 6, 1901.

Address to Long Island Bible Society, Oyster Bay, New York, June 11, 1901.

Address at Harvard Class Dinner, Boston, Massachusetts, June 26, 1901.

Applied Decency in Public Life, Oyster Bay, New York, June 29, 1901.

Manhood and Statehood, Colorado Quarter-Centennial Celebration of Statehood, Colorado Springs, Colorado, August 2, 1901.

Address at Hutchinson, Kansas, August 14, 1901.

National Duties, Minnesota State Fair, Minneapolis, Minnesota,

September 2, 1901.

Brotherhood and Heroic Virtue, Veterans' Reunion, Burlington, Vermont, September 5, 1901.

Address at Annual Outing of Fish and Game League, Isle La Motte, Vermont, September 6, 1901.

Address at Reunion of Department of the Potomac, G. A. R., Washington, D.C., February 19, 1902.

Response to toast of Prince Henry of Prussia, New York City, February 25, 1902.

Address at Charleston Exposition, Charleston, South Carolina, April 9, 1902.

Address at dinner in honor of Nicholas Murray Butler, New York City, April 19, 1902.

Address to the graduating class, United States Naval Academy, Annapolis, Maryland, May 2, 1902.

Address at cornerstone laying, McKinley Memorial, Washington, D.C., May 14, 1902.

The Church and Our Industrial Problems, Centennial Meeting Presbyterian Church Board of Home Missions, New York City, May 20, 1902.

Address at the unveiling of the Soldiers' and Sailors' Monument to the Colonial Dames of America, Arlington, Virginia, May 21, 1902.

Memorial Day Address, Arlington, Virginia, May 30, 1902.

Address to Junior Order of United American Mechanics, Washington, D.C., June 4, 1902.

Address to the National Association of Military Surgeons, Washington, D.C. June 5, 1902.

Address at the Centennial Celebration of the Establishment of the United States Military Academy, West Point, New York, June 11, 1902.

Address to Alumni Banquet, Harvard University, Cambridge, Massachusetts, June 25, 1902.

Commencement Dinner Address, Harvard University, Cambridge, Massachusetts, June 28, 1902.

Address at Schenley Park, Pittsburgh, Pennsylvania, July 4, 1902.

Address at Sea Girt, New Jersey, July 24, 1902.

The Right Attitude Toward Labor Problems, Hartford, Connecticut, August 22, 1902.

Addresses at Willimantic, Baltic, and Plainfield, Connecticut, August 23, 1902.

Necessity of Establishing Sovereignty Over Trusts, Providence, Rhode Island, August 23, 1902.

Addresses at Nahant and Lynn, Massachusetts, August 25, 1902.

Relations of Corporations to the Public, Boston, Massachusetts, August 25, 1902.

Addresses at Lowell, and Haverhill, Massachusetts, Dover, New
    Hampshire, Old Orchard, Portland, and Augusta, Maine,
    August 26, 1902.
Addresses at Bangor, and Ellsworth, Maine, August 27, 1902.
Addresses at Nashua, Manchester, Concord, Newbury, and
    Weirs, New Hampshire, August 28, 1902.
Wise and Unwise Methods for Remedying Trust Evils, Fitchburg,
    Massachusetts, September 2, 1902.
Limitations on the Aid Government Can Give the Individual,
    Dalton, Massachusetts, September 3, 1902.
Problems Growing out of Modern Industrial Revolutions,
    Wheeling, West Virginia, September 6, 1902.
The Organization of Labor, Chattanooga, Tennessee, September
    8, 1902.
Addresses at Ashville and Greensboro, North Carolina,
    September 9, 1902.
The Trusts and the Tariff, Cincinnati, Ohio, September 20, 1902.
Address at Detroit, Michigan, September 22, 1902.
Tarriff Reform and Business Stablility, Logansport, Indiana,
    September 23, 1902.
Address to Representatives and Operators of Mines, Washington,
    D.C. , October 3, 1902.
Address in Honor of George Washington's SesquiCentennial
    Masonic Initiation, Philadelphia, Pennsylvania, November
    5, 1902.
Address to New York State Chamber of Commerce, New York
    City, November 11, 1902.
Address at Memphis, Tennessee, November 19, 1902.
President McKinley's Policy, Union League, Philadelphia,
    Pennsylvania, November 22, 1902.
Address at high school building dedication exercise,
    Philadelphia, Pennsylvania, November 22, 1902.
Address to English Industrial Association Representatives,
    Washington, D.C., November 24, 1902.
Address at banquet for Justice Harlan, Washington, D.C.,
    December 9, 1902.
Address at the dedication of the Public Library Building,
    Washington, D.C., January 7, 1903.
Address to National Board of Trade, Washington, D.C., January
    5, 1903.
Address to YMCA, Washington, D. C., January 19, 1903.
Address at banquet in honor of the birthday of President
    William McKinley, Canton, Ohio, January 27, 1903.
Address opening Annual Convention of the Canning and Allied
    Industries, Washington, D.C., February 9, 1903.
Address at the Army War College cornerstone laying,
    Washington, D.C., February 21, 1903.
Address at the Bicentennial Celebration of the birth of John

Wesley, New York City, February 26, 1903.

Address to Society of American Foresters, Washington, D.C. March 26, 1903.

Address at Baltimore, Maryland and Harrisburg, Pennsylvania, March 1, 1903.

The Monroe Doctrine, Chicago, April 2, 1903.

Progress Made Toward Federal Control of Corporations, Milwaukee, Wisconsin, April 3, 1903.

Addresses at Madison and Waukesha, Wisconsin, April 3, 1903.

Prosperity and the Tariff, Minneapolis, Minnesota, April 4, 1903.

Addresses at Yankton, Mitchell, Aberdeen, South Dakota, April 6, 1903.

The Wage Earner and the Tiller of the Soil, Sioux Falls, South Dakota, April 6, 1903.

The Philippine Islands and the Army, Fargo, North Dakota, April 7, 1903.

Trust Legislation, Jamestown, North Dakota, April 7, 1903.

Addresses at a variety of unidentified cities in Nebraska, and Edgemont and Ardmore, South Dakota, April 25, 1903.

Addresses at Hastings, Fairmont, Crete, and Lincoln, Nebraska, April 27, 1903.

The Coal Strike Commission, Omaha, Nebraska, April 27, 1903.

Addresses at Des Moines and Ottumwa, Iowa, April 28, 1903.

Address to the National and International Good Roads Convention, St. Louis, Missouri, April 29, 1903.

Address at St. Louis University, St. Louis, Missouri, April 29, 1903.

Address at the opening of the Louisiana Purchase Exposition, April 30, 1903.

Address at Topeka, Kansas, May 1, 1903.

Addresses at Abilene, Salina, and Ellsworth, Kansas, May 2, 1903.

Address at Denver, Colorado, May 4, 1903.

Addresses at Santa Fe and Albuquerque, New Mexico, May 4, 1903.

Address at the Grand Canyon, Grand Canyon, Arizona, May 6, 1903.

Addresses at Riverside, Barstow, Redlands, and San Bernardino, California, May 7, 1903.

Addresses at Claremont, Los Angeles, and Pasadena, California, May 8, 1903.

Addresses at Oxnard, Paso Robles, Santa Barbara, San Luis Obispo, Surf, and Ventura, California, May 9, 1903.

Addresses at Campbell, Pajuro, San Jose, Santa Cruz, and Watsonville, California, May 11, 1903.

Addresses at Burlington, Palo Alto, and San Francisco (3), California, May 12, 1903.

Addresses at San Francisco, California (4), May 13, 1903.

Addresses at San Francisco (3), Berkley Oakland, and Velljo, California, May 14, 1903.

Address at Raymond, California, May 15, 1903.

Addresses at Berenda and Merced, California, May 18, 1903.

Addresses at Auburn, Colfax, Truskee, and Sacramento (3), California, Reno and Carson City, Nevada, May 19, 1903.

Addresses at Dunsmuir, Hornbrook, Montague, Redding, and Sisson, California, May 20, 1903.

Addresses at Olympia and Tacoma, Washington, May 22, 1903.

Address to the Arctic Brotherhood, Seattle, Washington, May 23, 1903.

Addresses at Clellum, North Yakima, Ellensburg, Pasco, Wallula, and Walla Walla, Washington, May 25, 1903.

Liberty Through Law, Spokane, Washington, May 26, 1903.

Supremacy of the Law, Butte, Montana, May 27, 1903.

Addresses at Shoshone, Glenns Ferry, and Mountain Home, Idaho, May 28, 1903.

Address at Salt Lake City, Utah, May 29, 1903.

Address at the University of Wyoming, Laramie, Wyoming, May 31, 1903.

Address at Denison, Iowa, June 2, 1903.

Addresses at Freeport, Aurora, Joliet, Lexington, and Bloomington, Illinois, June 3, 1903.

Addresses at Springfield, Lincoln, Decatur, and Danville, Illinois, June 4, 1903.

Address at the Consecration of Grace Memorial Reformed Church, Washington, D.C., June 7, 1903.

Address at Baltimore, Maryland, June 15, 1903.

Address at University of Virginia Commencement, Charlottesville, Virginia, June 16, 1903.

Address at Huntington, New York, July 4, 1903.

American Manhood, Holy Name Societies of New York City, Oyster Bay, New York, August 16, 1903.

Class Government, Syracuse, New York, September 7, 1903.

Address at Antietam, Maryland, September 17, 1903.

Address at the unveiling of Sherman Statue, Washington, D.C., October 15, 1903.

Address to the Pan American-Missionary Service, Washington, D.C., October 25, 1903.

Address at New York Avenue Presbyterian Church, Washington, D.C., November 16, 1903.

Address to the German Societies of Washington, D.C., Washington D.C., November 19, 1903.

Address to National Republican Editorial Association, Washington, D.C., February 5, 1904.

Address to National Wholesale Lumber Dealers' Association, Washington, D.C., March 2, 1904.

Address to the Periodical Publishers' Association of America,

Washington, D.C., April 7, 1904.

Address at Groton School, Groton, Massachusetts, May 24, 1904.

Memorial Day Address, Gettysburg, Pennsylvania, May 30, 1904.

Address at Valley Forge, Pennsylvania, June 19, 1904.

Address upon receiving Cardinal Satolli, Washington, D.C., June 21, 1904.

Address at College Point, New York, June 23, 1904.

Address accepting the Republican party nomination for the presidency, Oyster Bay, New York, July 27, 1904.

Address to Porto Rican teachers, Washington, D.C., August 12, 1904.

Address to the Interparlimentary Union, Washington, D.C., September 24, 1904.

Address at the unveiling of Frederick the Great Statue, Washington, D.C., November 19, 1904.

Address at St. Patrick's Roman Catholic Church, Washington, D.C., November 20, 1904.

Addresses at YMCA of Washington, D.C. and The Lafayette Opera House, Washington, D.C., November 22, 1904.

Address at Richmond, Indiana, November 25, 1904.

Address at the Louisiana Purchase Exposition, St. Louis, Missouri, November 26, 1904.

Address at Grace Reformed Church, Washington, D.C., December 15, 1904.

Address to the Forest Council, Washington, D.C., January 5, 1905.

Address at Interchurch Conference, Washington, D.C. January 26, 1905.

Address at the United States Naval Academy, Annapolis, Maryland, January 30, 1905.

Address to the Union League Club, Philadelphia, Pennsylvania, January 30, 1905.

Addresses to the Press Club and the Republican Club, New York City, February 13, 1905.

Address to Hungarian Republican Club, New York City, February 14, 1905.

Address at delivery of the portrait of the Empress Dowager of China, Washington, D.C., February 18, 1905.

Address at the University of Pennsylvania, Philadelphia, Pennsylvania, February 22, 1905.

Inaugural Address, Washington, D.C., March 4, 1905.

Address to the American Tract Society, Washington, D.C., March 12, 1905.

Address to National Congress of Mothers, Washington, D.C., March 13, 1905.

Address to the Friendly Sons of St. Patrick, New York City, March 17, 1905.

Address at Louisville, Kentucky, April 4, 1905.
The Square Deal, Dallas, Texas, April 5, 1905.
Railroad Legislation, Austin, Texas, April 6, 1905.
Address at San Antonio, Texas, April 7, 1905.
Addresses at Fort Worth, Texas, Wichita, Kansas, April 8, 1905.
Address at Glenwood Spring, Colorado, May 6, 1905.
Addresses at Denver Colorado, Omaha, Nebraska, and Council
    Bluffs, Iowa, May 9, 1905.
Addresses at Chicago (2), May 10, 1905.
Addresses at Alliance, Canton, Ohio, and Pittsburgh,
    Pennsylvania, May 11, 1905.
Address to Naval Branch YMCA, Brooklyn, New York, May 30,
    1905.
Address at Worcester, Massachusetts, June 21, 1905.
Commencement Address at Williams College, Williamstown,
    Massachussetts, June 22, 1905.
The Harvard Spirit, Cambridge, Massachusetts, June 28, 1905.
Address to the National Education Association, Asbury Park,
    New Jersey, July 7, 1905.
Address to United Mine Workers Convention, Wilkesbarre,
    Pennsylvania, August 10, 1905.
Address at Chautauqua, New York, August 11, 1905.
Address at Richmond, Virginia, October 18, 1905.
Addresses at Charlotte, Durham, and Raleigh, North Carolina,
    October 19, 1905.
Address at Atlanta, Georgia, October 20, 1905.
Address at Florida Baptist College, Jacksonville, Florida,
    October 21, 1905.
Address at Tuskegee Institute, Tuskegee, Alabama, October 24,
    1905.
Address at Little Rock, Arkansas, October 25, 1905.
Address at New Orleans, Louisiana, October 26, 1905.
Address to Railway employees, Washington, D.C., November 14,
    1905.
Address to the National Boot and Shoe Manufacturing
Association,
    Washington, D.C., November 15, 1905.
Address to Central Juvenile Reformatory Committee,
    Washington, D.C., December 15, 1905.
Address to District of Columbia Board of Education,
    Washington, D.C., December 18, 1905.
Addresss on presenting Medal of Honor to Captain James R.
    Church, Washington, D.C., January 10, 1906.
Address to Improved Order of Rodmen, Washington D.C.,
    January 11, 1906.
Address to National Rivers and Harbors Congress, Washington,
    D.C., January 16, 1906.

Address to National Board of Trade, Washington, D.C., January 17, 1906

Address to Virginia Theological Seminary students and faculty, Washington, D.C., January 17, 1906.

Address to the Interstate National Guard Association, Washington, D.C., January 22, 1906.

Address to students of Manassa, Virginia, Industrial School, Washington, D.C., February 14, 1906.

Address to the National Lumberman's Association, Washington, D.C., March 8, 1906.

Address to the Consular Reform Committee, Washington D.C., March 14, 1906.

Address to the Committee and Assistant Committees on Department Methods, Washington, D.C. , March 20, 1906.

Address to Executive Council, American Federation of Labor, Washington, D.C., March 21, 1906.

Address to German Veterans, Washington, D.C., April 12, 1906.

Address to National Playgrounds Council, Washington, D.C., April 12, 1906.

The Man with the Muck-rake, Washington, D.C., April 14, 1906.

Address at the reinterment of the remains of John Paul Jones, Annapolis, Maryland, April 24, 1906.

Address to Civil Service Conference, Washington, D.C., May 15, 1906.

Addresses at Portsmouth, Virginia, and at the Hampton Normal and Agricultural Institute, Hampton, Virginia, May 30, 1906.

Address at Dinner for Associate Justice Brown, Washington, D.C., May 31, 1906.

Commencement Address, Howard University, Washington, D.C., June 1, 1906.

Commencement Address, National Cathedral School, Washington, D.C., June 3, 1906.

Commencement Address, Georgetown University, Washington, D.C., June 14, 1906.

Address at District of Columbia National Guard Review, Washington, D.C., June 28, 1906.

Address at Oyster Bay, New York, July 4, 1906.

Address at the Bicentenary Celebration of Christ Church Parish, Oyster Bay, New York, September 8, 1906.

Addresses at York and Harrisburg, Pennsylvania, October 4, 1906.

Address at Colon, Panama, November 17, 1906.

Address on board U.S.S. Louisiana, November 24, 1906.

Address to Waterways Convention, Washington, D.C., December 7, 1906.

Address to the Archaeological Institute of America and Philological Society, Washington, D.C., January 4, 1907.

Address at One-Hundredth Anniversary of the Birth of Lincoln Celebration, Hodgenville, Kentucky, February 12, 1907.

Address to the Naval League of the United States, Washington, D.C., February 22, 1907.

Address at the Harvard Union, February 23, 1907.

Address to teachers visiting from Toronto, Canada, Washington, D.C., March 30, 1907.

Address at unveiling of monument to the dead of the Rough Riders Arlington, Virginia, April 12, 1907.

Address at the opening of the Jamestown Exposition, Norfolk, Virginia, April 26, 1907.

Address at the unveiling of the statute of General George B. McClellan, Washington, D.C., May 2, 1907.

Address to Friends Select School, Washington, D.C., May 25, 1907

Address at the unveiling of monument to General Lawton, Indianapolis, Indiana, May 30, 1907.

Address at the Semicentennial of the Founding of Agricultural Colleges in the United States, Lansing, Michigan, May 31, 1907.

Address to National Editorial Assocation, Jamestown, Virginia, June 10, 1907.

Address at the cornerstone laying, Pilgrim Memorial Monument, Provincetown, Massachusetts, August 20, 1907.

Address at the cornerstone laying, Cathedral of Saints Peter and Paul, Washington, D.C., September 29, 1907.

Address at the unveiling of monument to President McKinley, Canton, Ohio, September 30, 1907.

Addresses at Meridosia, Illinois, and Keokuk, Iowa, October 1, 1907.

Address at St. Louis, Missouri, October 2, 1907.

Address at Cairo, Illinois, October 3, 1907.

Address to the Deep Waterway Convention, Memphis, Tennessee, October 4, 1907.

Address at Vicksburg, Mississippi, October 21, 1907.

Addresses at Nashville and Chattanooga, Tennessee, October 22, 1907.

Address at the installation of Wilbur Patterson Thirkield as president of Howard University, Washington, D.C., November 15, 1907.

Address on the departure of the fleet, Hampton Roads, Virginia, December 16, 1907.

Address to Committee of the Arlington Confederate Monument Association, Washington, D.C., February 6, 1908.

Address to the Religious Education Association, Washington, D.C., February 12, 1908.

Address to the National Education Association, Washington, D.C., February 26, 1908.

Address to the National Congress of Mothers, Washington, D.C., March 10, 1908.

Address to the Tulsa, Oklahoma, Commercial Club, Washington, D.C., April 17, 1908.

Address to the Twenty-fifth Anniversary of the National Florence Crittenden Mission, Washington, D.C., April 27, 1908.

Address to the National League of Woman Workers, Washington, D.C., May 1, 1908.

Address to the Welfare Department of the Civic League, Washington, D.C., May 11, 1908.

Address at Cornerstone Laying, Bureau of American Republics Building, Washington, D.C., May 11, 1908.

Address at the Opening of Conference on the Conservation of National Resources, Washington, D.C., May 13, 1908.

Address at Governors Conference, Washington, D.C., May 15, 1908.

Address to Members of the Methodist Episcopal General Conference, Washington, D.C., May 16, 1908.

Address at the Unveiling of Monument to Captain John Underhill, Matinecock, New York, July 11, 1908.

Address at the Naval War College, Newport, Rhode Island, July 22, 1908.

Address to American Olympic Team, Oyster Bay, New York, August 31, 1908.

Address to German Singing Society, Oyster Bay, New York, September 17, 1908.

Address to International Congress On Tuberculosis, Washington, D.C., October 3, 1908.

Address to delegations from three Railroad Workers Associations, Washington, D.C., October 14, 1908.

Address to the Vermont Regiment Association, Washington, D.C., October 19, 1908.

Address at Episcopal High School, Alexandria, Virginia, November 14, 1908.

Address to gathering of prominent Washington women, Washington, D.C., November 17, 1908.

Address at the unveiling of General Sheridan Monument, Washington, D.C., November 25, 1908.

Address at the cornerstone laying, Colored Young Men's Christian Association Building, Washington, D.C., November 26, 1908.

Address to Conservationists, Washington, D.C., December 8, 1908.

Address at the Saint Gaudens Exhibition, Cocoran Art Gallery, Washington, D.C., December 15, 1908.

Address to American Irish Historical Society, Washington, D.C.,

January 16, 1909.

Address at opening of Conference on Dependent Children, Washington, D.C., January 25, 1909

Address at Banquet of Conference on Dependent Children, Washington D.C., January 26, 1909.

Attitude of the Progressive Party Toward the Colored Race, Chicago, February 9, 1909.

Address at the cornerstone laying, Lincoln Birthplace Memorial, Hodgensville, Kentucky, February 12, 1909.

Address to the Conference on the Natural Resources of North America, Washington, D.C., February 18, 1909.

Address to "Tennis Cabinet," Washington, D.C., March 1, 1909.

Education in Africa, Nairobi, Kenya, August 3, 1909.

Address at Gordon Memorial College, Khartoum, Sudan, March 15, 1910.

Peace and Justice in the Sudan, Khartoum, Sudan, March 16, 1910.

Address at Egyptian Officer's Club, Khartoum, Sudan, March 17, 1910.

Addresses at American Girl's College, and National University, Cairo, Egypt, March 28, 1910.

Citizenship in a Republic, Sorbonne, Paris, France, April 23, 1910.

International Peace, Nobel Prize Speech, Christiana, Norway, May 5, 1910.

Colonial Policy of the United States, Christiana, Norway, May 5, 1910.

World Movement, Berlin, Germany, May 12, 1910.

Conditions of Success, Cambridge, England, May 26, 1910.

British Rule in Africa, London, England, May 31, 1910.

Biological Analogies in History, Oxford, England, June 7, 1910.

Address to Camp Fire Club, Oyster Bay, New York, June 22, 1910.

Address to Harvard Law School Alumni, Cambridge, Massachusetts, June 28, 1910.

Address to Negro Business Men's League, New York City, August 19, 1910.

Addresses at Albany and Utica, New York, August 23, 1910.

Addresses at Dunkirk, Buffalo, New York, Astabula, and Toledo, Ohio, and Chicago, Illinois, August 25, 1910.

Address in Council Bluffs and Carroll, Iowa, and Fremont, Nebraska, August 26, 1910.

Address at Cheyenne, Wyoming, August 27, 1910.

Addresses to the Colorado Legislature and the Colorado Livestock Association, Denver, Colorado, August 29, 1910.

Addresses at Colorado Springs and Pueblo, Colorado, August 30, 1910.

The New Nationalism, Osawatamie, Kansas, August 31, 1910.

Addresses at Kansas City, Kansas, and Kansas City, Missouri, September 1, 1910.
Address at Omaha, Nebraska, September 2, 1910.
Address at Sioux City, Iowa, and Sioux Falls, South Dakota, September 3, 1910.
Address at Willmar, Minnesota, September 4, 1910.
Address at cornerstone laying, Carnegie Library Building, Fargo, North Dakota, September 5, 1910.
Address at St. Paul, Minnesota, September 6, 1910.
Address at Milwaukee, Wisconsin, September 7, 1910.
Addresses at Freeport and Chicago, Illinois, September 8, 1910.
Address to Ohio Valley Exposition, Cincinnati, Ohio, September 9, 1910.
Addresses at Pittsburgh, Pennsylvania, September 10, 1910.
Address at Suffolk County Fair, Riverhead, New York, September 15, 1910
Address at New York State Fair, Syracuse, New York, September 17, 1910.
Address to New York State Republican Convention, Saratoga, New York, September 27, 1910.
Address at Dutchess County Fair, Poughkeepsie, New York, September 29, 1910.
Address to the New York Volunteer Fireman's Association, Oyster Bay, New York, October 4, 1910.
Address at Brooklyn, New York, October 5, 1910.
Addresses in Bristol, Jefferson City, Johnson City, and Knoxville, Tennessee, October 7, 1910.
Addresses at Berry School, Rome, and Atlanta, Georgia, October 8, 1910.
Addresses at unidentified cities in Tennessee, Alabama, Mississippi, October 9, 1910.
Address at Hot Springs, Arkansas, October 10, 1910.
Addresses at Clayton, St. Louis, Missouri, October 11, 1910.
Address to the Knights of Columbus, Peoria, Ilinois, October 12, 1910.
Addresses at Covington, Anderson, Muncie, Richmond, and Indianapolis, Indiana, October 13, 1910.
Addresses at Corning, Dunkirk, Elmira (2), Fredonia, Hornell, Jamestown, Sinclairville, and Wellerville, New York, October 14, 1910.
Addresses at Schenectady (2), Troy, Albany, and Hudson, New York, October 17, 1910.
Addresses at Brooklyn, New York City (2), New York, October 20, 1910.
Address at Boston Massachusetts, October 21, 1910.
Addresses in Concord, Manchester, and Nashua, New Hampshire, October 22, 1910.

Addresses at Binghampton, Ithaca, Newfield, Oswego, and Spensor, New York, October 24, 1910.

Addresses at Penn Yan, Canadaigua, Geneva, Waterloo, Seneca Falls, Auburn, and Syracuse, New York, October 25, 1910.

Addresses at Phoenix, Fulton, Oswego, Watertown, and Ogdensburg,New York, October 26, 1910.

Addresses at Fonda, Johnstown, Amsterdam, Gloversville, Little Falls, and Utica, New York, October 27, 1910.

Addresses at Brownsville, Rome, Lyons, and Rochester, New York, October 28, 1910.

Addresses at Brooklyn (2), Kingston, and Mineola, New York, October 29, 1910.

Addresses at New York City (3), October 31, 1910.

Addresses at Albion, Lockport, Buffalo (2), New York, November 1, 1910.

Addresses at Baltimore (2), Maryland, November 2, 1910.

Addresses at Des Moines, Davenport, and West Liberty City, Iowa, November 4, 1910.

Addresses at Cleveland and Toledo, Ohio, November 5, 1910.

Addresses in New York City (7), November 7, 1910.

Wild Man and Wild Beast in Africa, National Geographic Society, Washington, D.C., November 18, 1910.

Address to New Haven Chamber of Commerce, New Haven, Connecticut, December 13, 1910.

Applied Ethics, Cambridge, Massachusetts, December 15, 1910.

Address to National Civic Federation, New York City, January 13, 1911.

Address to the Council of the Union of American Hebrew Congregations, New York City, January 18, 1911.

Address at Grand Rapids, Michigan, February 11, 1911.

Address to the Republican Club of the City of New York, New York City, February 12, 1911.

Address to Harvard Club of Chicago, February 21, 1911.

Addresses in Commeration of George Washington, Chicago (4) February 22, 1911.

Address to Southern Commercial Congress, Atlanta, Georgia, March 9, 1911.

Addresses at Birmingham (3), Alabama, March 10, 1911.

Addresses at Jackson and McComb, Mississippi, and New Orleans, Louisiana, March 11, 1911.

Addresses at Houston and Beaumont, Texas, March 12, 1911.

Addresses at San Antonio, Austin, Fort Worth, Dallas and Waco, Texas, March 13, 1911.

Addresses at El Paso (2), Texas, and Albuquerque, New Mexico, March 15, 1911.

Addresses at Williams and Flagstaff, Arizona, March 16, 1911.

Address at Dedication of Roosevelt Dam, Roosevelt, Arizona,

March 18, 1911.

Address at Phoenix, Arizona, March 18, 1911.

Address at Throop Polytechnic Institute, Pasadena, California, March 21, 1911.

Address at Occidental College, Los Angeles, California, March 22, 1911.

Address at Charter Day Exercise, University of California, Berkeley, California, March 23, 1911.

Realizable Ideas, Berkeley, California, March 24, 1911.

The Home and the Child, Berkeley, California, March 25, 1911.

The Bible and the Life of the People, Berkeley, California, March 26, 1911.

The Public Servant and the Eighth Commandment, Berkeley, California, March 27, 1911.

The Shaping of Public Opinion and the Ninth Commandment, Berkeley, California, March 28, 1911.

Address at San Francisco, California, March 29, 1911.

Address at Reno, Nevada, April 3, 1911.

Address to state legislature, Sacramento, California, April 4, 1911.

Addresses at Roseberg, Euguene, and Portland, Oregon, April 5, 1911.

Addresses at Seattle, and Tacoma, Washington, April 6, 1911.

Address at Spokane, Washington, April 8, 1911.

Addresses at Moscow and Sandpoint, Idaho, April 9, 1911.

Address at Missoula, Montana, April 11, 1911.

Addresses at Madison (2), Wisconsin, April 15, 1911.

Address at New York City, May 12, 1911.

Address to Berry School Association, New York City, April 25, 1911.

Address at DeWitte Clinton High School, New York City, May 12, 1911.

Address to Federation of Churches, New York City, May 16, 1911.

Address at Naturalization Ceremony, New York City, May 19, 1911.

Addresses at Newark, New Jersey and New York City, May 30, 1911.

Address at Cardinal Gibbons Jubilee, Baltimore, Maryland, June 6, 1911.

Address (testimony) to U.S. Congressional Committee investigating the U.S. Steel Corporation, New York City, August 5, 1911.

Conservation of Womanhood and Childhood, New York City, October 12, 1911.

Address at Groton School, Groton, Massachusetts, November 29, 1911.

Address at St. Marks School, Southboro, Massachusetts,
    November 30, 1911.
Applied Christianity, New York City, December 17, 1911.
A Charter of Democracy, Columbus, Ohio, February 21, 1912.
Address to the Massachusetts General Assembly, Boston,
    February 26, 1912.
The Right of the People to Rule, New York City, March 20, 1912.
Address at Portland, Maine, March 23, 1912.
Addresses at New York City (3), March 25, 1912.
A Charter on Business Prosperity, Chicago, March 27, 1912.
Address at St. Louis, Missouri, March 28, 1912.
Addresses at Cedar Rapids, Vinton, Waterloo, and Cedar Falls,
    Iowa, and Faribault, Owatonna, Northfield, Albert Lea,
    and St. Paul, Minnesota, March 29, 1912.
Addresses at Kalamazoo, Dowagiac, Ann Arbor, Battle Creek,
    and Detroit, Michigan, March 30, 1912.
What a Progressive Is, Louisville, Kentucky, April 3, 1912.
Addresses at Point Pleasant, Huntington, and Parkersburg, West
    Virginia, and Covington, Augusta, and Maysville,
    Kentucky, April 4, 1912.
Address at Martinsburg, West Virginia, April 5, 1912.
Addresses at Rockford, Freeport, Polo, Dixon, Amboy, Mendota,
    Minonk, Pontiac, Bloomington, and Springfield, Illinois,
    April 6, 1912.
Addresses at Danville, Decatur, Clinton, Sullivan, Mattoon,
    Tuscola, and Urbana, Illinois, and Peru and Fort Wayne,
    Indiana, April 8, 1912.
Addresses in Pittsburgh, Pennsylvania, April 9, 1912.
Addresses at Jeannette, Greensburg, Latrobe, Blairsville,
    Johnstown, Cresson, Altoona, Huntingdon, Harrisburg,
    Lancaster, and Coatesville, Pennsylvania, April 10, 1912.
Recall of Judges and Referendum of Decision, Philadelphia,
    Pennsylvania, April 10, 1912.
Addresses in Reading, Allentown, and Easton, Pennsylvania,
    April 11, 1912.
Address at Springfield, Massachusetts, April 12, 1912.
Addresses at Worchester, Clinton, Ayer, Massachusetts, Nashua,
    Concord, and Manchester, New Hampshire, April 13,
    1912.
Addresses at Aurora, Mendota, Princeton, and Galesburg,
    Illinois, and Burlington, Mount Pleasant, Fairfield,
    Ottumwa, Albia, Chariton, Osceola, Iowa, April 16, 1912.
Addresses at Hastings and Omaha, Nebraska, April 17, 1912.
Addresses at Lincoln, Wilber, Auburn Falls, Pawnee City,
    Tecumseh, Beatrice, Wynmore, Crete, Nebraska, April 18,
    1912.
Addresses at unidentified cities in Nebraska and Kansas, April
    19, 1912.

Address at Fort Smith, Ozark, and Little Rock, Arkansaw, April 20, 1912.

Addresses in Greensboro and Salisbury, North Carolina, April 22, 1912.

Address at Worchester, Massachusetts, April 26, 1912.

Addresses at Worchester, Brockton, Tauton, Bridgewater, Middleboro, New Bedford, Fall River and Boston, Massachusetts, April 27, 1912.

Addresses at Lowell, Lawrence, North Adams, Pittsfield, Massachusetts, April 29, 1912.

Addresses at Havre de Grace, Baltimore, and Salisbury, Maryland, April 3, 1912.

Addresses at Westminister, Frederick, Baltimore, Hagerstown, and Cumberland Falls, Maryland, May 4, 1912.

Addresses at Alliance, Canton, East Liverpool, Niles, Warren, Bellaire, Youngstown, and Steubenville, Ohio, May 14, 1912.

Addresses at Kenton, Elyria, Bellevue, Norwalk, Sandusky, Freemont, Findlay, Fostoria, Oberlin, Springfield, Bellefontaine, Urbana, Kenton, Norwalk, Xenia, and Dayton, Ohio, May 15, 1912.

Addresses at Defiance, Lima, Paulding, Sidney, Wapakoneta, Greenville, Picqua, and Toledo, Ohio, May 16, 1912.

Addresses at Chillicothe, Ironton, Portsmouth, Jackson, Athens, Nelsonville, Logan, Lancaster, and Columbus, Ohio, May 17, 1912.

Addresses at Delaware, Elyria, Galion, Marion, Mansfield, Akron, and Cleveland, Ohio, May 18, 1912.

Addresses at Caldwell, Marietta, Cambridge, Zanesville, Newark, Coshhocton, Newcomerstown, and New Philadelphia, Ohio, May 20, 1912.

Addresses at Paterson, Passaic, Lodi, Hackensack, Hasborouck Heights, Rutherford, Belleville, Bloomfield, Montclair, West Orange, Newark, and Jersey City, New Jersey, May 23, 1912.

Addresses at Burlington, Egg Harbor, Atlantic City, Camden, Trenton, New Jersey, April 24, 1912.

Addresses at Trenton, Freehold, Lakewood, New Brunswick, Long Branch, Red Bank, Perth Amboy, Rahway, Bound Brook, Plainfield, and Elizabeth, New Jersey, April 25, 1912.

Addresses at Hoboken, West Hoboken, Somerville, Princeton, Bayonne, Morristown, Dover, Newton, Hackettstown, Washington, Phillipsburg, and Lambertville, New Jersy, April 26, 1912.

Address at Gettysburg, Pennsylvania, May 30, 1912.

Address at Congress Hotel, Chicago, June 15, 1912.

We Stand at Armageddon, Chicago, June 17, 1912.

A Confession of Faith, Chicago, August 6, 1912.

Address at Providence, Rhode Island, August 16, 1912.

Addresses at Point of Pines, Boston, Massachusetts, August 17, 1912.

Address at Wilkes-Barre, Pennsylvania, August 22, 1912.

Addresses at Bennington, Manchester, Rutland, Middlebury, Brandon, and Burlington, Vermont, August 29, 1912.

Addresses at St Johnsbury, St. Albans, Morrisville, Barton and Hardwick, Vermont, August 30, 1912.

Addresses at Barre, Randolph, Bellows Falls, Windsor, Brattleboro, Vermont, August 31, 1912.

Addresses in Samford, Hartford, New Haven, and Bridgeport, Connecticut, September 2, 1912.

Addresses at Mattoon, Illinois, Indianpolis, Indiana, and St. Louis, Missouri, September 3, 1912.

Address in Keokuk and Des Moines, Iowa, September 4, 1912.

Addresses at St. Paul, Minneapolis, Minnesota, September 5, 1912.

Addresses at Grand Forks, Fargo, and Jamestown, North Dakota, September 6, 1912.

Addresses at Miles City, Billings, Livingston, Bozeman, and Helena, Montana, September 7, 1912.

Address at Spokane, Washington, September 9, 1912.

Addresses at Seattle and Tacoma, Washington, September 10, 1912.

Addresses at Portland, Oregon, September 11, 1912.

Addresses at unidentified cities in Oregon and Idaho, including Boise, Idaho, September 12, 1912.

Addresses at Blackfoot and Pocatello, Idaho, and Ogden, Utah, September 13, 1912.

Addresses at Reno, Nevada and Oakland, Sacramento, and San Francisco, California, September 14, 1912.

Address at Los Angeles, Santa Barbara, California, September 16, 1912.

Address at Phoenix, Arizona, September 17, 1912.

Addresses at Laguna and Albuquerque, New Mexico, September 18, 1912.

Addresses at Trinidad, Pueblo, Colorado Springs, La Junta, Rock Ford, and Denver, Colorado, September 19, 1912.

Addresses at Hastings, Lincoln, Minden, and Omaha, Nebraska, September 20, 1912.

Addresses at Ottawa and Topeka, Kansas, September 21, 1912.

Addresses at Kansas City, Pittsburg, and Liberal, Kansas and Lamar, Springfield, Aurora, Monett, Joplin, Missouri, September 23, 1912.

Addresses at Tulsa, Chandler, Oklahoma City, and McAlester, Oklahoma, September 24, 1912.

Address to the Lakes-to-Gulf Deeper Waterways Association, Little Rock, Arkansas, September 25, 1912.

Addresses in Memphis and Jackson, Tennessee, September 26, 1912.

Address at New Orleans, Louisiana, September 27, 1912.

Addresses at Montgomery, Opelika, Alabama, Macon, Columbus, and Atlanta, Georgia, September 28, 1912.

Addresses at Chattanooga, Cleveland, Lenoir City, and Knoxville, Tennessee, September 30, 1912.

Addresses at Hickory, Asheville, Salisbury, Greensboro, Burlington, Durham, and Raleigh, North Carolina, October 1. 1912.

Addresses at Detroit, Flint, Saginaw, and Bay City, Michigan, October 8, 1912.

Addresses at Marquette, Cheboygan, Houghton, and Calumet, Michigan, October 9, 1912.

Addresses in Minnesota, including Duluth, October 10, 1912.

Addresses in Wisconsin, including Oshkosh, October 11, 1912.

Address at Chicago, October 12, 1912.

Progressive Cause Greater Than Any Individual, Milwaukee, Wisconsin, October 14, 1912.

Address at New York City, October 30, 1912.

Address at New York City, November 1, 1912.

Addresses in Oyster Bay and Mineola, New York, November 4, 1912.

Address at New York City, November 19, 1912.

Address to the Progressive Members of the Illinois State Legislature, Chicago, December 9, 1912.

Addresss to the National Committee of the Progressive Party, Chicago, December 10, 1912.

History as Literature, Presidential Address, American Historical Association, Boston, Massachusetts, December 27, 1912.

Address to the Military Historical Society, Boston, Massachusetts, December 28, 1912.

Address at Lincoln Day Dinner, Progressive party, New York City, February 12, 1913.

Address to Rough Rider dinner, New York City, February 14, 1913.

Progressive Service, Philadelphia, Pennsylvania, March 13, 1913.

Address to the Electoral College Association of Pennsylvania, Philadelphia, Pennsylvania, March 14, 1913.

Address to New York Progressives, Albany, New York, March 28, 1913.

Address to Michigan Progressives, Detroit, Michigan, March 29, 1913.

Woman Suffrage Demanded in the Interests of Good Government, New York City, May 2, 1913.

Address to the Men's League for Woman Suffrage, Plainfield, New Jersey, May 16, 1913.

Commencement Address, Hill School, Pottstown, Pennsylvania, June 9, 1913.

Address to Buffalo Progressive Club, Buffalo, New York, June 10, 1913.

Address at Rochester, New York, June 11, 1913.

Address at Pittsburgh, Pennsylvania, June 12, 1913.

Address to Alumni Luncheon, Phillips Academy, Andover, Massachusetts, June 13, 1913.

Address at Boston, Massachussets, June 16, 1913.

The American Navy, Newport, Rhode Island, July 2, 1913.

Address to the National Conference of the Progressive Service, Portsmouth, Rhode Island, July 2, 1913.

Address to the Progressive Club, Chicago, August 25, 1913.

Address at Rochester, New York, September 27, 1913.

Address at Farewell Dinner, October 2, 1913.

Address to the YMCA, Rio de Janeiro, Brazil, October 22, 1913.

American Internationalism, Rio de Janeiro, Brazil, October 24, 1913.

Character and Civilization, Sao Paulo, Brazil, October 27, 1913.

Democratic Ideals, Buenos Aires, Argentina, November 7, 1913.

Truths and Half Truths, Buenos Aires, Argentina, November 10, 1913.

American Ideals, Buenos Aires, Argentina, November 12, 1913.

The Democratic Movement In A Republic, Santiago, Chile, November 22, 1913.

Address to the National Geographic Society, Washington, D.C., May 26, 1914

Address to the Royal Geographic Society, London, England, June 16, 1914.

Address to the Progressive League of Pittsburgh, Pittsburgh, Pennsylvania, June 30, 1914.

Address at Hartford, Connecticut, August 15, 1914.

Address at Boston, Massachussets, August 17, 1914.

Addresses at Lewiston and Portland, Maine, August 18, 1914

Address at New Orleans, Louisiana, September 7, 1914.

Addresses at Franklin, Jeanerette, and New Iberia, Louisiana, September 8, 1914.

Addresses at Wichita and Hutchinson, Kansas, September 19, 1914.

Addresses at Kansas City, Kansas and Kansas City, Missouri, September 21, 1914.

Address at Lincoln, Nebraska, September 22, 1914.

Addresses at Des Moines and Boone, Iowa, September 23, 1914.

Addresses at Rock Island, Galesburg, and Peoria, Illinois, September 24, 1914.

Addresses at Marion and East St. Louis, Illinois, September 25, 1914.

Addresses at Indianapolis and Terre Haute, Indiana, September 26, 1914.

Addresses at Cleveland and Columbus, Ohio, September 28, 1914.

Address at Toledo, Ohio, September 29, 1914.

Address at Bay City, Michigan, September 30, 1914.

Address at Philadelphia, Pennsylvania, October 1, 1914.

Addresses at Yonkers, Cold Spring, Beacon, Wappingers Falls, and Poughkeepsie, New York, October 5, 1914.

Addresses at Kingston, Saugerties, Catskill, Athens, Hudson, and Troy, New York, October 6, 1914.

Addresses at Schenectady, Ballston Spa, Saratoga, Hudson Falls, and Glens Falls, New York, October 7, 1914.

Addresses at Ticonderoga, Port Henry, Keeseville, and Plattsburgh, New York, October 8, 1914.

Addresses at Malone, Potsdam, Canton, and Ogdensburg, New York, October 9, 1914.

Addresses at Gouverneur, Watertown, and Utica, New York, October 10, 1914.

Addresses at Herkimer and Gloversville, New York, October 12, 1914.

Addresses at Cobleskill, Cooperstown, and Oneonta, New York, October, 13, 1914.

Address at Syracuse, New York, October 14, 1914.

Address at Auburn, New York, October 15, 1914.

Address at Rochester, New York, October 16, 1914.

Addresses in Gary, Indiana and Chicago, Illinois, October 19, 1914

Addresses at Westfield and Chautaugua, New York, October 20, 1914.

Addresses at Ithaca and Binghamton, New York, October 22, 1914.

Addresses at Liberty, Monticello, and Middletown, New York, October 23, 1914.

Addresses at Goshen and Newburgh, New York, October 24, 1914.

Addresses at Williamsport and Pottsville, Pennsylvania, October, 26, 1914.

Addresses at Johnstown and Altonna, Pennsylvania, October 27, 1914.

Addresses at Reading, Wilkes-Barre, Hazleton, and Lancaster, Pennsylvania, October 28, 1914.

Addresses at New York City, October 29, 1914.

Addresses at Elizabeth, Princeton, and Trenton, New Jersey, October 30, 1914.

Addresses at New York City, October 31, 1914.

Address to the American Museum of Natural History, New York City, December 10, 1914.
Address to the Brooklyn Institute of Arts and Sciences, Brooklyn, New York, December 17, 1914.
Address to Episcopal Church, Oyster Bay, New York, December 24, 1914.
Address to Interchurch Committee on Unemployment, New York City, January 26, 1915.
Address at Philadelphia, Pennsylvania, April 7, 1915.
Address in Atlanta, Georgia, June 13, 1915.
Address to Panama Pacific International Exposition, San Francisco, California, July 21, 1915.
Address to the American Historical Congress, San Francisco, California, July 23, 1915.
Address at War Department Student Instruction Camp, San Francisco, July 24, 1915.
Address at Panama California Exposition, San Diego, California, July 27, 1915.
This Nation's Needs, Plattsburgh, New York, August 25, 1915.
Americanism, New York City, October 12, 1915.
Address at Tuskegee Institute, Tuskegee, Alabama, December 12, 1915.
Address at Philadelphia, Pennsylvania, January 10, 1916.
Address to Brooklyn Academy of Arts and Sciences, Brooklyn, New York, January 30, 1916.
Address at Dedication of new wing, New York Orthopaedic Dispensary and Hospital, January 31, 1916.
Address to National Americanization Committee, New York City, February 1, 1916.
Address at Jewish Bazaar, New York City, March 30, 1916.
Address to Methodist Social Union, New York City, March 27, 1916.
National Duty and International Ideals, Chicago, April 29, 1916.
Address at Cove School, Oyster Bay, New York, May 5, 1916.
Address to Oyster Bay Boy Scouts, Oyster Bay, New York, May 13, 1916.
Righteous Peace and National Unity, Detroit, Michigan, May 19, 1916.
Address to Delegation from Roosevelt Non-Partisian League, May 27, 1916.
National Preparedness, Kansas City, Nebraska, May 30, 1916.
The Weasel Words of Mr. Wilson, St. Louis, Missouri, May 31, 1916.
America for Americans, St. Louis, Missouri, May 31, 1916.
Address at Newark, New Jersey, June 1, 1916.
Address at Oyster Bay, New York, July 4, 1916.
Address at Fort Terry, New York, July 25, 1916.
Duty First, Lewiston, Maine, August 31, 1916.

Address at Battle Creek, Michigan, September 30, 1916.
Address at New York City, October 3, 1916.
Address at Wilkes-Barre, Pennsylvania, October 14, 1916.
Addresses in Louisville, Paris, Cynthiana, Wincester, and Richmond, Kentucky, October 18, 1916.
Address at Phoenix, Arizona, October 21, 1916.
Address at Albuquerque, New Mexico and Las Vegas, Nevada, October 23, 1916.
Address at Denver, Colorado, October 23, 1916.
Address at Chicago, October 26, 1916.
Address at South Bend, Indiana, October 27, 1916.
Address at Brooklyn Academy of Music, New York City, October 28, 1916.
Addresses at Toledo and Cleveland, Ohio, November 1, 1916.
Addresses at New York City (2), November 3, 1916.
Address at Bridgeport, Connecticut, November 4, 1916.
Address at Oyster Bay, November 6, 1916.
Address to the Joint Meeting of American Academy of Arts and Letters and the National Institute of Arts and Letters, New York City, November 16, 1916.
Belgian Relief, Oyster Bay, New York, March 4, 1917.
Address to the Union League Club, New York City, March 20, 1917.
Address at Jacksonville, Florida, March 24, 1917.
Addresses at Lakeland and Punta Gorda, Florida, April 1, 1917
Address to Long Island Farmers Club, Oyster Bay, New York, April 21, 1917.
Address to the National Security League, Chicago, April 28, 1917.
Address to the Brooklyn Republican Club, Brooklyn, New York, May 8, 1917.
Address to Yale Club, New York City, May 28, 1917.
Address at Mineola, New York, May 30, 1917.
Address to the American Medical Association, New York City, June 7, 1917.
Address at the Memorial Service of Railroad Brotherhood and Order of Railroad Telegraphers, Philadelphia, Pennsylvania, June 10, 1917.
Nine-Tenths of Wisdom is Being Wise in Time, Lincoln, Nebraska, June 14, 1917.
Trinity College Commencement Address, Hartford, Connecticut, June 16, 1917.
Address to Red Cross, Oyster Bay, New York, June 24, 1917.
Address at Forest Hills, New York, July 4, 1917.
Address to American Friends of Russian Freedom, New York City, July 6, 1917.
Wake Up America, Pittsburgh, Pennsylvania, July 27, 1917.
Address to the Columbia County Fair, Chatham, New York,

September 5, 1917.
Address at Oyster Bay, New York City, August 15, 1917.
Address at Columbia County Fair, Chatham, New York, September 5, 1917.
Address to Woman's Suffrage Meeting, Oyster Bay, New York, September 8, 1917.
Why We are at War, Kansas City, Missouri, September 24, 1917.
Address at Chicago and Rockford, Illinois, September 26, 1917.
Addresses at Fort Sheridan, Illinois and Great Lakes Naval Training Station, Illinois, September 27, 1917.
The Hun Within our Gates, Racine, Wisconsin, September 27, 1917.
True Democracy and the Conscientious Objector, Minneapolis, Minnoseta, September 28, 1917.
How to Save Others by Saving Ourselves, Johnstown, Pennsylvania, September 30, 1917.
Address at New York City, October 1, 1917.
Address to Social Service Commission, Methodist Episcopal Church, October 4, 1917.
The Duty of the Hour, New York City, October 5, 1917.
Address at Oyster Bay, New York, October 24, 1917.
Address at New York City, October 29, 1917.
Address at New York City, November 1, 1917.
Address at Hartford, Connecticut, November 2, 1917.
Address at Bridgeport, Connecticut, November 3, 1917.
National Strength and International Duty, Princeton, New Jersey, November 17, 1917.
Address at Yaphank, New York, November 18, 1917.
Address to New York State Woman's Suffrage Party, New York City, November 20, 1917.
Addresses at Hamilton, Ontario, and Toronto, Canada, November 26, 1917.
Address to Allied War Bazaar, New York City, December 6, 1917.
Address to the Pennsylvania Society, New York City, December 8, 1917.
Address at Cincinnati, Ohio, December 14, 1917.
Address for the Nassau County Red Cross, Hempstead, New York, December 16, 1917.
Address at Episcopal Church Christmas Party, Oyster Bay, December 24, 1917.
Speed Up the War, Philadelphia, Pennsylvania, January 9, 1918.
Address to the Ohio Society, New York City, January 12, 1918.
Address to the Trustees of the American Defense Society, New York City, January 16, 1918.
Addresses at New York City (2), January 19, 1918.
Address to National Security League, January 20, 1918.
Address at National Press Club, Washington, D.C., January

24, 1918.

Address at New Building Dedication, Camp Merritt, New Jersey,
January 30, 1918.

Address to the Maine Convention of the Republican Party,
March 28, 1918.

Address at Oyster Bay, New York, April 2, 1918.

Address to Women's Civic League, Oyster Bay, New York, April
18, 1918.

Address at Fort Totten, New York, April 26, 1918.

Address to Hampton County Improvement League, Springfield,
Massachusetts, May 1, 1918.

Address at Boston, Massachusetts, May 2, 1918.

Address at New York City (2), May 7, 1918.

Address at opening of Nassau County Red Cross Drive, Garden
City, New York, May 14, 1918.

Address to Needle Work Guild of America, Oyster Bay, New
York, May 17, 1918.

Address at New York City, May 18, 1918.

Address at Carnegie Hall, New York City, May 21, 1918.

Address at Wittenberg College, Springfield, Ohio, May 25, 1918.

Addresses at Des Moines, Iowa (3), May 27, 1918.

Address at Madison, Wisconsin, May 28, 1918.

Addresses at Milwaukee, Wisconsin (2), May 29, 1918.

Address at Detroit, Michigan, May 30, 1918.

Address at New York City, June 5, 1918.

Address at Omaha, Nebraska, June 8, 1918.

Address at St Louis, Missouri, June 10, 1918.

Straightforward Americanism, Indianapolis, Indiana, June 11,
1918.

Addresses at Indianapolis and Bloomington, Indiana, June 12,
1918.

Address at Trinty College, Hartford, Connecticut, June 16, 1918.

Address at Passaic, New Jersey, July 4, 1918.

Address at Saratoga, New York, July 18, 1918.

Address to Japanese Red Cross Mission, Oyster Bay, New York,
July 20, 1918.

Address at Dark Harbor, Maine, August 4, 1918.

Yankee Blood vs. German Blood, Springfield, Illinois, August 26,
1918.

Labor Day Address, Newburgh, New York, September 2, 1918.

The Terms of Peace, New York City, September 6, 1918.

Address to National League for Women's Service, New York City,
September 18, 1918.

Address at the opening of the Fourth Liberty Loan Campaign,
Baltimore, Maryland, September 28, 1918.

Address at Columbus, Ohio, September 30, 1918.

Address at Alliance, Nebraska, October 4, 1918.

Address at Billings, Montana, October 5, 1918.

Address at Oyster Bay, New York, October 12, 1918.
Addresses at New York City (2), October 15, 1918.
What Wilson Did and Lincoln Didn't, New York City, October 28, 1918.
Address to Boys' Victory Mobilization Meeting, New York City, November 1, 1918.
Address to the Circle for Negro War Relief, November 2, 1918.

Bibliography

The researcher investigating Roosevelt's speaking can become overwhelmed by the enormous quantity of material that is available. This bibliography is broken into three sections: an essay on primary sources, a listing of books and major essays, and a listing of major articles.

SELECTED PRIMARY SOURCES

The principal Roosevelt collections are those found at the Library of Congress and at Harvard University. Much of the Library of Congress collection, which centers on Roosevelt's presidential years, is available on microfilm. The Library of Congress collection includes draft manuscripts that illustrate the evolution of some Roosevelt speeches.

The Roosevelt collection at Harvard is based upon the library of the Theodore Roosevelt Memorial Association, which was given to Harvard in the 1940s and has since been kept up to date. It is an exceptional collection that is especially rich in contemporary periodical accounts of Roosevelt's speaking. It also includes speech manuscripts, Roosevelt diaries, and scrapbooks. The latter are especially helpful for newspaper accounts of Roosevelt's speaking.

The principal published primary source for the scholar interested in Roosevelt's speaking are the two editions of The Works of Theodore Roosevelt. The minor differences between the twenty-four volume Memorial Edition (New York: Charles Scribner's Sons, 1923-1926) and the twenty volume National Edition (New York: Charles Scribner's Sons, 1926) are not critical for the scholar interested in Roosevelt's speaking.

The first difference between the two editions is that Roosevelt's work has been organized slightly differently. Hence materials are not always in the same volume of each edition. Second, the Memorial edition concludes with a two volume biography, Theodore Roosevelt and His Time by Joseph B. Bishop. Both editions include virtually all of Roosevelt's best-known speeches, well over a hundred of his lesser addresses and virtually all of his major published works, including his biographies of Benton and Morris, his account of the Naval War of 1812, his study of western expansion, his key works as a naturalist, and his own autobiography. Moreover, both editions include all of the more popular collections of his speeches and essays, which were published periodically throughout Roosevelt's career. They include American Ideals, The Strenuous Life, Realizable Ideals, America and the World War, Fear God and Take Your Own Part, and The Great Adventure. The editors have generally included appropriate introductory essays and bibliographical notes for each volume.

The second principal published source of primary materials of interest to the Roosevelt researcher is The Letters of Theodore Roosevelt, edited by Elting E. Morison. (Cambridge, Mass.: Harvard University Press, 1951-54). The researcher interested in Roosevelt's speaking will find much valuable material in the Roosevelt letters, including the reactions of many of his associates to Roosevelt's speeches, and Roosevelt's own explanations of his meaning and/or intent. Morison and his staff have done an excellent job of indexing, footnoting, and providing several exceptionally useful interpretative essays.

SELECTED BOOKS AND MAJOR ESSAYS

Aaron, Daniel. Men of Good Hope: A Story of American
    Progressives. New York: Oxford University Press, 1951.
Abbott, Lyman. Silhouettes of My Contemporaries. New York:
    Doubleday Page and Company, 1921.
Anderson, Walt. Campaigns: Cases in Political Conflict.
    Pacific Palisades: Goodyear Publishing, 1970.
Beale, Howard K. Theodore Roosevelt and the Rise of America
    to World Power. Baltimore, Md.: Johns Hopkins, 1956.
Blum, John M. The Republican Roosevelt. Cambridge, Mass.:
    Harvard University Press, 1954.
_____. "Theodore Roosevelt and the Legislative Process: Tariff
    Revision and Railroad Regulation, 1904-1906." In The
    Letters of Theodore Roosevelt 4. Edited by Elting E.
    Morison. Cambridge, Mass.: Harvard University Press,
    1951.
_____. "Theodore Roosevelt: The Years of Decision." In The
    Letters of Theodore Roosevelt 1. Edited by Elting
    E. Morison. Cambridge, Mass.: Harvard University Press,
    1951.

Boorstin, Daniel J.   The Americans: The Democratic Experience.   New York: Random House, 1973.

Braden, Waldo W. "Theodore Roosevelt" In American Orators of the Twentieth Century. Edited by Burnard Duffy and Halford Ryan.
Westport Conn.: Greenwood Press, 1987.

Burton, David H.   Theodore Roosevelt.   New York: Twayne Publishers, 1972.

_____. Theodore Roosevelt: Confident Imperialist.   Philadelphia: University of Pennsylvania Press, 1968.

_____.   The Learned Presidency.   Rutherford, N. J.: Fairleigh Dickinson   University Press and Associated University Presses, 1988.

Chessmen, C. Wallace.   Theodore Roosevelt and the Politics of Power.   Boston: Little Brown and Company, 1969.

Collin, Richard H. Theodore Roosevelt, Culture, Diplomacy and Expansion.   Baton Rouge, La.: LSU Press, 1985.

Cotton, Edward H.   The Ideals of Theodore Roosevelt.   New York: Appleton and Company, 1923.

Current, Richard, Garraty, John and Julius Weinberg.   Words That Made American History.   Boston: Little Brown and Company, 1972

Dalinger, Carl A.   "Theodore Roosevelt: The Preacher Militant." In American Public Address: Studies in Honor of Albert Craig Baird   Edited by Loren Reid.   Columbia, Missouri: University of Missouri Press, 1961.

Felsenthal, Carol. Alice Longworth Roosevelt.   New York: G.P. Putnam's and Sons, 1988.

Gardner, Joseph L.   Departing Glory: Theodore Roosevelt as Ex-President.   New York: Charles Scribner's Sons, 1973.

Goldman, Eric.   Rendezvous with Destiny.   New York: Vintage Books, 1956.

Gould, Lewis L.   Reform and Regulation: American Politics from Roosevelt to Wilson.   New York: Alfred A. Knopf, 1986.

Harbaugh, William H.   The Life and Times of Theodore Roosevelt.   New York: Collier Books, 1963.

Hart, Wilbert Bushnell and Herbert Ferleger, editors. Theodore Roosevelt Cyclopedia.   New York: Theodore Roosevelt Association, 1941.

Hofstadter, Richard.   The American Political Tradition.   New York: Vintage Books, 1948.

_____.   Anti-Intellectualism in American Life.   New York: Alfred Knopf, 1970.

Holland, Dewitte, editor.   Preaching in American History.   Nashville, Tenn.: Abington Press, 1969.

Marks, Frederick. Velvet on Iron: The Diplomacy of Theodore Roosevelt.   Lincoln: University of Nebraska Press, 1979.

Matthews, Brander. The Tocsin of Revolt and Other Essays.
    New York: Charles Scribner's Sons, 1922.
Miller, Raymond C. "Theodore Roosevelt: Historian." In Medieval
    History and Historiographic Essays in Honor of James
    Westfall Thompson. Edited by James Lea Cate and
    Eugene Anderson. Chicago: University of Chicago Press,
    1938.
Morris, Edmund. The Rise of Theodore Roosevelt. New York:
    Coward, McCann and Geoghegan Inc., 1979.
Murphy, Richard. "Theodore Roosevelt." In A History and
    Criticism of American Public Address. Edited by Marie
    Hochmuth. New York: Russell and Russell, 1965.
Norton, Aloysius A. Theodore Roosevelt. Boston: Twayne
    Publishers, 1980.
Perry, Ralph Barton. The Plattsburgh Movement. New York:
    E.P. Dutton and Company, 1921.
Pollard, James E. The Presidents and the Press. New York:
    Macmillian Company, 1947.
Pringle, Henry F. Theodore Roosevelt: A Biography. New York:
    Harcourt Brace Janovich, 1956.
Putnam, Carleton. Theodore Roosevelt: The Formative Years.
    New York: Charles Scribner's Sons, 1958.
Reisner, Christian F. Roosevelt's Religion. New York: Abington
    Press, 1922.
Republican National Committee. Our Patriotic President: His Life
    In Pictures, Famous Words and Maxims. New York:
    Columbia Press, 1904.
Richardson, William H. Theodore Roosevelt: One Day of His
    Life. New Jersey Printing Company, 1921.
Riis, Jacob A. Theodore Roosevelt the Citizen. New York: The
    Outlook Company, 1904.
Steel, Ronald. Walter Lippman and the American Century.
    New York: Vintage Books, 1981.
Straus, Roger Williams. Religious Liberty and Democracy.
    Chicago and New York: Willett Clark and Company,
    1939.
Washburn, Charles C. Theodore Roosevelt: The Logic of his
    Career. Boston: Houghton Mifflin, Company, 1916.
Wister, Owen. Roosevelt: The Story of a Friendship. New York:
    Macmillian, 1930.
Wolf, Simon. The Presidents I Have Known: From 1860-1918.
    Washington, D.C.: Bryan Adams Press, 1918.

SELECTED ARTICLES

Behl, William B. "Theodore Roosevelt's Principles of Speech
    Preparation and Delivery." Speech Monographs (1945):
    112-22.

_____. "Theodore Roosevelt's Principles of Invention." Speech Monographs (1947): 93-110.

Beltz, Lynda. "Theodore Roosevelt's 'Man with the Muck-rake'." Central States Speech Journal (Summer 1969): 97-103.

Beveridge, Albert J. "The Roosevelt Period." Saturday Evening Post (April 5, 1919): 10, 49-53.

Brigance, William Norwood. "In the Workshop of Great Speakers." American Speech (August, 1926): 589-95.

Ceaser, James W.; Thurow, Glen E.; Tulis, Jeffrey; and Bessette, Joseph M. "The Rise of the Rhetorical Presidency." Presidential Studies Quarterly (Spring 1981): 158-71.

"The Ex-Presidential War on the War Department." Literary Digest (September 11, 1915): 514-15.

Grantham, Dewey W. Jr. "Theodore Roosevelt in American Historical Writing, 1945-1960." Mid-America (January 1961): 3-35.

Hale, William Baynard. "Friends and Fellow Citizens: Our Political Orators of All Parties and the Ways They Use to Win Us." The World's Work (April 1912): 673-83.

Karsten, Peter. "The Nature of 'Influence': Roosevelt, Mahan and the Concept of Sea Power." American Quarterly (October 1971): 585-600.

Lucas, Stephen E. "Theodore Roosevelt's 'The Man with the Muck-rake': A Reinterpretation." Quarterly Journal of Speech (December 1973): 452-62.

Moers, Ellen. "Teddy Roosevelt: Literary Feller." Columbia University Forum (Summer 1963): 10-16.

Morris, Edmund. "The Many Words and Works of Theodore Roosevelt." Smithsonian (November 1983): 86-97.

Nye, Russell B. "Theodore Roosevelt as a Historian." The Nassau County Historical Journal (Fall-Winter 1939-40): 1-7.

"President Roosevelt on Muck-rakers." Harpers Weekly (April 28 1906): 580.

Putnam, George. "Roosevelt As a Man Of Letters." Review of Reviews (September 1900): 377-78.

"A Review of the World." Current Literature (October 1910):39-62.

Robinson, Elwyn B. "Theodore Roosevelt: Amateur Historian." North Dakota History (January 1958): 5-13.

Sellen, Robert W. "Theodore Roosevelt: Historian With A Moral." Mid-America (October 1959): 223-40.

Semonche, John E. "Theodore Roosevelt's 'Muck-rake' Speech: A Reassessment." Mid-America (April 1964): 114-25.

Silvestri, Vito N. "Theodore Roosevelt's Preparedness Oratory: The Minority Voice of an Ex-President." Central States Speech Journal (Fall 1969): 179-86.

Straus, Oscar W. "Theodore Roosevelt and Religion." The Forum (February 1923): 1191-97.

"Theodore Roosevelt-By Himself." Cosmopolitan (November 1907): 38-46.

"Theodore Roosevelt's Religion." Current Opinion (January 1922): 82-83.

Whitingale, John L. "Theodore Roosevelt-His Face." Metropolitan Magazine (December 1902): 619-27.

Williams, Mark Wayne. "Preaching Presidents." Homiletic Review (August 1934): 90-96.

Zyskind, Harold. "A Case Study of Philosophical Rhetoric: Theodore Roosevelt." Philosophy and Rhetoric (Summer 1968): 228-54.

Index

Addams, Jane, 95
Altgeld, John Peter, 21

Bailey, Thomas, 37
Bellamy, Edward, 21
Benton, Thomas Hart, 39
Blum, John Morton, 5, 9, 17, 29
Bryan, William Jennings, 21, 46
Bulloch, Annie, 2-3
Bunyan, John, 75
Butler, Nicholas Murray, 15

Cadenhead, I. E., 37
Cambridge University, 15
Charles, Robert, 7-8
Columbia University Law School, 7-8
Conwell, Russell, 25
Cooper, James Fenimore, 4
Crane, Stephen, 21
Croly, Herbert, 81, 87, 89
Cushing, 43
Cutler, Arthur, 2

Davis, Richard Harding, 21
Debating, 5-7, 10
Debs, Eugene, 21
Dickens, Charles, 5

Farragut, Admiral David, 43

Garland, Hamlin, 21

Garrison, Lindley M., 46-47
George, Henry, 21
Gorki, Maxim, 29
Grant, President Ulysses, 63, 67

Hagedorn, Hermann, 29
Hart, Albert Bushnell, 6
Harvard University, 2, 5-7, 9-10, 19, 26
Haywood, William, 21
Herron, George, 25
Hofstadter, Richard, 22, 37
Howells, William Dean, 21
Hunt, Isaac, 9

Jefferson, President Thomas, 19

Knox, Philander, 15

Lee, Alice, 7. See also Roosevelt, Alice
Lincoln, Abraham, 27, 41, 48, 61-63, 67, 82, 88
Lodge, Henry Cabot, 24, 90
Longfellow, William, 4
Lowell, James Russell, 40, 58
Lucas, Stephen, 78
Luce, Rear Admiral Stephen B., 39
Lynch, John R., 27

Macaulay, Thomas Babington, 4-5
Madison, President James, 19
Marks, Frederick W., 38
Matthews, Brander, 21
McKinley, President William, 17, 45
Morris, Edmund, 39, 63
Morris, Gouverneur, 39
Mowry, George, 90

Naismith, James, 18
Nobel Peace Prize, 20

Pinchot, Gifford, 95

Quintilian, 97-98

Rauschenbush, Walter, 25
Rhodes, James Ford, 4
Riis, Jacob, 21
Roosevelt, Alice, 7. See also Lee, Alice
Roosevelt, Martha, 2-3

Roosevelt, Theodore: influences of early reading, 3-5; influences of family, 1-3,5; influences of Harvard, 5-7; influences of New York legislature, 7-11.   Public speaking: basic themes of, 17-30, 37-42, 57, 59, 61, 63-66, 69, 75-80, 83-87, 97; characteristics of, 15-17; rhetorical practices of, 43-44, 51, 61-63, 66-69, 79-81, 88-90, 96-97. <u>See also</u> Speeches of Theodore Roosevelt
Roosevelt, Theodore (Sr.), 1-4, 7-8
Root, Elihu, 30
Ryan, John, 25

Speeches of Theodore Roosevelt: to Republican National Convention (June 3, 1884), 27; "The Duties of American Citizenship" (January 26, 1893), 57; analyses of, 58-63, 69; "Washington's Forgotten Maxim" (June 2, 1897), analysis of, 39-44; reactions to, 44-45; significance of, 45-46; "The Strenuous Life" (April 10, 1899), 57-58; analysis of, 63-69; at the Quarter-centennial celebration of Statehood for Colorado (August 2, 1901), 23; to the New York Chamber of Commerce banquet (November 11, 1902), 57; "The Man with the Muck-rake" (April 14, 1906), 85, 90; analysis of, 74-81; reactions to, 78-79; at Harvard Union (February 23, 1907), 26; "The New Nationalism" (August 31, 1910), 74, 81; analysis of, 82-90; to the Republican Convention (June 17, 1912), 26; "This Nation's Needs" (August 25, 1915), analysis of, 46-52
Steffens, Lincoln, 21
Straus, Oscar, 27

Taft, President William Howard, 74
Tammany Hall, 9
Treyelyan, George Otto, 5

Washington, Booker T., 27
Washington, President George, 39-41, 75
White, William Allan, 15, 17
Wilson, President Woodrow, 46, 48, 50
Wister, Owen, 4
Wood, Leonard, 46-47, 49

About the Author

ROBERT V. FRIEDENBERG is Professor of Communication at Miami University, Ohio. He is coauthor of *Political Campaign Communication: Principles and Practices* (Praeger, 1983) and editor of *Rhetorical Studies of National Political Debates: 1960-1988* (Praeger, 1990). In 1989 he received the "Outstanding Book of the Year Award" from the Religious Speech Communication Association for *"Hear O Israel": The History of American Jewish Preaching, 1654-1970*.

Great American Orators

Defender of the Union: The Oratory of Daniel Webster
Craig R. Smith

Harry Emerson Fosdick: Persuasive Preacher
Halford R. Ryan

Eugene Talmadge: Rhetoric and Response
Calvin McLeod Logue

The Search of Self-Sovereignty: The Oratory of Elizabeth Cady Stanton
Beth M. Waggenspack

Richard Nixon: Rhetorical Strategist
Hal W. Bochin

Henry Ward Beecher: Peripatetic Preacher
Halford R. Ryan

Edward Everett: Unionist Orator
Ronald F. Reid